the unbeatable Squirrel Girl
welcome to Earth KIT

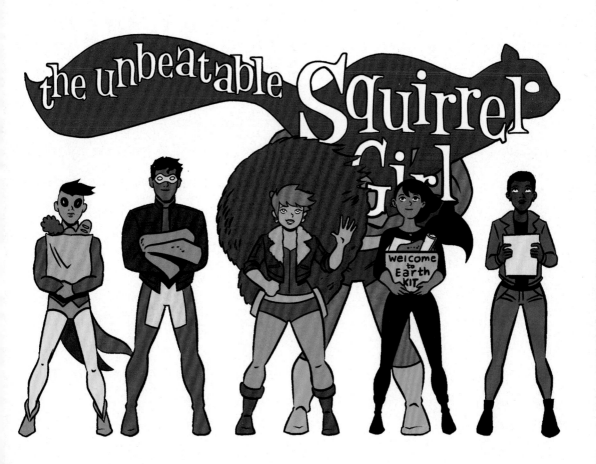

COLLECTION EDITOR: **JENNIFER GRÜNWALD**
ASSISTANT EDITOR: **CAITLIN O'CONNELL**
ASSOCIATE MANAGING EDITOR: **KATERI WOODY**
EDITOR, SPECIAL PROJECTS: **MARK D. BEAZLEY**
VP PRODUCTION & SPECIAL PROJECTS: **JEFF YOUNGQUIST**
SVP PRINT, SALES & MARKETING: **DAVID GABRIEL**
BOOK DESIGNER: **JAY BOWEN**

EDITOR IN CHIEF: **C. B. CEBULSKI**
CHIEF CREATIVE OFFICER: **JOE QUESADA**
PRESIDENT: **DAN BUCKLEY**
EXECUTIVE PRODUCER: **ALAN FINE**

THE UNBEATABLE SQUIRREL GIRL VOL. 10: LIFE IS TOO SHORT, SQUIRREL. Contains material originally published in magazine form as THE UNBEATABLE SQUIRREL GIRL #37-41. First printing 2019. ISBN 978-1-302-91447-9. Published by MARVEL WORLDWIDE, INC., a subsidiary of MARVEL ENTERTAINMENT, LLC. OFFICE OF PUBLICATION: 135 West 50th Street, New York, NY 10020. Copyright © 2019 MARVEL No similarity between any of the names, characters, persons, and/or institutions in this magazine with those of any living or dead person or institution is intended, and any such similarity which may exist is purely coincidental. **Printed in Canada.** DAN BUCKLEY, President, Marvel Entertainment; JOHN NEE, Publisher; JOE QUESADA, Chief Creative Officer; TOM BREVOORT, SVP of Publishing; DAVID BOGART, SVP of Business Affairs & Operations, Publishing & Partnership; DAVID GABRIEL, SVP of Sales & Marketing, Publishing; JEFF YOUNGQUIST, VP of Production & Special Projects; DAN CARR, Executive Director of Publishing Technology; ALEX MORALES, Director of Publishing Operations; DAN EDINGTON, Managing Editor; SUSAN CRESPI, Production Manager; STAN LEE, Chairman Emeritus. For information regarding advertising in Marvel Comics or on Marvel.com, please contact Vit DeBellis, Custom Solutions & Integrated Advertising Manager, at vdebellis@marvel.com. For Marvel subscription inquiries, please call 888-511-5480.

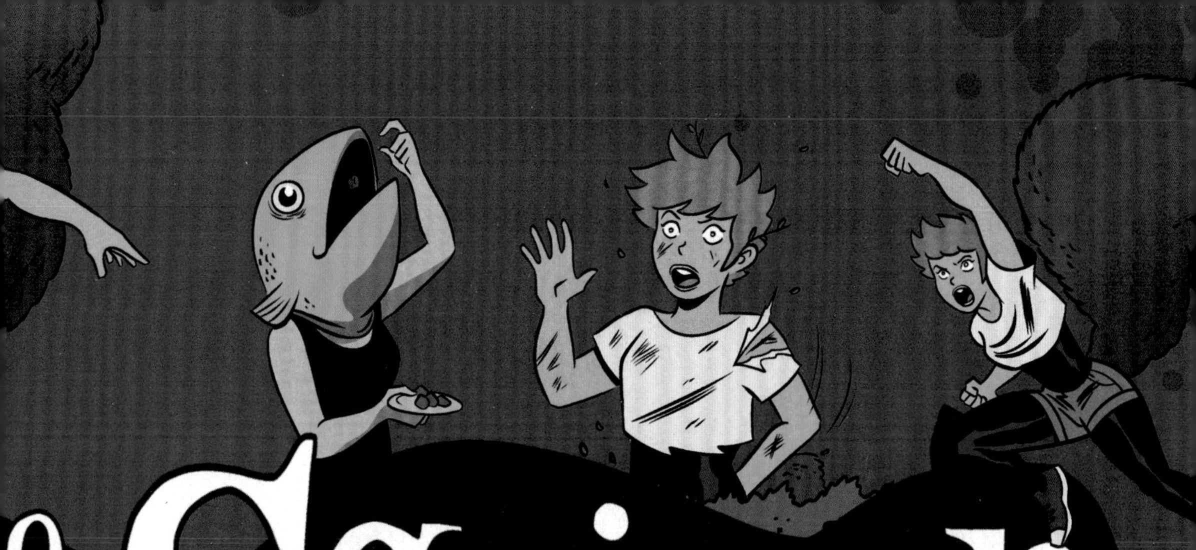

e Squirrel Girl

Life Is Too Short, Squirrel

Ryan North
WRITER

Derek Charm (#37-40) &
Naomi Franquiz (#41)
ARTISTS

Rico Renzi
COLOR ARTIST & TRADING CARD ARTIST

VC's Travis Lanham
LETTERER

Erica Henderson
COVER ART

Michael Allred
LOGO

Sarah Brunstad
ASSOCIATE EDITOR

Wil Moss
EDITOR

SQUIRREL GIRL CREATED BY WILL MURRAY & STEVE DITKO

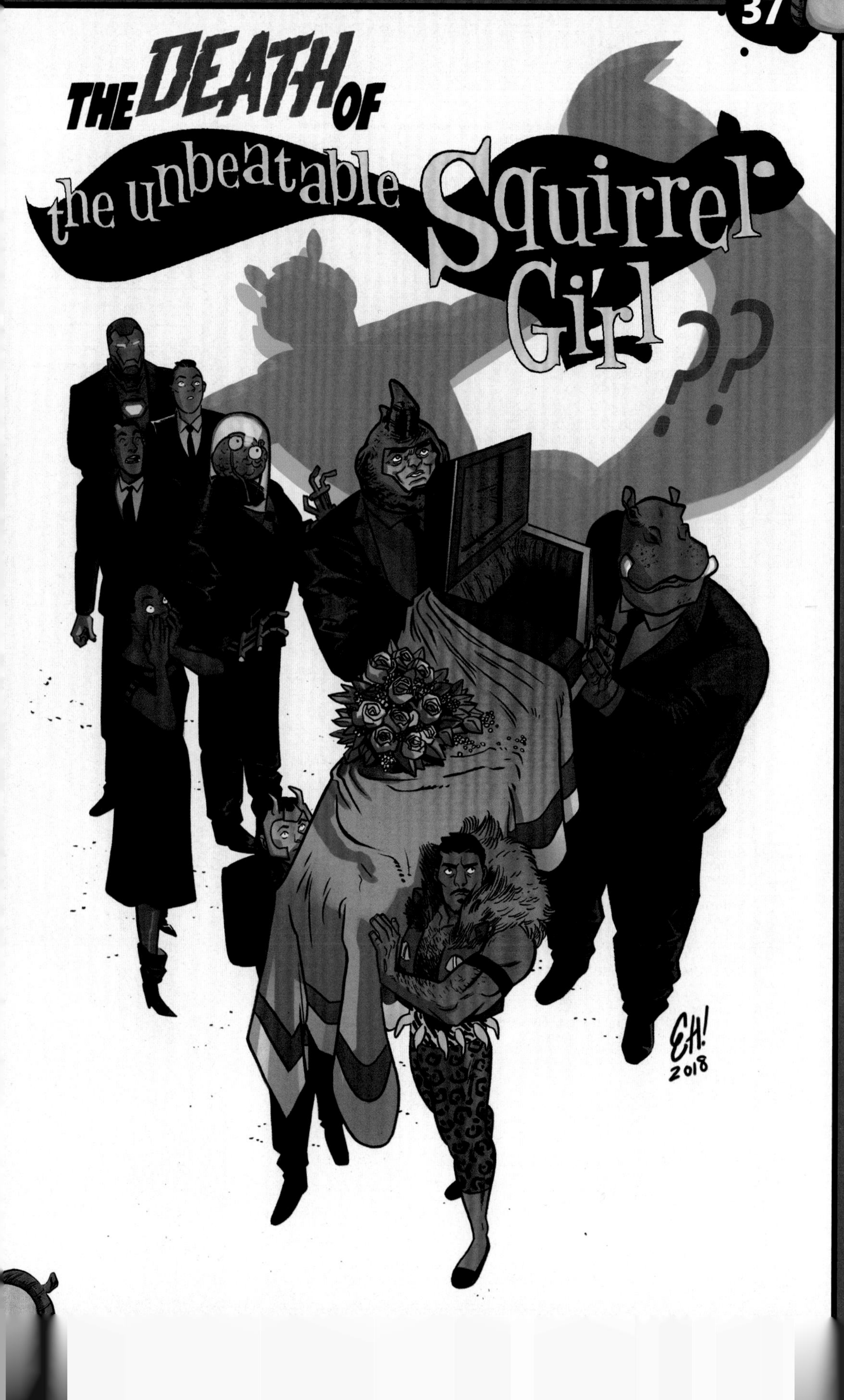
THE DEATH OF
the unbeatable Squirrel Girl
??
EH! 2018

Doreen Green isn't just a second-year computer science student: she secretly also has all the powers of both squirrel *and* girl! She uses her amazing abilities to fight crime **and** be as awesome as possible. You know her as...The Unbeatable Squirrel Girl! Find out what she's been up to, with...

Squirrel Girl *in a nutshell*

search!

#octobliterator

#coolcars

#rip

#riproaringadventure

#speeches

Squirrel Girl @unbeatablesg
New York has been silenced by a spooky ghost! Literally! She's generating a weird field around the city that's preventing anyone from talking!

Squirrel Girl @unbeatablesg
Out loud, I mean! We can still talk online as much as we want. So that's good.

Nancy W. @sewwiththeflo
@unbeatablesg I will say this: there were YEARS in my life where I wouldn't have even noticed anything changed.

Squirrel Girl @unbeatablesg
@sewwiththeflo haha internet friends can be the best friends!! but in other news: IS TEXTING BY MILLENNIALS KILLING SPEAKING??

Nancy W. @sewwiththeflo
@unbeatablesg As a millennial may I just say: only once napkins, top sheets, and mayo are forever destroyed will I be satisfied. Also: chain restaurants.

Squirrel Girl @unbeatablesg
@sewwiththeflo haha

Squirrel Girl @unbeatablesg
@sewwiththeflo We should really go get on this silence thing though

Squirrel Girl @unbeatablesg
Don't worry, citizens! Your friendly neighborhood Unbeatable Squirrel Girl is on the case!!

Squirrel Girl @unbeatablesg
UPDATE: WE DID NOT SOLVE THE CASE AND NEW YORK REMAINS SILENT, SORRY, BUT I'M SURE TONIGHT I'LL BE ABLE TO FIX IT

Tony Stark @starkmantony ✓
@unbeatablesg Got a plan for tonight.

Squirrel Girl @unbeatablesg
@starkmantony I've got a plan for tonight too! They're not going to interfere with each other are they?

Tony Stark @starkmantony ✓
@unbeatablesg Absolutely not.

Tony Stark @starkmantony ✓
@unbeatablesg ...Okay, um, apparently there was a sliiiiight chance they could cancel each other out.

Squirrel Girl @unbeatablesg
@starkmantony ANTHONY EDWARD "TONY" STARK.

Squirrel Girl @unbeatablesg
UPDATE: WE DID NOT SOLVE THE CASE AGAIN AND NEW YORK STILL REMAINS SILENT, BUT I FEEL REAL GOOD ABOUT TONIGHT

Squirrel Girl @unbeatablesg
UPDATE: CASE STILL NOT SOLVED BUT I ASSURE YOU I REMAIN UNBEATABLE AND TONIGHT WILL DEFINITELY DO THE TRICK

Squirrel Girl @unbeatablesg
OKAY, TONIGHT FOR SURE, FOR REAL THIS TIME

Squirrel Girl @unbeatablesg
UPDATE: CASE SOLVED!! The ghost just wanted silence and we managed to find a new place for her to volunteer--at the library! She now assures silence for all patrons--AND it means the library is now open overnight! Thanks, Ms. Chloe, library ghost!!

Squirrel Girl @unbeatablesg
Also: she fights crime now too. So that and running a library are TWO things you can look forward to when you become a ghost, if you're lucky!! also apparently ghosts are real but let's all deal with the implications of that later!!

Squirrel Girl @unbeatablesg
thanks for following me everyone, let's hang out online soon!!

New York Bulletin @ny_bulletin
BREAKING NEWS!

New York Bulletin @ny_bulletin
LOCAL HERO FALLS! CITY MOURNS LOSS OF ONE OF ITS OWN AS AVENGER DIES SAVING EVERYONE. SADNESS BEFALLS ALL, FOR TODAY IS THE DAY WE HAVE WITNESSED...

New York Bulletin @ny_bulletin
THE DEATH OF SQUIRREL GIRL

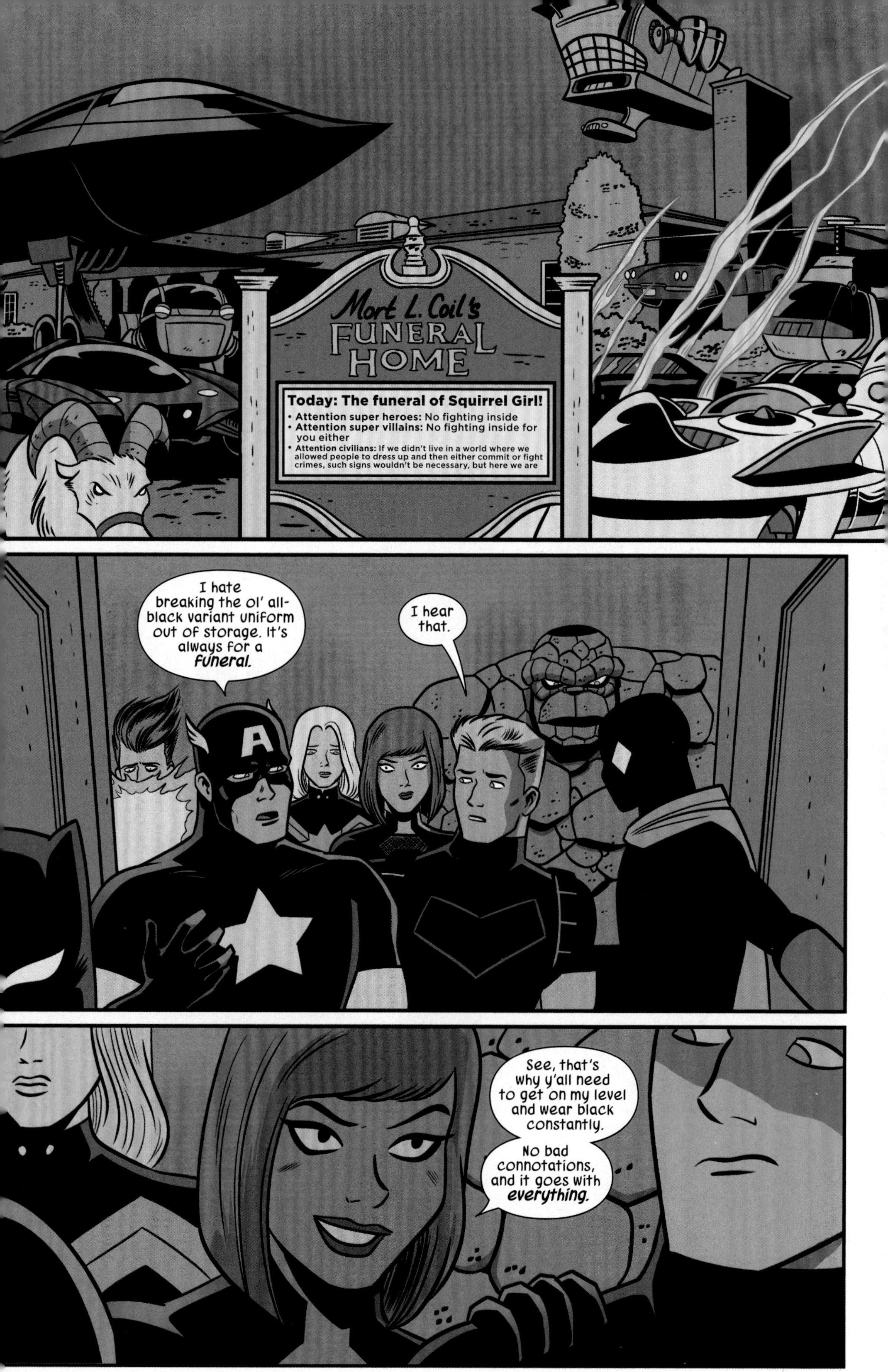

Mort L. Coil's
FUNERAL HOME
Today: The funeral of Squirrel Girl!
• Attention super heroes: No fighting inside
• Attention super villains: No fighting inside for you either
• Attention civilians: If we didn't live in a world where we allowed people to dress up and then either commit or fight crimes, such signs wouldn't be necessary, but here we are
I hate breaking the ol' all-black variant uniform out of storage. It's always for a *funeral.*
I hear that.
See, that's why y'all need to get on my level and wear black constantly.
No bad connotations, and it goes with *everything.*

That's right! It's the funeral of ***Squirrel Girl!*** Were we ***really*** so bold as to kill her, off-panel, between issues? For those of you who have never read a comic before and are thus inexperienced and therefore credulous toward these sorts of stunts, let me answer my own rhetorical question with an enthusiastic ***"maybe??"***

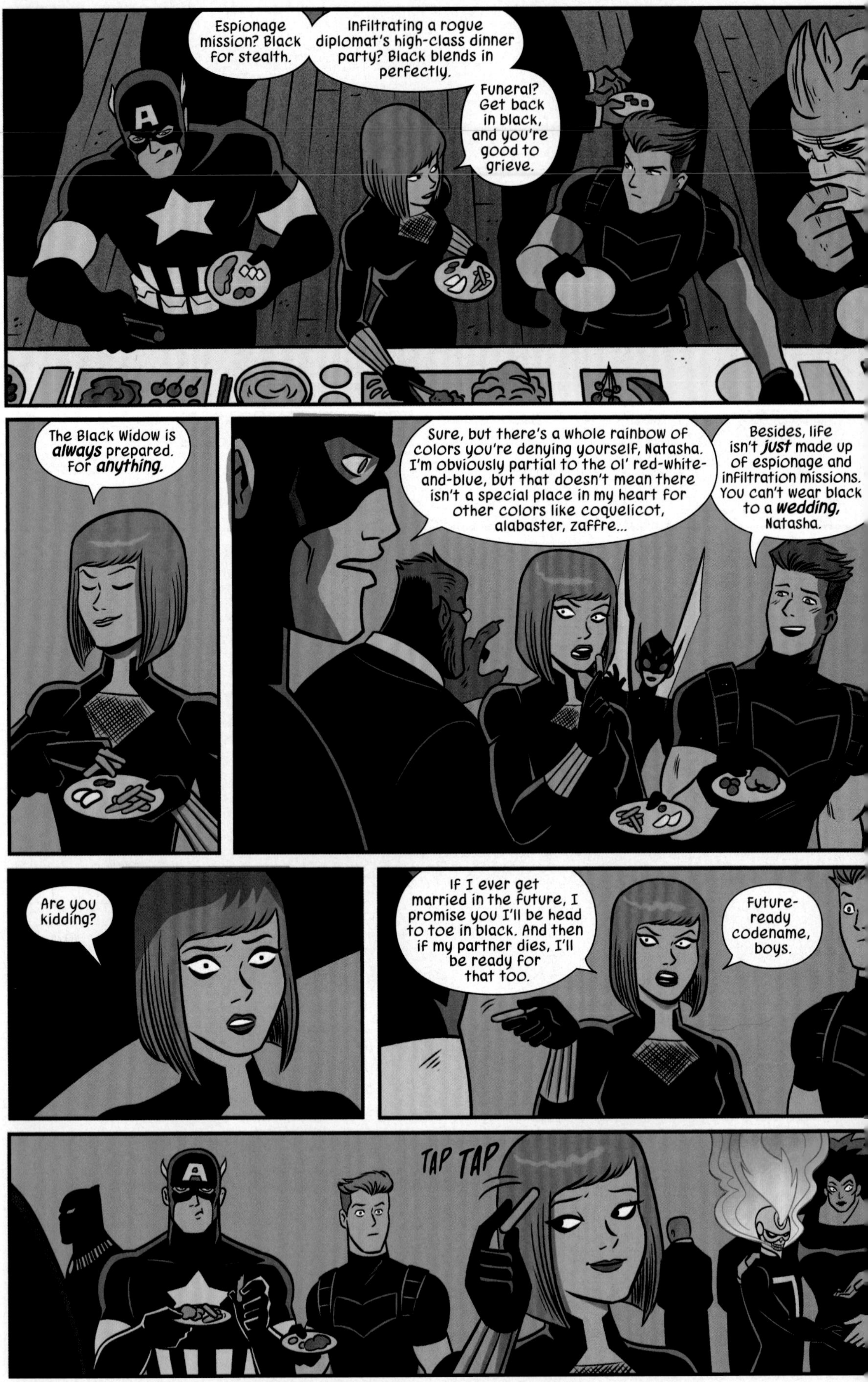
Espionage mission? Black for stealth.
Infiltrating a rogue diplomat's high-class dinner party? Black blends in perfectly.
Funeral? Get back in black, and you're good to grieve.
The Black Widow is *always* prepared. For *anything.*
Sure, but there's a whole rainbow of colors you're denying yourself, Natasha. I'm obviously partial to the ol' red-white-and-blue, but that doesn't mean there isn't a special place in my heart for other colors like coquelicot, alabaster, zaffre...
Besides, life isn't *just* made up of espionage and infiltration missions. You can't wear black to a *wedding,* Natasha.
Are you kidding?
If I ever get married in the future, I promise you I'll be head to toe in black. And then if my partner dies, I'll be ready for that too.
Future-ready codename, boys.
TAP TAP

Black Widow has clearly never been on a construction site at night and wanted to stay visible for safety! Fashion demands you accessorize with a high-visibility vest at the *very* least.

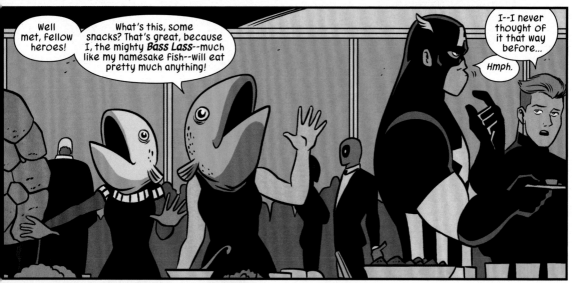

Well met, fellow heroes!

What's this, some snacks? That's great, because I, the mighty **Bass Lass**--much like my namesake fish--will eat pretty much anything!

I--I never thought of it that way before...

Hmph.

This is weird.

This is mega weird.

Big turn-out though, huh??

I'm just relieved the doorman didn't have a guest list. I don't think "Bass Lass and Fish Miss" would've been on it.

Snap, **Bi-Beast** showed up? Nice!

Don't say his name! Remember: We're just some regular run-of-the-mill super heroes who are **definitely real**, showing up to pay our respects and have some sad funeral times.

I know, I know! It's just--oh man, the **Walrus** is here too?

I barely even talked with him the one time we fought, and he still made the time! What a class act!!

Ahem.

Sad Funeral times.

Right, right. I got it. But come on...

Fun Fact about the Walrus: He has the proportional speed, strength, and agility of a walrus! But as walruses are actually *larger* than humans, technically that makes him slower and weaker than even a regular person. THAT'S JUST HOW PROPORTIONALITY WORKS, SORRY THE WALRUS

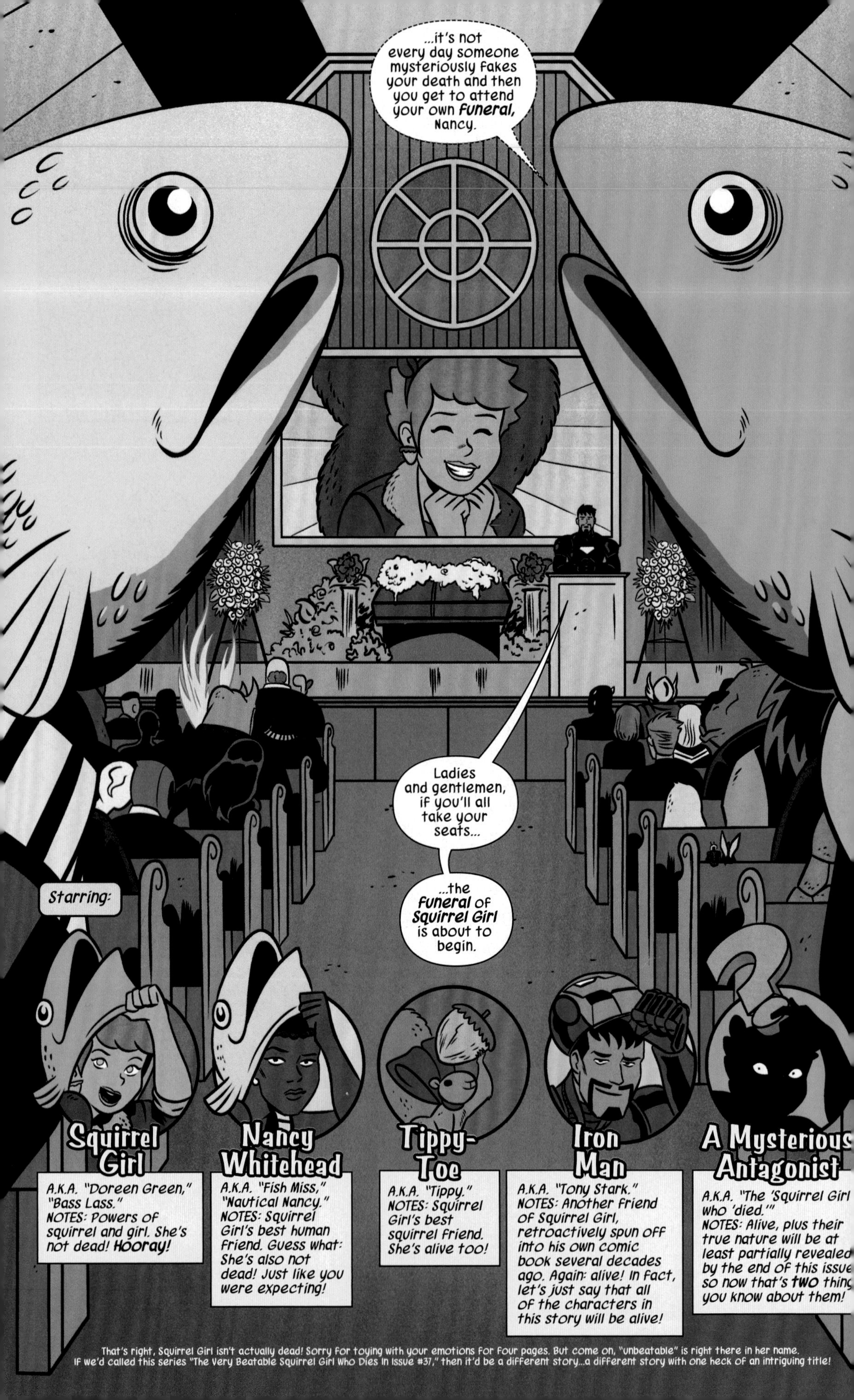
...it's not every day someone mysteriously fakes your death and then you get to attend your own funeral, Nancy.
Ladies and gentlemen, if you'll all take your seats...
...the funeral of Squirrel Girl is about to begin.
Starring:
Squirrel Girl
A.K.A. "Doreen Green," "Bass Lass." NOTES: Powers of squirrel and girl. She's not dead! HOORAY!
Nancy Whitehead
A.K.A. "Fish Miss," "Nautical Nancy." NOTES: Squirrel Girl's best human friend. Guess what: She's also not dead! Just like you were expecting!
Tippy-Toe
A.K.A. "Tippy." NOTES: Squirrel Girl's best squirrel friend. She's alive too!
Iron Man
A.K.A. "Tony Stark." NOTES: Another friend of Squirrel Girl, retroactively spun off into his own comic book several decades ago. Again: alive! In fact, let's just say that all of the characters in this story will be alive!
A Mysterious Antagonist
A.K.A. "The 'Squirrel Girl who 'died.'" NOTES: Alive, plus their true nature will be at least partially revealed by the end of this issue so now that's two thing you know about them!
That's right, Squirrel Girl isn't actually dead! Sorry for toying with your emotions for four pages. But come on, "unbeatable" is right there in her name. If we'd called this series "The Very Beatable Squirrel Girl Who Dies In Issue #37," then it'd be a different story...a different story with one heck of an intriguing title!

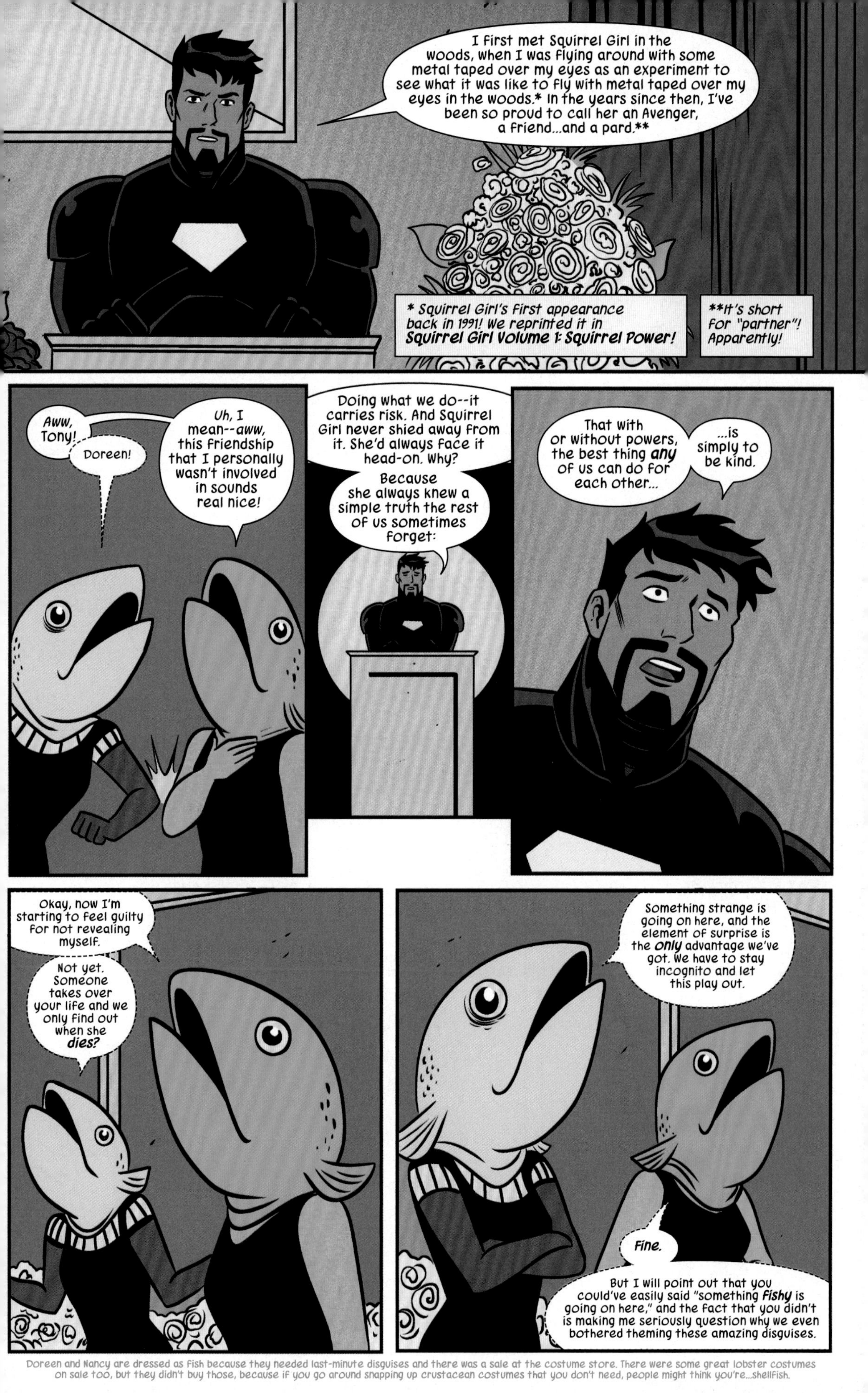
I first met Squirrel Girl in the woods, when I was flying around with some metal taped over my eyes as an experiment to see what it was like to fly with metal taped over my eyes in the woods.* In the years since then, I've been so proud to call her an Avenger, a friend...and a pard.**
* Squirrel Girl's first appearance back in 1991! We reprinted it in Squirrel Girl Volume 1: Squirrel Power!
**It's short for "partner"! Apparently!
Aww, Tony!
Doreen!
Uh, I mean--aww, this friendship that I personally wasn't involved in sounds real nice!
Doing what we do--it carries risk. And Squirrel Girl never shied away from it. She'd always face it head-on. Why?
Because she always knew a simple truth the rest of us sometimes forget:
That with or without powers, the best thing any of us can do for each other...
...is simply to be kind.
Okay, now I'm starting to feel guilty for not revealing myself.
Not yet. Someone takes over your life and we only find out when she dies?
Something strange is going on here, and the element of surprise is the only advantage we've got. We have to stay incognito and let this play out.
Fine.
But I will point out that you could've easily said "something fishy is going on here," and the fact that you didn't is making me seriously question why we even bothered theming these amazing disguises.

Doreen and Nancy are dressed as fish because they needed last-minute disguises and there was a sale at the costume store. There were some great lobster costumes on sale too, but they didn't buy those, because if you go around snapping up crustacean costumes that you don't need, people might think you're...shellfish.

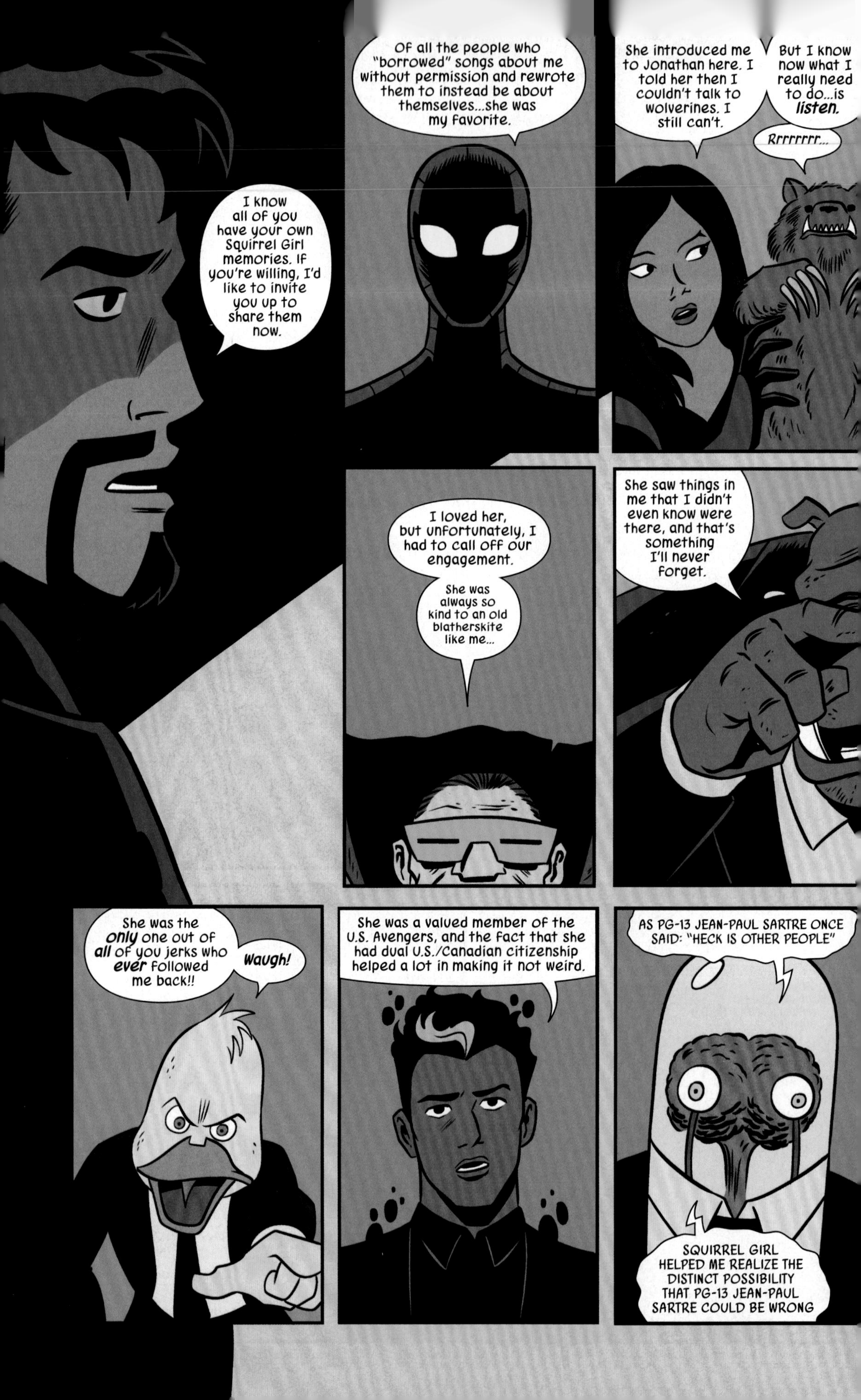
I know all of you have your own Squirrel Girl memories. If you're willing, I'd like to invite you up to share them now.
Of all the people who "borrowed" songs about me without permission and rewrote them to instead be about themselves...she was my favorite.
She introduced me to Jonathan here. I told her then I couldn't talk to wolverines. I still can't.
But I know now what I really need to do...is listen.
Rrrrrrrr...
I loved her, but unfortunately, I had to call off our engagement.
She was always so kind to an old blatherskite like me...
She saw things in me that I didn't even know were there, and that's something I'll never forget.
She was the only one out of all of you jerks who ever followed me back!!
Waugh!
She was a valued member of the U.S. Avengers, and the fact that she had dual U.S./Canadian citizenship helped a lot in making it not weird.
AS PG-13 JEAN-PAUL SARTRE ONCE SAID: "HECK IS OTHER PEOPLE"
SQUIRREL GIRL HELPED ME REALIZE THE DISTINCT POSSIBILITY THAT PG-13 JEAN-PAUL SARTRE COULD BE WRONG

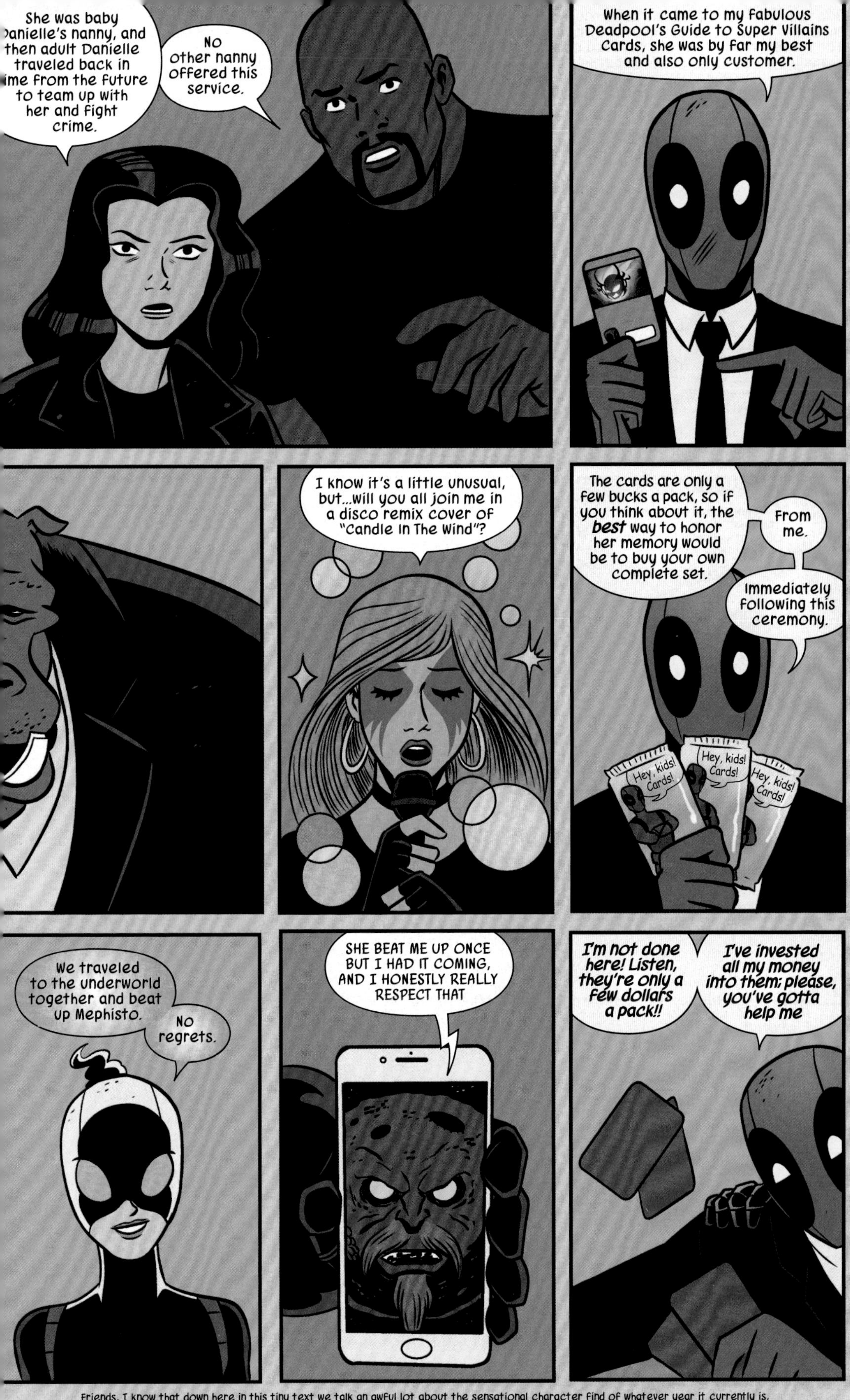
She was baby)anielle's nanny, and then adult Danielle traveled back in ime from the future to team up with her and fight crime.
No other nanny offered this service.
When it came to my fabulous Deadpool's Guide to Super Villains Cards, she was by far my best and also only customer.
I know it's a little unusual, but...will you all join me in a disco remix cover of "Candle In The Wind"?
The cards are only a few bucks a pack, so if you think about it, the *best* way to honor her memory would be to buy your own complete set.
From me.
Immediately following this ceremony.
Hey, kids! Cards!
Hey, kids! Cards!
Hey, kids! Cards!
We traveled to the underworld together and beat up Mephisto.
No regrets.
SHE BEAT ME UP ONCE BUT I HAD IT COMING, AND I HONESTLY REALLY RESPECT THAT
I'm not done here! Listen, they're only a few dollars a pack!!
I've invested all my money into them; please, you've gotta help me

Friends, I know that down here in this tiny text we talk an awful lot about the sensational character find of whatever year it currently is, but I am here once again to tell you that PG-13 Jean-Paul Sartre is absolutely the sensational character find of whatever year it currently is!!

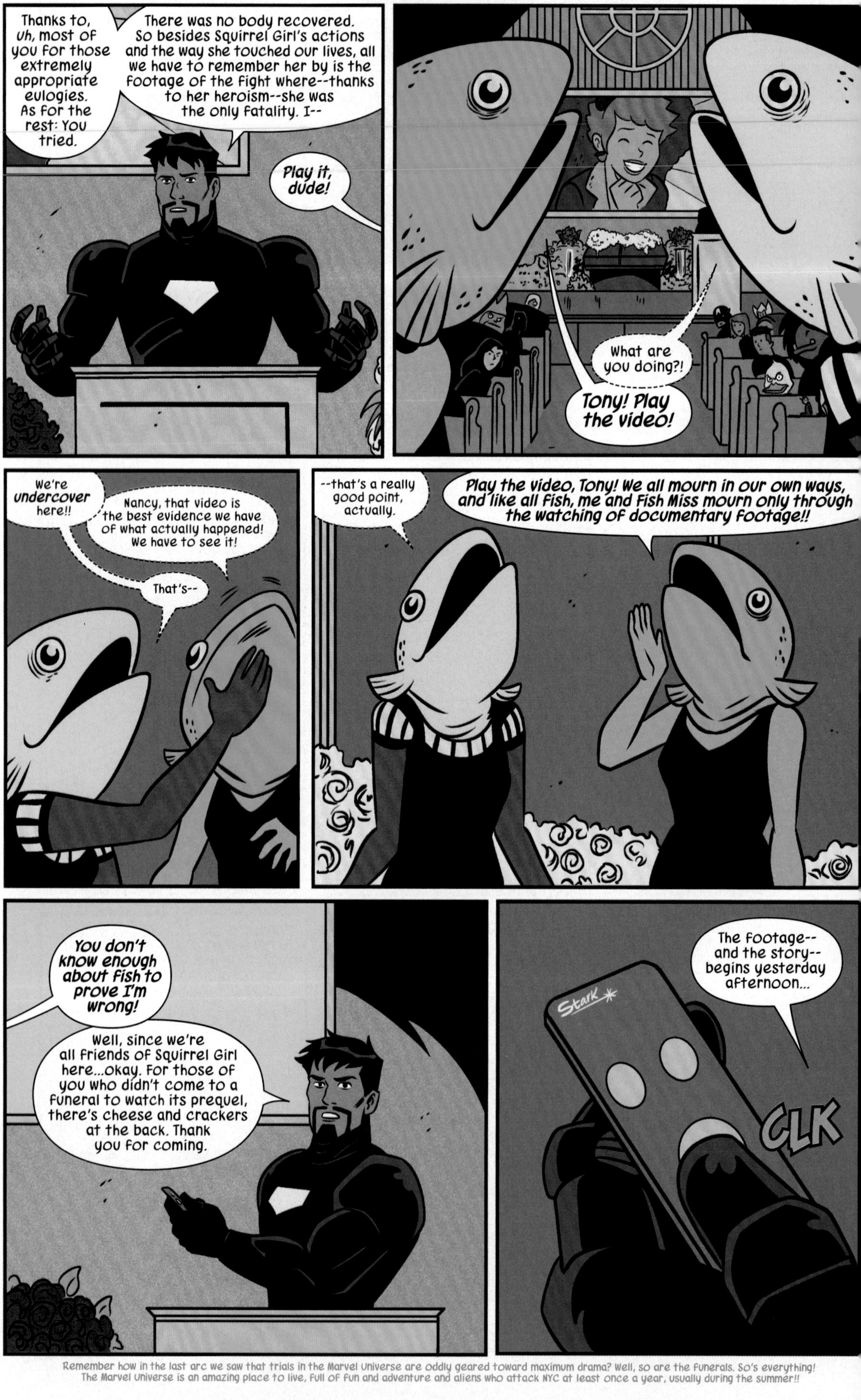

Thanks to, uh, most of you for those extremely appropriate eulogies. As for the rest: You tried.
There was no body recovered. So besides Squirrel Girl's actions and the way she touched our lives, all we have to remember her by is the footage of the fight where--thanks to her heroism--she was the only fatality. I--
Play it, dude!
What are you doing?!
Tony! Play the video!
We're undercover here!!
Nancy, that video is the best evidence we have of what actually happened! We have to see it!
That's--
--that's a really good point, actually.
Play the video, Tony! We all mourn in our own ways, and like all fish, me and Fish Miss mourn only through the watching of documentary footage!!
You don't know enough about fish to prove I'm wrong!
Well, since we're all friends of Squirrel Girl here...okay. For those of you who didn't come to a funeral to watch its prequel, there's cheese and crackers at the back. Thank you for coming.
Stark
The footage--and the story--begins yesterday afternoon...
CLK

Remember how in the last arc we saw that trials in the Marvel Universe are oddly geared toward maximum drama? Well, so are the funerals. So's everything! The Marvel Universe is an amazing place to live, full of fun and adventure and aliens who attack NYC at least once a year, usually during the summer!!

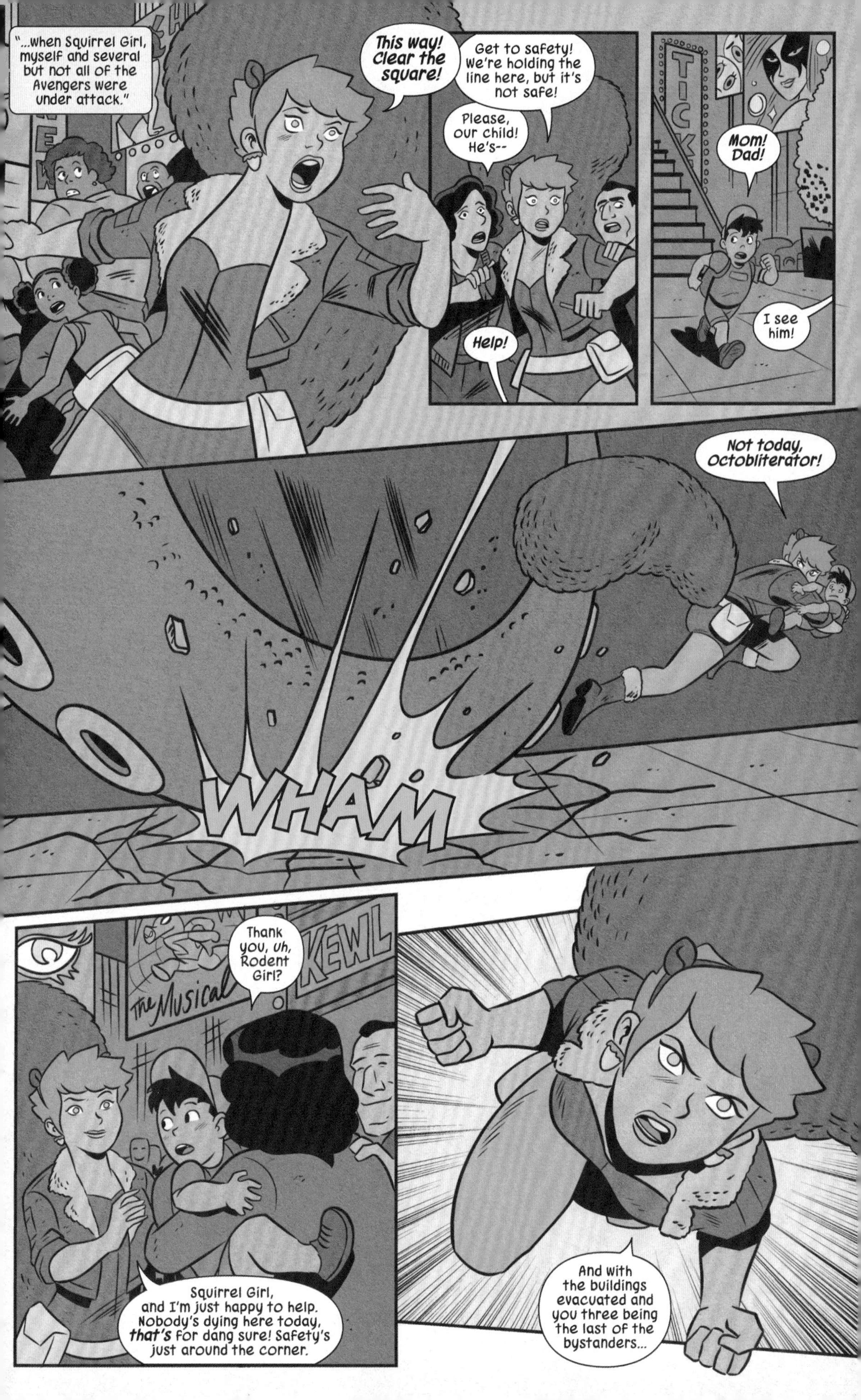

"...when Squirrel Girl, myself and several but not all of the Avengers were under attack."
This way! Clear the square!
Get to safety! We're holding the line here, but it's not safe!
Please, our child! He's--
Help!
Mom! Dad!
I see him!
Not today, Octobliterator!
WHAM
Thank you, uh, Rodent Girl?
KEWL
The Musical
Squirrel Girl, and I'm just happy to help. Nobody's dying here today, *that's* for dang sure! Safety's just around the corner.
And with the buildings evacuated and you three being the last of the bystanders...

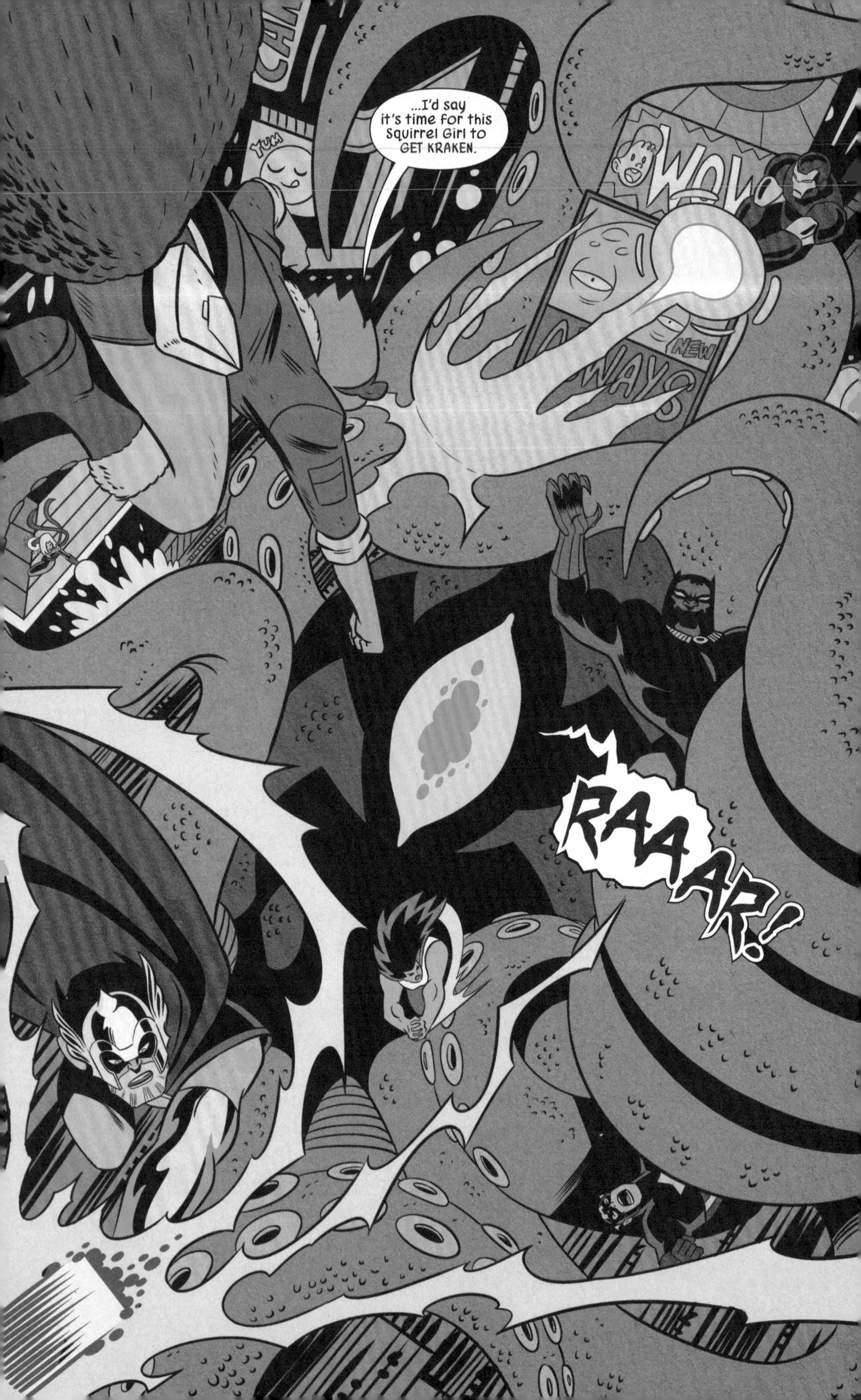
...I'd say it's time for this Squirrel Girl to GET KRAKEN.
YUM
WOW
NEW
WAYS
RAAAR!

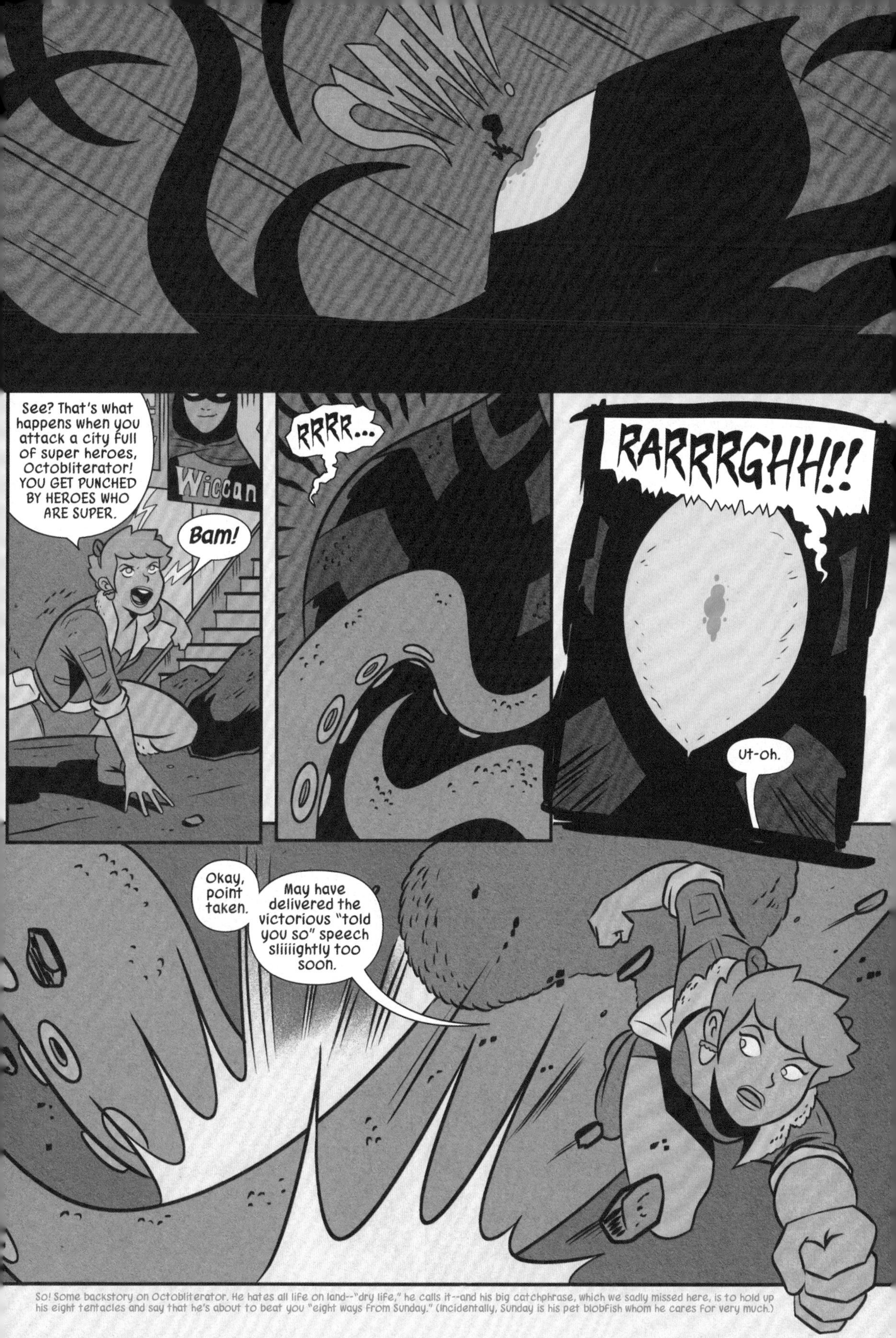
See? That's what happens when you attack a city full of super heroes, Octobliterator! YOU GET PUNCHED BY HEROES WHO ARE SUPER.
Wiccan
Bam!
RRRR...
RARRRGHH!!
Ut-oh.
Okay, point taken.
May have delivered the victorious "told you so" speech sliiiightly too soon.

So! Some backstory on Octobliterator. He hates all life on land--"dry life," he calls it--and his big catchphrase, which we sadly missed here, is to hold up his eight tentacles and say that he's about to beat you "eight ways from Sunday." (Incidentally, Sunday is his pet blobfish whom he cares for very much.)

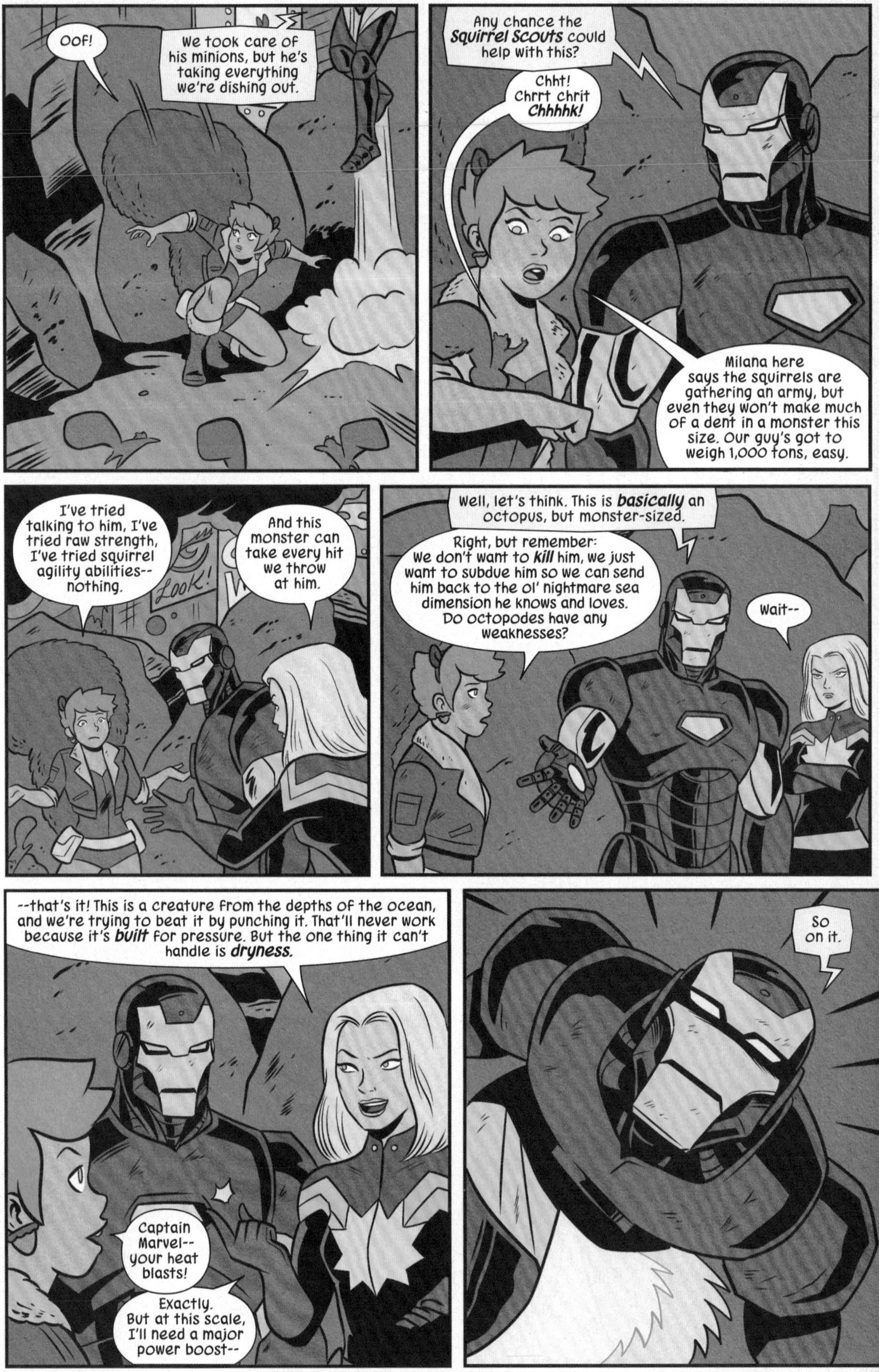
Oof!
We took care of his minions, but he's taking everything we're dishing out.
Any chance the ***Squirrel Scouts*** could help with this?
Chht! Chrrt chrit ***Chhhhk!***
Milana here says the squirrels are gathering an army, but even they won't make much of a dent in a monster this size. Our guy's got to weigh 1,000 tons, easy.
I've tried talking to him, I've tried raw strength, I've tried squirrel agility abilities--nothing.
And this monster can take every hit we throw at him.
Well, let's think. This is ***basically*** an octopus, but monster-sized.
Right, but remember: We don't want to ***kill*** him, we just want to subdue him so we can send him back to the ol' nightmare sea dimension he knows and loves. Do octopodes have any weaknesses?
Wait--
--that's it! This is a creature from the depths of the ocean, and we're trying to beat it by punching it. That'll never work because it's ***built*** for pressure. But the one thing it can't handle is ***dryness.***
Captain Marvel--your heat blasts!
Exactly. But at this scale, I'll need a major power boost--
So on it.

Oh! Also, Sunday is secretly evil, and ***he's*** the one who originally convinced Octobliterator to hate all surface life and to change his name from "Quiet Harold" to ***"Octobliterator."*** Poor Octobliterator--he just fell in with the wrong crowd! And now he's in...***deep.***

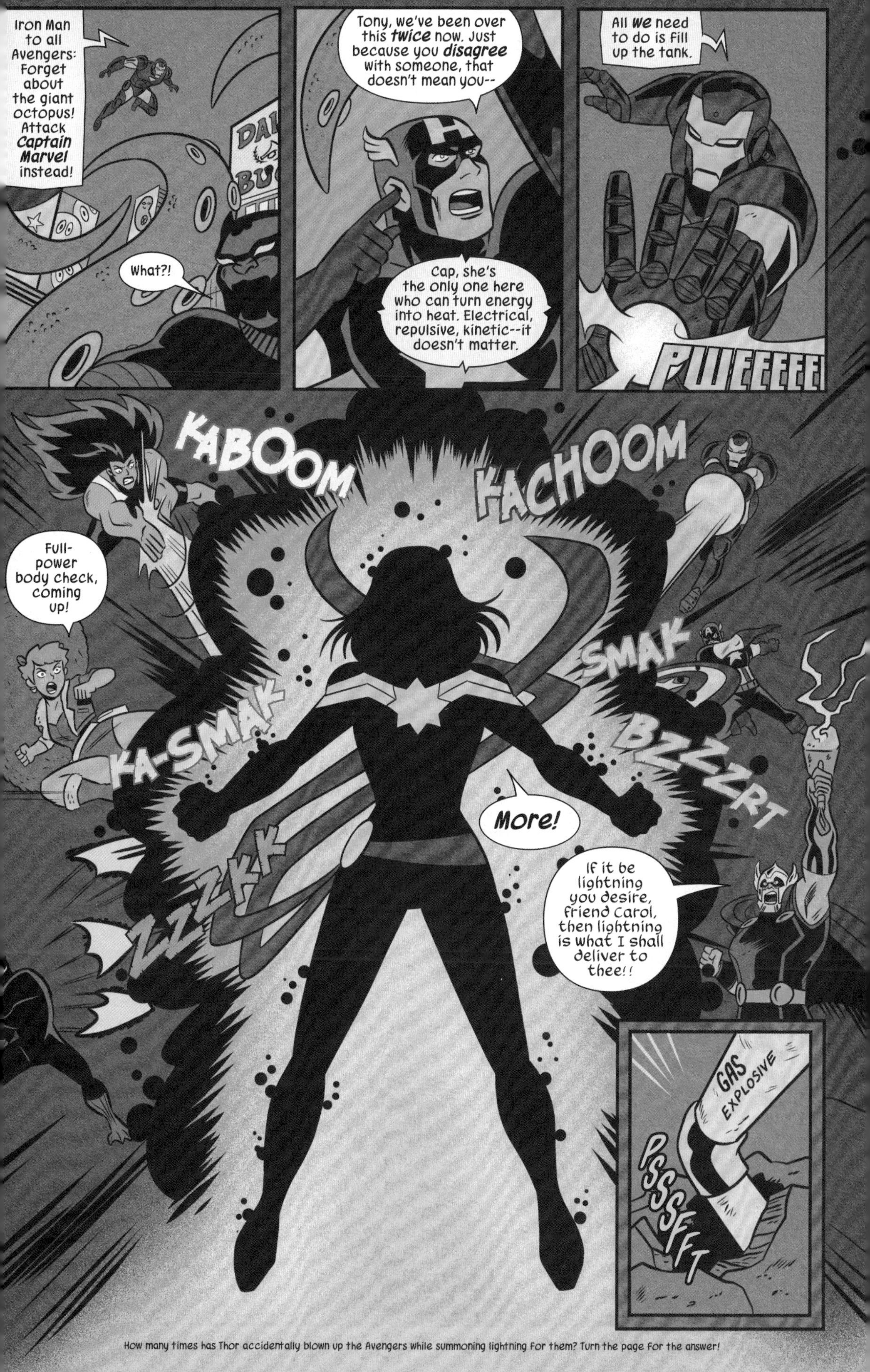
Iron Man to all Avengers: Forget about the giant octopus! Attack Captain Marvel instead!
What?!
Tony, we've been over this twice now. Just because you disagree with someone, that doesn't mean you--
Cap, she's the only one here who can turn energy into heat. Electrical, repulsive, kinetic--it doesn't matter.
All we need to do is fill up the tank.
PWEEEEE
KABOOM
KACHOOM
Full-power body check, coming up!
SMAK
KA-SMAK
BZZZZRT
More!
ZZZZKK
If it be lightning you desire, friend Carol, then lightning is what I shall deliver to thee!!
GAS
EXPLOSIVE
PSSSFFT

How many times has Thor accidentally blown up the Avengers while summoning lightning for them? Turn the page for the answer!

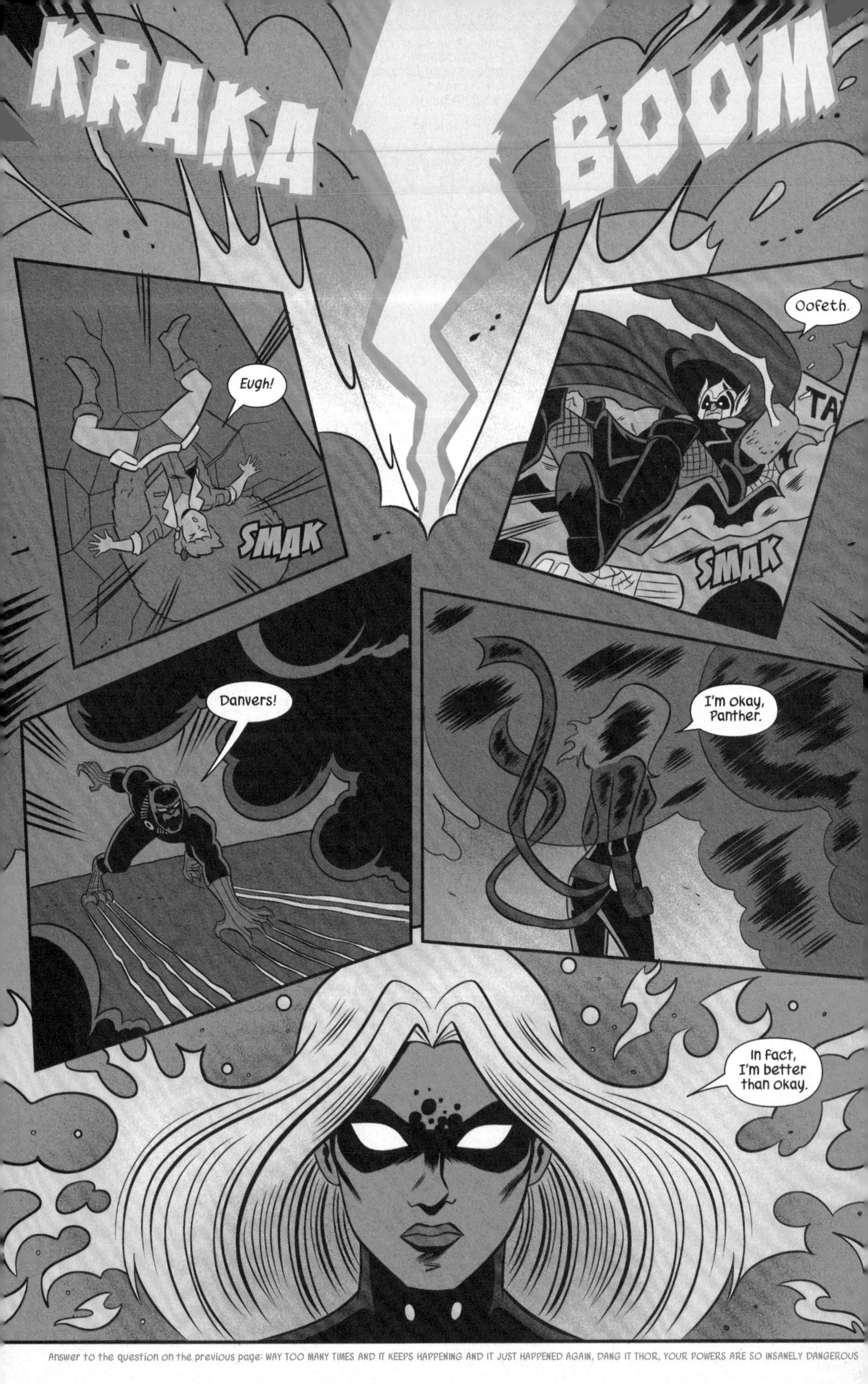
KRAKA
BOOM
Eugh!
SMAK
Oofeth.
SMAK
Danvers!
I'm okay, Panther.
In fact, I'm better than okay.

Answer to the question on the previous page: WAY TOO MANY TIMES AND IT KEEPS HAPPENING AND IT JUST HAPPENED AGAIN, DANG IT THOR, YOUR POWERS ARE SO INSANELY DANGEROUS

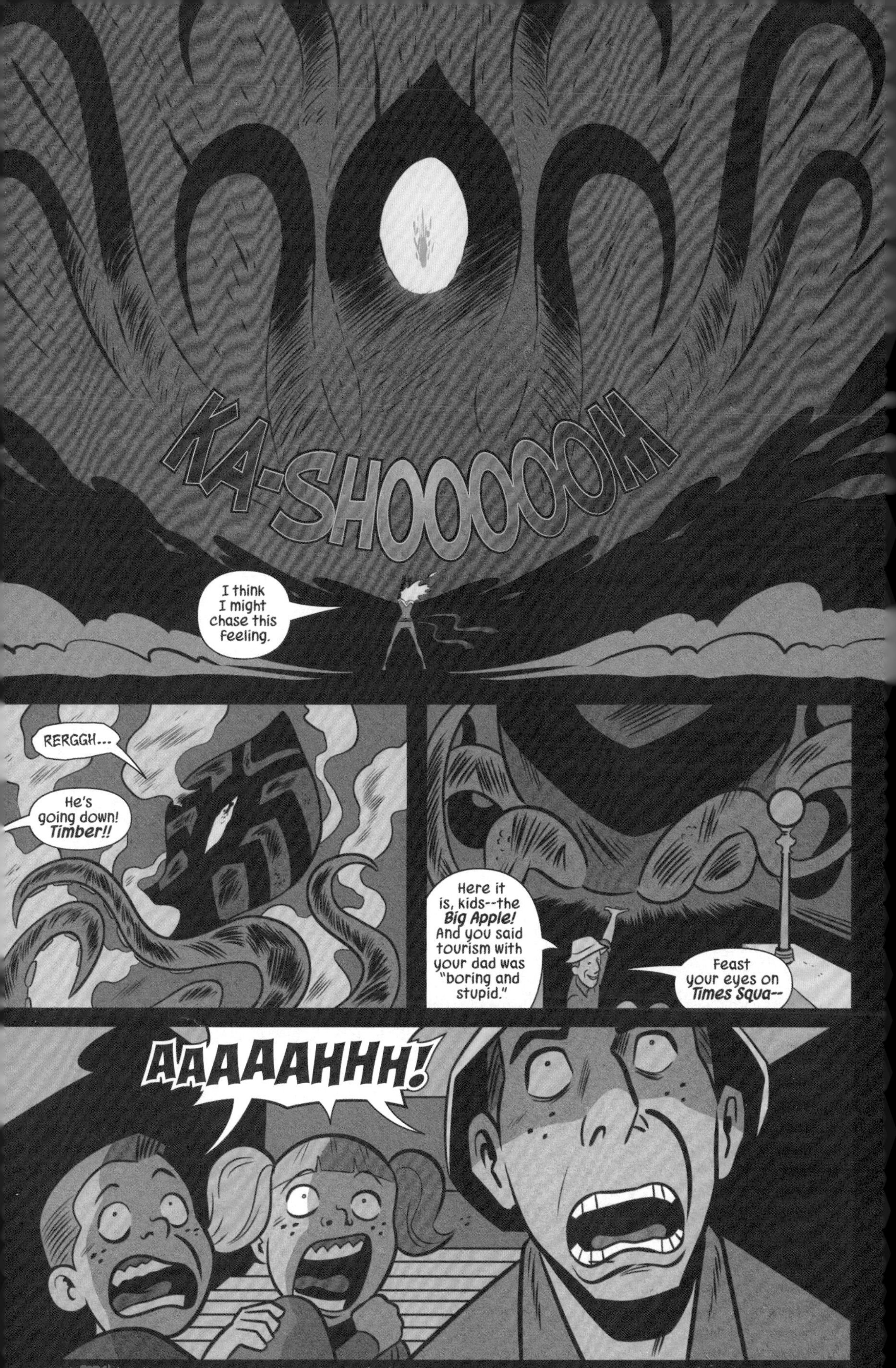
KA-SHOOOOOOM
I think I might chase this feeling.
RERGGH...
He's going down! Timber!!
Here it is, kids--the Big Apple! And you said tourism with your dad was "boring and stupid."
Feast your eyes on Times Squa--
AAAAAHHH!

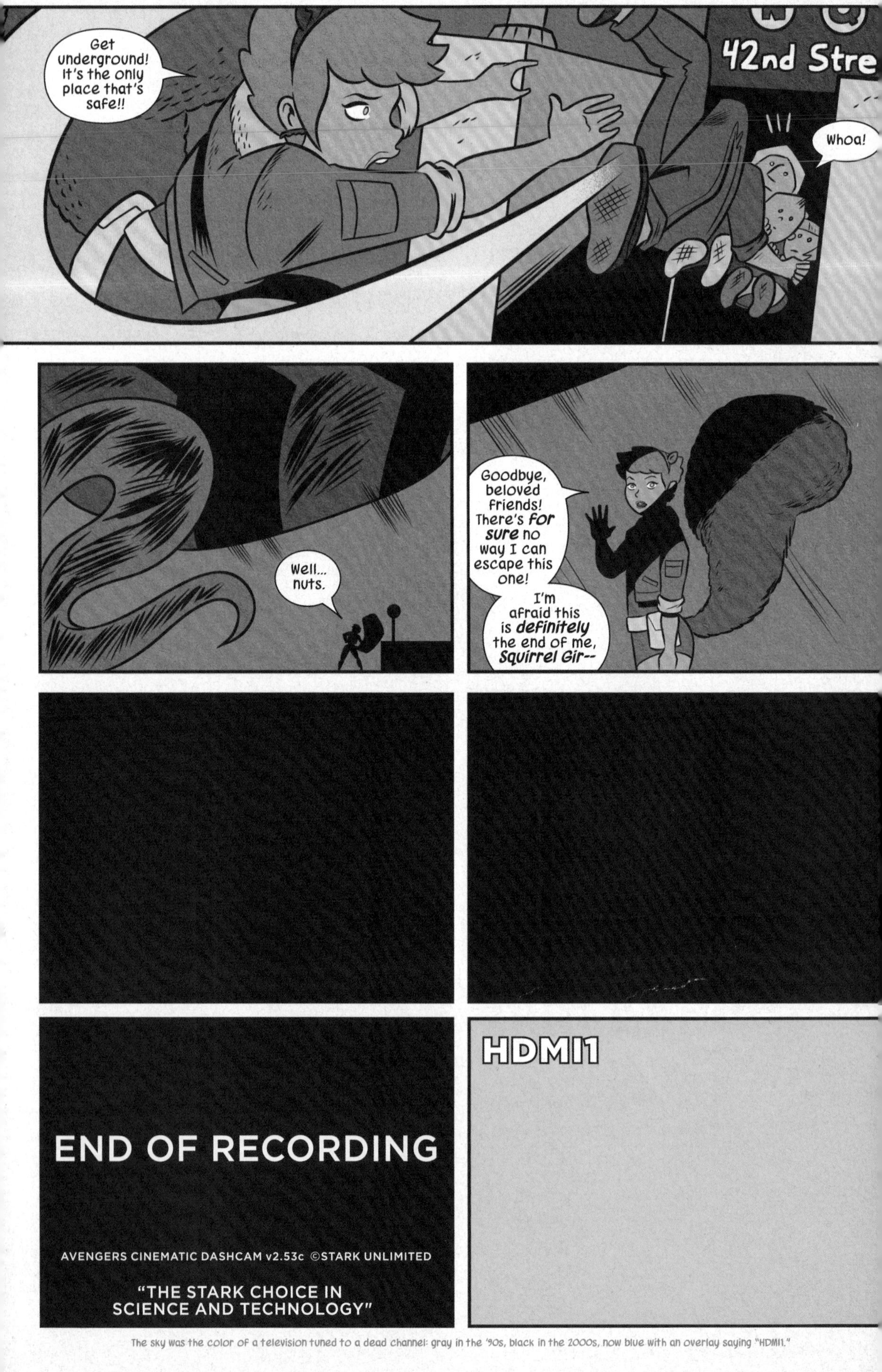
Get underground! It's the only place that's safe!!
42nd Stre
Whoa!
Well... nuts.
Goodbye, beloved friends! There's *for sure* no way I can escape this one!
I'm afraid this is *definitely* the end of me, *Squirrel Gir--*
END OF RECORDING
AVENGERS CINEMATIC DASHCAM v2.53c ©STARK UNLIMITED
“THE STARK CHOICE IN SCIENCE AND TECHNOLOGY”
HDMI1

The sky was the color of a television tuned to a dead channel: gray in the '90s, black in the 2000s, now blue with an overlay saying "HDMI1."

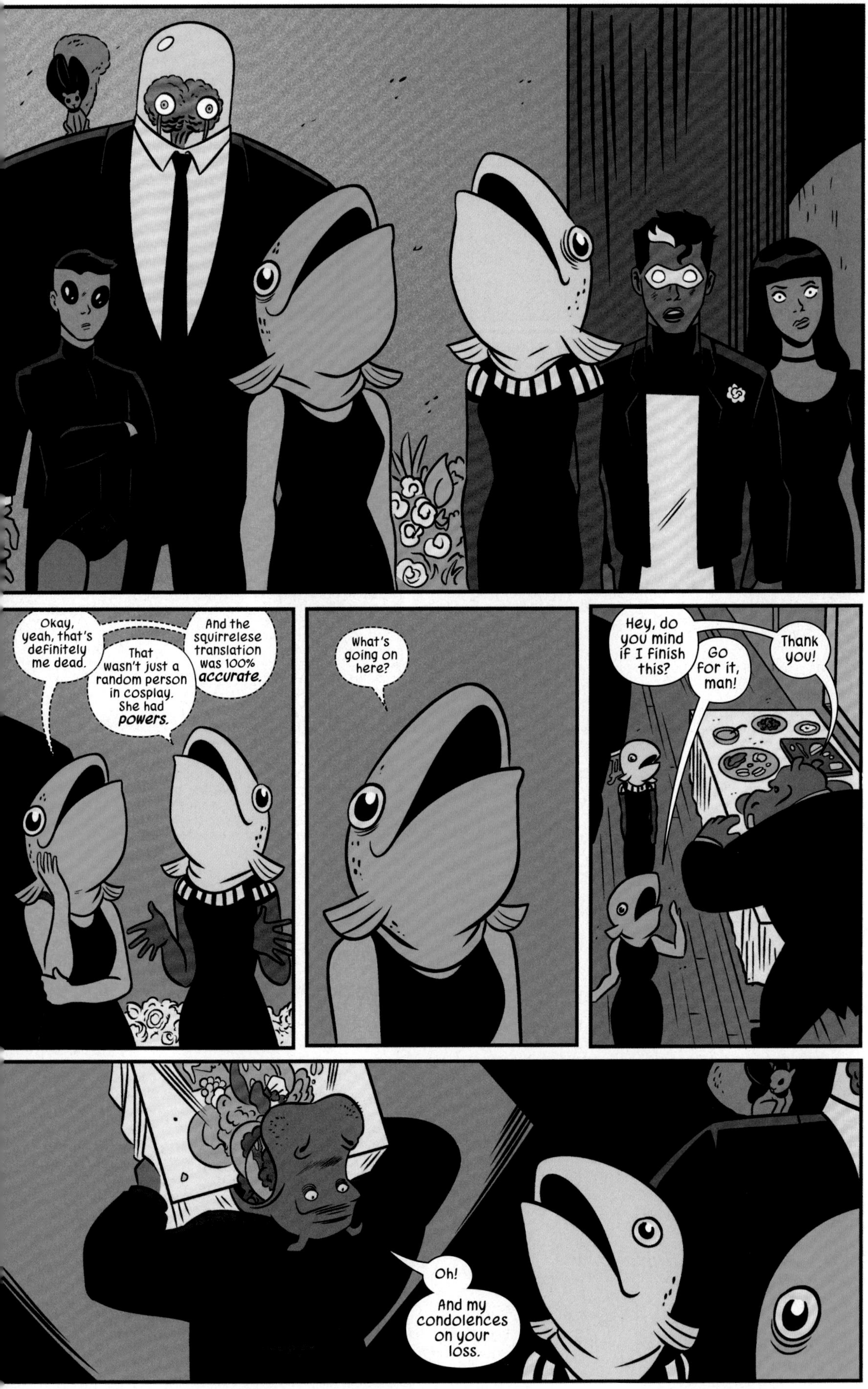

Okay, yeah, that's definitely me dead.
That wasn't just a random person in cosplay. She had *powers.*
And the squirrelese translation was 100% *accurate.*
What's going on here?
Hey, do you mind if I finish this?
Go for it, man!
Thank you!
Oh!
And my condolences on your loss.

I, Ryan, also operate under Hippo's theory: If food is going to go to waste, ***especially*** in a buffet situation, then it's absolutely ethical to gobble it. A perhaps not-unrelated anecdote: Watching me eat the scraps off of other friends' plates at breakfast, a friend once described me as "the place where food goes to die."

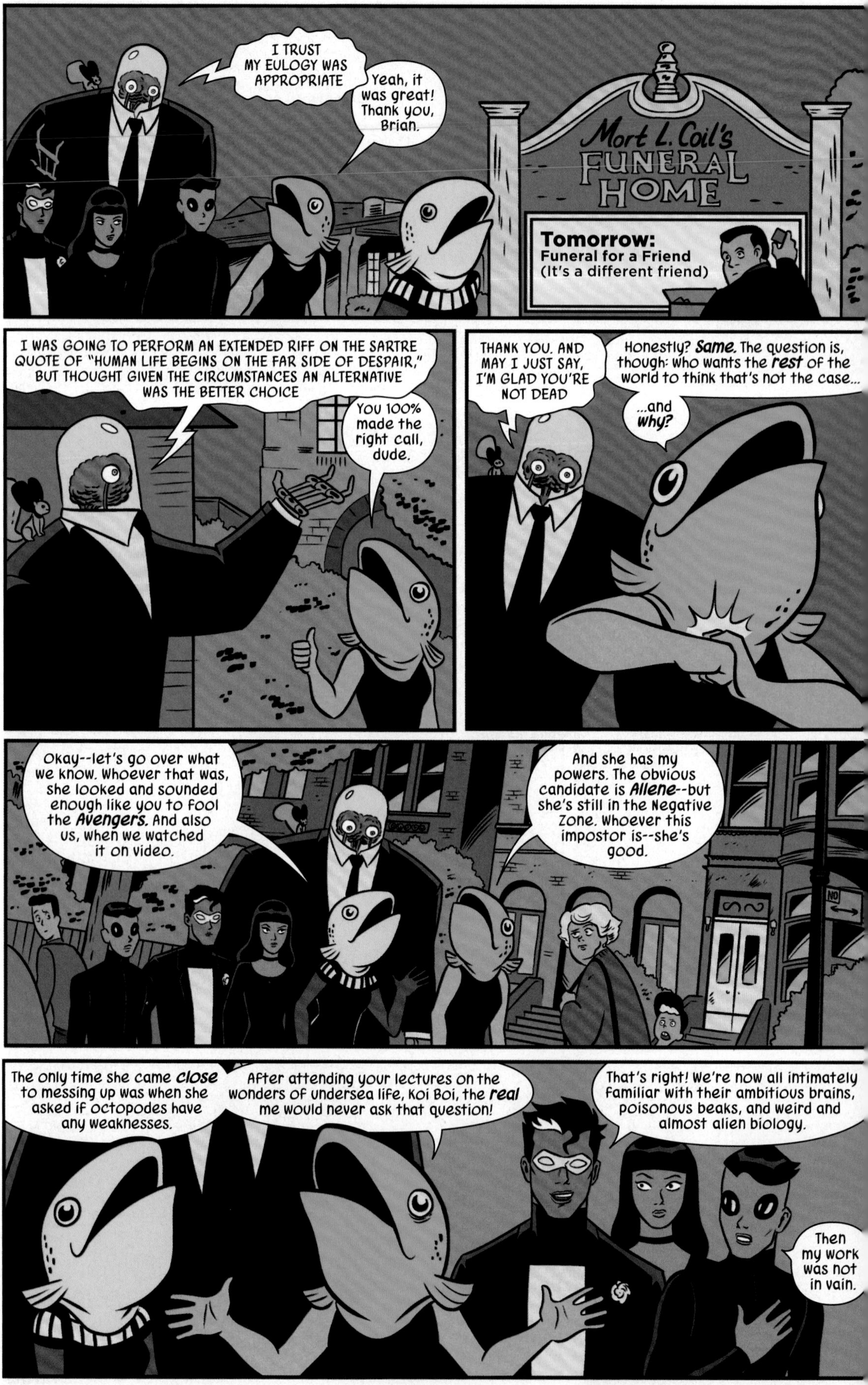
I TRUST MY EULOGY WAS APPROPRIATE
Yeah, it was great! Thank you, Brian.
Mort L. Coil's FUNERAL HOME
Tomorrow: Funeral for a Friend (It's a different friend)
I WAS GOING TO PERFORM AN EXTENDED RIFF ON THE SARTRE QUOTE OF "HUMAN LIFE BEGINS ON THE FAR SIDE OF DESPAIR," BUT THOUGHT GIVEN THE CIRCUMSTANCES AN ALTERNATIVE WAS THE BETTER CHOICE
You 100% made the right call, dude.
THANK YOU. AND MAY I JUST SAY, I'M GLAD YOU'RE NOT DEAD
Honestly? *Same.* The question is, though: who wants the *rest* of the world to think that's not the case...
...and *why?*
Okay--let's go over what we know. Whoever that was, she looked and sounded enough like you to fool the *Avengers.* And also us, when we watched it on video.
And she has my powers. The obvious candidate is *Allene*--but she's still in the Negative Zone. Whoever this impostor is--she's good.
NO
The only time she came *close* to messing up was when she asked if octopodes have any weaknesses.
After attending your lectures on the wonders of undersea life, Koi Boi, the *real* me would never ask that question!
That's right! We're now all intimately familiar with their ambitious brains, poisonous beaks, and weird and almost alien biology.
Then my work was not in vain.

I CAN ALSO DISCOURSE ON "WE DO NOT KNOW WHAT WE WANT AND YET WE ARE RESPONSIBLE FOR WHAT WE ARE" AT SOME POINT IN THE FUTURE. TO BE HONEST, I AM JUST WAITING FOR AN EXCU

But all that tells us is that it wasn't *really* you who died, which everyone who knows Doreen Green already knows.

COULD IT BE A ROBOT DUPLICATE?

But why build an android me just to kill her? And Tony would've detected that anyway--the heat signature would be all wrong.

That rules out hard-light simulations too.

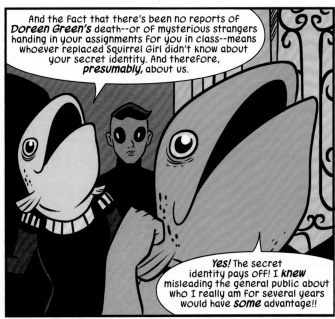

And the fact that there's been no reports of *Doreen Green's* death--or of mysterious strangers handing in your assignments for you in class--means whoever replaced Squirrel Girl didn't *know* about your secret identity. And therefore, *presumably*, about us.

Yes! The secret identity pays off! I *knew* misleading the general public about who I really am for several years would have *some* advantage!!

So our suspect is someone who knows you well enough to perfectly duplicate Squirrel Girl, but *not* well enough to even *know* about Doreen Green.

That doesn't really suggest anyone to me. *Hm.*

Me neither. And the thing I can't get past is how my *powers* were duplicated.

But if it's not me...

AND IT'S NOT A ROBOT...

And it's not a clone...

And it's not a simulacrum...

Oh *dang.* Of course! I should've seen it sooner.

Friends, whoever's impersonating me can only be *one thing*...

CONTINUED NEXT MONTH! Naw, I'm kidding, we wouldn't end the comic on such an unfair cliffhanger! We'll give you another page and end it on a more fair but still conceptually adjacent cliffhanger instead!

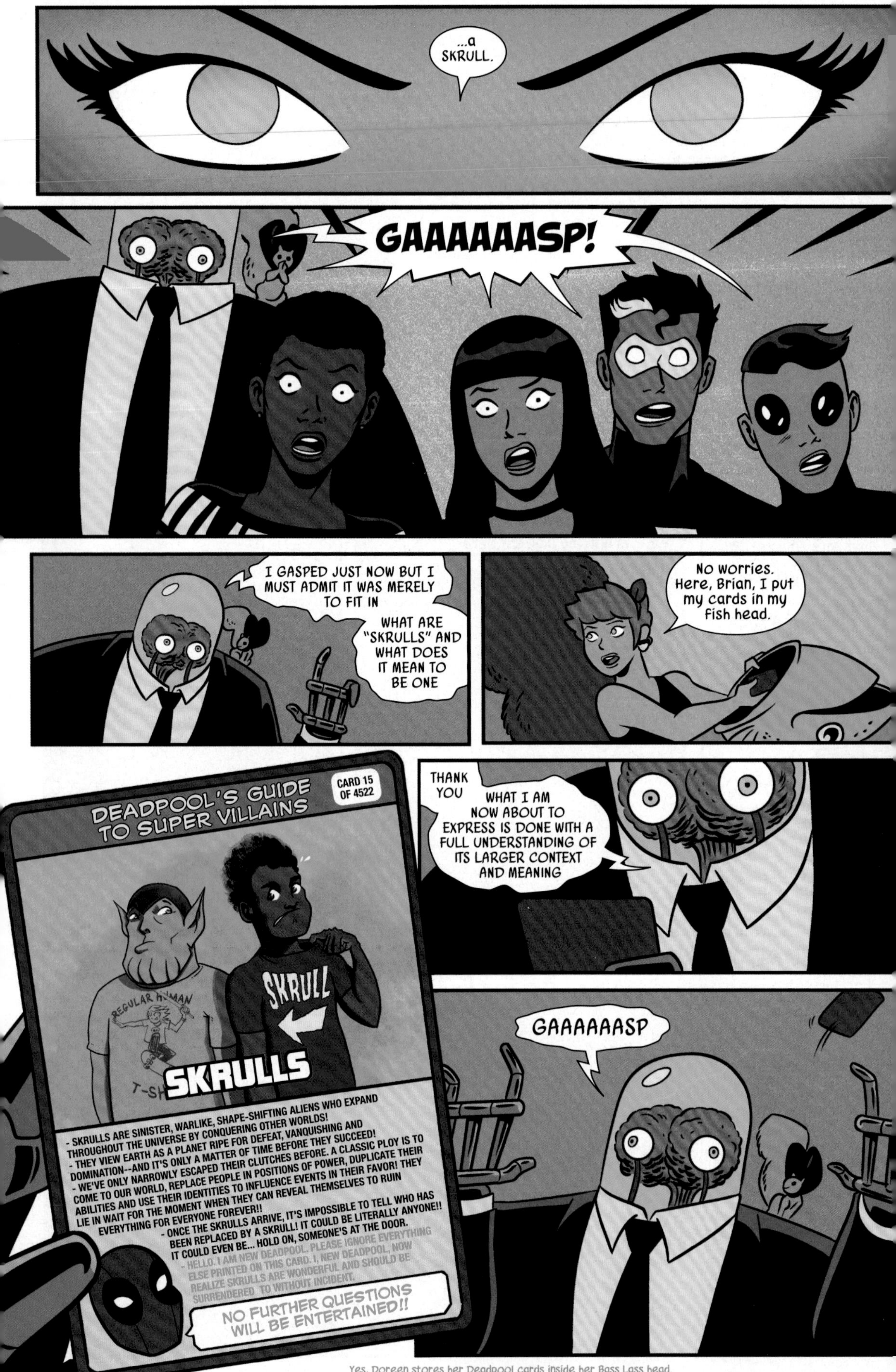
...a SKRULL.
GAAAAAASP!
I GASPED JUST NOW BUT I MUST ADMIT IT WAS MERELY TO FIT IN
WHAT ARE "SKRULLS" AND WHAT DOES IT MEAN TO BE ONE
No worries. Here, Brian, I put my cards in my fish head.
DEADPOOL'S GUIDE TO SUPER VILLAINS
CARD 15 OF 4522
REGULAR HUMAN
SKRULL
SKRULLS
- SKRULLS ARE SINISTER, WARLIKE, SHAPE-SHIFTING ALIENS WHO EXPAND THROUGHOUT THE UNIVERSE BY CONQUERING OTHER WORLDS!
- THEY VIEW EARTH AS A PLANET RIPE FOR DEFEAT, VANQUISHING AND DOMINATION--AND IT'S ONLY A MATTER OF TIME BEFORE THEY SUCCEED!
- WE'VE ONLY NARROWLY ESCAPED THEIR CLUTCHES BEFORE. A CLASSIC PLOY IS TO COME TO OUR WORLD, REPLACE PEOPLE IN POSITIONS OF POWER, DUPLICATE THEIR ABILITIES AND USE THEIR IDENTITIES TO INFLUENCE EVENTS IN THEIR FAVOR! THEY LIE IN WAIT FOR THE MOMENT WHEN THEY CAN REVEAL THEMSELVES TO RUIN EVERYTHING FOR EVERYONE FOREVER!!
- ONCE THE SKRULLS ARRIVE, IT'S IMPOSSIBLE TO TELL WHO HAS BEEN REPLACED BY A SKRULL! IT COULD BE LITERALLY ANYONE!! IT COULD EVEN BE... HOLD ON, SOMEONE'S AT THE DOOR.
- HELLO. I AM NEW DEADPOOL. PLEASE IGNORE EVERYTHING ELSE PRINTED ON THIS CARD. I, NEW DEADPOOL, NOW REALIZE SKRULLS ARE WONDERFUL AND SHOULD BE SURRENDERED TO WITHOUT INCIDENT.
NO FURTHER QUESTIONS WILL BE ENTERTAINED!!
THANK YOU
WHAT I AM NOW ABOUT TO EXPRESS IS DONE WITH A FULL UNDERSTANDING OF ITS LARGER CONTEXT AND MEANING
GAAAAAASP

Yes, Doreen stores her Deadpool cards inside her Bass Lass head.
It's cavernous and Bass Lass' outfit doesn't come with a belt! You gotta make do with what you got!

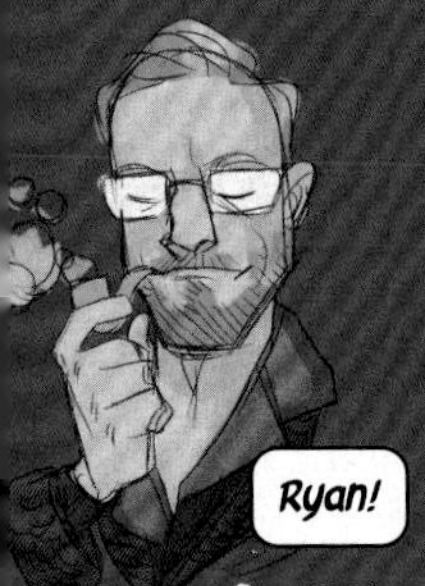

Ryan!

Letters From Nuts

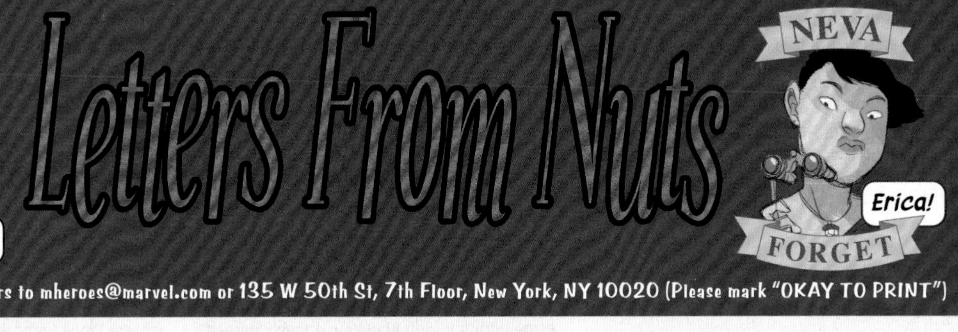

NEVA
Erica!
FORGET

Send letters to mheroes@marvel.com or 135 W 50th St, 7th Floor, New York, NY 10020 (Please mark "OKAY TO PRINT")

Hello there! I very much enjoy your marvelous comic with its increasingly tortuous puns (which just sound peculiar to me because around here we pronounce "squirrel" to rhyme with "Cyril"). I've introduced my sister and nieces to it (hello, Louise, Nieve, Amy and Lucy!). I feel USG isn't just funny and charming; it also has a laudable and healthy approach for young readers. For instance, the Mole Man story wasn't just whimsically hilarious but also had something to say about Doreen's self-determination.

You exceeded yourselves with issue #31. I'm sure I wasn't the only person choking up at "you're not getting rid of me that easily"...

My good wishes to Ryan and to Erica for her sterling and delightful work!

Now for the ridiculous part... I went to a fancy dress party recently, the theme of which was "Literary Heroes." Of course, Brain Drain was the only possible choice. You'll be pleased that I was indeed recognized (by Winston Smith from *1984*).

More power to your cerebellums and I look forward to reading what's next!

John Callaghan
London

P.S. "Cerebella" seemed pretentious and wasn't recognized by my spell-checker anyway.

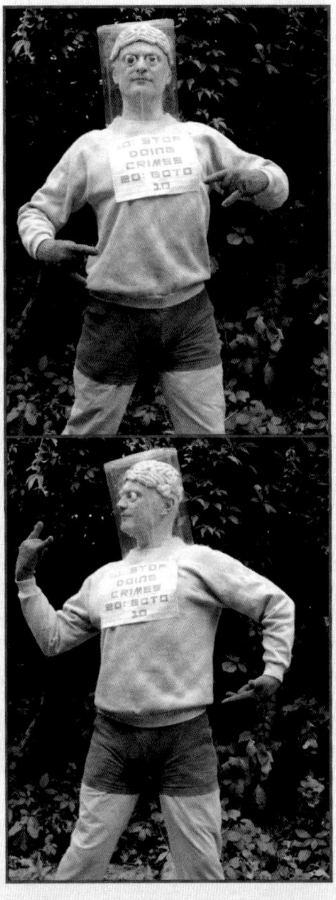

RYAN: I think the best thing about Brain Drain (okay, ONE of the best things about Brain Drain) is this costume. It's somehow so great, so insane and so Brian Drayne. It's PERFECT, John, and there is no greater literary hero. One time I went to a "good vs. evil" party and I dressed as half Bruce Banner, half Hulk. Basically I just cut up half of my clothes, covered half my body in green makeup, and messed up half my hair. I recommend this costume to those who find themselves in similar circumstances. Also: Hello, Louise, Nieve, Amy and Lucy! Your names are in a comic book now!

Dear Justice Pals,

Now that convention season is finally winding down--it is never over--I had the time to finish the Ryan and Erica figures Ms. Henderson requested. I want to point out that Little Plastic Ryan is in fact "freakishly tall," but Little Plastic Erica is wearing platforms under that dress.

On a complete unrelated note, I am glad to see that Kraven is still trying to work on being a better man. I am just sorry to see that he has once again fallen into the trap of trying to be a better SPIDER-man, rather than the better Sergei. He needs to do what he does best, hunting poachers. Or robots. Or robot poachers!

Until next month, keep eating nuts and kicking butts! And using existential angst to stop super hero fights!

Sincerely,

David Oakes
Chandler, AZ
Age 48

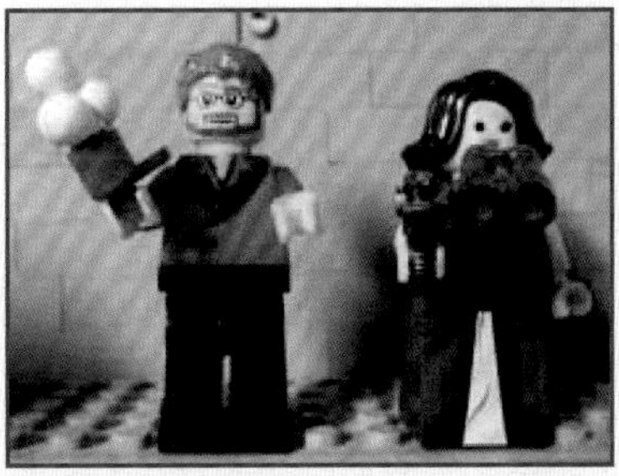

RYAN: David, these are AMAZING, and I love that they're not just us in LEGO form, but us as rendered in the letters page in LEGO form! I've got my bubble pipe, Erica's got her opera glasses, and we are READY for a night on the town. Thank you so much!! As for Kraven--I think (assuming you caught the verrrrry last page of that story after this letter was sent in!) that you'll agree he's on a path to becoming something that is, at its core, Very Kraven!

Dear Ryan and Erica,

I saw Squirrel Girl and instantly got her comics. I've collected ALL of her collections. I have a request: Please please PLEASE make a crossover with Ms. Marvel (Kamala Khan). She's also in *Lego Marvel Super Heroes 2* in a level with Koi Boi and Chipmunk Hunk. Also, I saw the COSMIC GHOST RIDER with Howard the Duck AND Ms. Marvel. To wrap up this email, I hope Nancy Whitehead and Squirrel Girl will fight crime together and be BFFs until time's end.

Sincerely,
Armyn Carpenter

RYAN: Armyn, thank you! As for the crossover--YOU ARE IN LUCK, because the MARVEL RISING comic is out now and features Squirrel Girl and Ms. Marvel teaming up! Also: There's a cartoon coming out very soon--you can watch an intro on YouTube--that is ALSO called *Marvel Rising* (thanks, corporate synergy!) and ALSO features Doreen and Kamala! So your wish is coming true EVEN AS WE SPEAK. Erica and I were super thrilled to see Team Doreen in *Lego Marvel Super Heroes 2* and I'm glad they got to save the day. As for Nancy and Doreen fighting crime together and being BFFs together until time's end: You got it!!

My favorite Squirrel Squad,

I used to live in a much sadder world where I did not name random squirrels I see on my walks. A time where I could not randomly yell "fun fact!" and tell those around me about how many different species of squirrels there are. Now I live in a much brighter place where all of these things happen. A world where my friends (shameless name drop) Chris and Sarah's 5-year-old daughter Mattie asks me to dress up as Squirrel Girl for her birthday party--a party where absolutely no one else wore a costume. My tail and ears prompted lots of conversation. I can only hope I would make Doreen Green proud. Thank you for making a story come to life that's brilliant for us 20-somethings and 5-year-olds alike.

Cyndi Kennerson
West Gardiner, ME

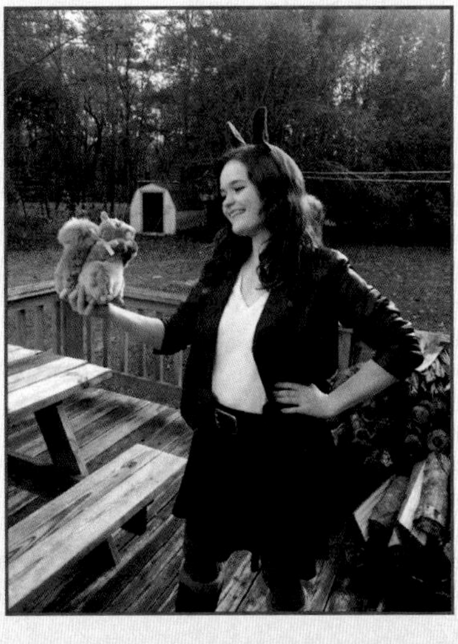

RYAN: CYNDI, WHAT A GREAT COSTUME, and what a great thing to do for Mattie! Though honestly, being the only one dressed as a super hero at a 5-year-old's birthday party sounds GREAT. You will absolutely be the center of attention and will for sure have lots of kids wanting to be around you and/or be you. I may just have to steal that move for the next 5-year-old's party I attend!

Is Doreen Green a mutant? I mean, she used to an unofficial member of the X-Men. When will the 2018 Great Lake Avengers comic come out?

Gajeena Rajeswaran
Scarborough, Ontario

RYAN: Hi, Gajeena--I live in Toronto, which is RIGHT BESIDE Scarborough, and I have been to your beautiful sandy cliffs. Here is a picture of me there as proof, so you know I'm not...bluffing.

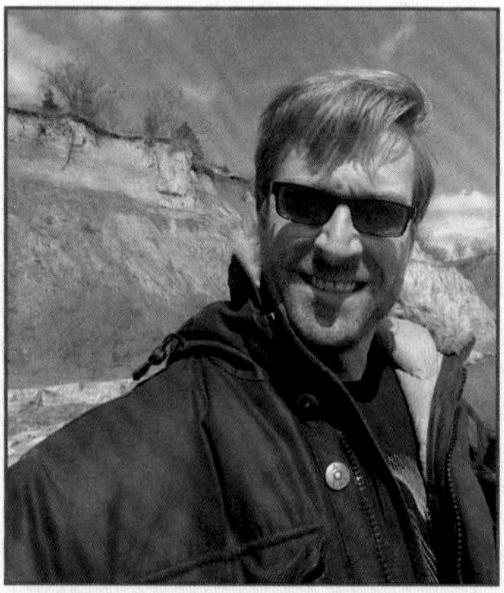

Now to the questions! Doreen Green is similar but legally distinct from a mutant, though she used to think she was one. And if you're talking about Zac Gorman and Will Robson's run on GREAT LAKES AVENGERS, that was collected in 2017! If there's ANOTHER Great Lakes Avengers comic you're talking about, then I am missing out and want to know when it's going to come out too.

Hello. My name is Simone Jenkins and I have just a few questions about some of the characters in the Marvel Universe.

1. Is the Ryan North who writes SQUIRREL GIRL the same Ryan North who did the *Dinosaur Comics* and is a friend of Andrew Hussie?

2. How is Loki the Sorcerer Supreme?

3. Does Peter Parker have ADHD?

3b. Can he have ADHD?

Thank you for taking the time to read my email.

P.S. I love Tom Holland's portrayal of Peter Parker and Spider-Man. He really has the whole "realistic teenage problems" thing going along with the supremely high IQ level.

RYAN: Hi Simone, I have answers for you! 1) Yes, I am the very same, and Andrew is a good friend who loaned me a painting of a muscley horse. 2) He won the role from Doctor Strange in a tournament of sorcerers! THIS IS WHY YOU SHOULDN'T GAMBLE. 3) I don't know! 3b) I don't know, why not!

Dear Ryan, Erica, Derek and Rico,

I've been reading SQUIRREL GIRL since your very first #1 after my friend Steve, who was working at Gosh! Comics in London at the time, suggested it to me as something I might enjoy. And boy was he right! Every issue since then has been a joy to read and guaranteed to make me laugh, a welcome relief among all those grim and gritty books out there. Doreen's compassion and positivity, even in the direst of situations, is infectious and it's refreshing to read about a hero who would rather talk through her problems, rather than hit them.

From the start, I was simply blown away by Erica's artwork, which felt fresh and unique from other comics on the shelves. Her sheer productivity was also inspirational to me as an artist, managing not only to consistently produce a 20-page comic month after month and cover art, but also somehow manage to draw and color an entire OGN alongside that already hefty workload! And so when it was suddenly announced that #31 was going to be Erica's last issue as artist, I felt genuinely sad that the two of you would no longer be working together to produce my favorite comic. Issue #31 was a fantastic swansong to your and Erica's run, and for a while I thought about dropping off the title too. Eventually #32 hit the shelves, and my desire for more Squirrel Girl and your writing won out. Reading through Doreen and the gang's adventures in the Escape Room, I couldn't believe I'd really thought about dropping the book.

Fast-forward a few months and after reading issue #34, can I just say that I am really loving Derek Charm's work on this book. There were just so many wonderful moments in that issue and genuinely funny visual moments that I felt like he was really making his mark on my favorite title. Around the same time, I also started re-reading from #1 and with it came the realization that Erica's work too had grown in leaps and bounds during her run on this book, and her work in #1 was very different to where she ended up in #31. With that in mind, I'm very excited to see how Derek's artwork will develop, and hope that he'll be sticking around on this book for the foreseeable future!

Talking about the arc in general, I love the dynamic between Doreen's circle of friends, and giving Kraven a more prominent role among that grouping was genius! I'd love an entire issue of Kraven and Brian discussing Russian philosophy...and fighting crime! And I got a huge kick out of seeing a genuine in-continuity Uncle Ben/Uncle Ben's reference from Spider-Man! Speaking of Spider-Man, another thing that I've loved about this book right from the start is how much it reflects the actual Marvel Universe! Thankfully without being constantly tied in to whatever crossover event is doing the rounds at the time, the regular appearances from various characters from all corners of the Marvel Universe make this feel like one of the best depictions of what it would be like to live in a world where you could end up bumping into Howard the Duck at an Escape Room and have She-Hulk as your lawyer. Doreen often feels like the true epicenter of the Marvel Universe, and I look forward to seeing who she runs into next.

Finally, it's also worth mentioning that while it might be Squirrel Girl's name on the cover, this book definitely feels like an ensemble piece, and you've created a great cast of characters to star alongside Doreen. Nancy, Koi Boi, Chipmunk Hunk, Brain Drain and the rest all have great moments of their own in each issue, and aren't just relegated to voiceless sidekicks. The issue where Koi Boi, Chipmunk Hunk and Brain Drain were left to their own devices while Doreen and Nancy went on holiday was a great example, and I love how Nancy has taken more and more of a starring role alongside Doreen. Issue #31 really said a lot about their friendship and love for each other.

Anyway, I'll wrap it up now. There's probably lots more I could say about how much I love this book, but hopefully I can save that for when you eventually reach #100!

Thanks!

Paul Shinn
London, UK

P.S. Oh, one more thing! The last page of #35 when the Unhuntable Sergei stood atop a building with lighting in the background--was that a *Batman: The Animated Series* reference? Nice touch!

RYAN: Wow, thank you, Paul! This was amazing to read, and I really appreciate it. I think the best thing about doing creative work--no matter what the medium--is that you get better at it the more you do it, almost without even trying. I can't think of a single artist who has worked on something for a while and that thing they're producing hasn't improved. I hold fast to that idea when I think that I'm not as good as I could be. We're always learning, and we're all always getting better! I've never heard Squirrel Girl described as the true epicenter of the Marvel Universe, but that's a great compliment, and I will take it. Thank you!

As for your P.S.: I may have mentioned something precisely along those lines to Derek in the script.

Next Issue:

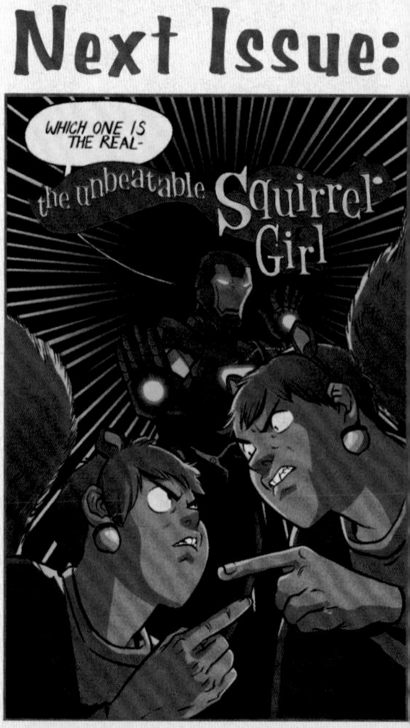
WHICH ONE IS THE REAL-
the unbeatable Squirrel Girl

Attention, Squirrel Scouts! Make sure to check out our production blog, **unbeatablesquirrelgirl.tumblr.com**, where we post behind-the-scenes stuff on how the book gets made, along with all sorts of cool things *you* make: fanart, cosplay, whatever!

Okay.

Let's go over what we know.

Not much. Someone replaced Squirrel Girl and then died, or at least made it look like that.

And they were probably a Skrull.

And if there was ONE Skrull around replacing people, it's overwhelmingly likely that there's others...

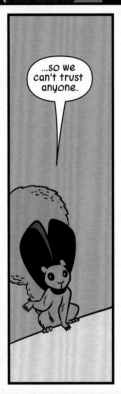

...so we can't trust anyone.

INCLUDING

(THOUGH I HESITATE TO SAY IT)

EACH OTHER

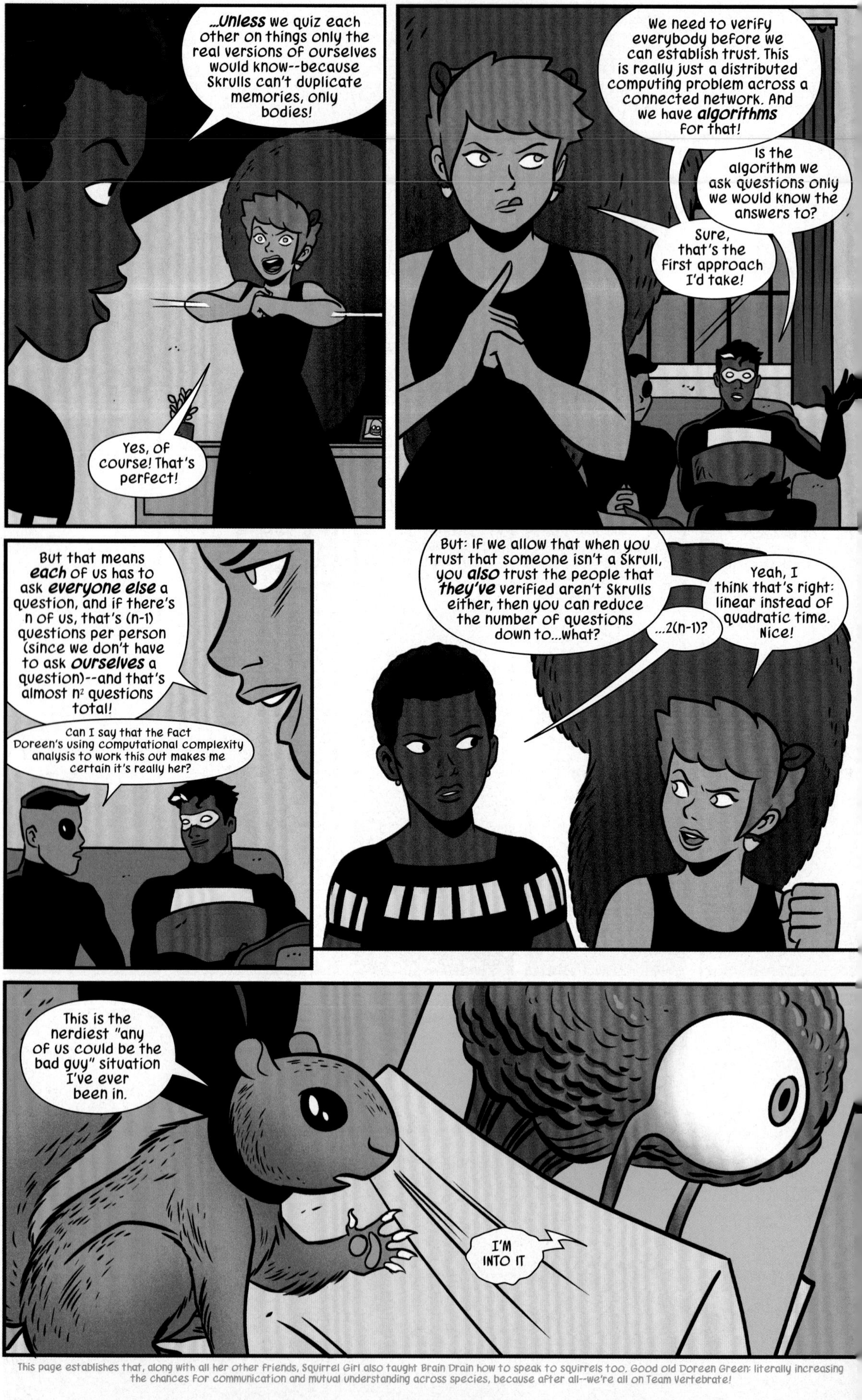
...Unless we quiz each other on things only the real versions of ourselves would know--because Skrulls can't duplicate memories, only bodies!
Yes, of course! That's perfect!
We need to verify everybody before we can establish trust. This is really just a distributed computing problem across a connected network. And we have algorithms for that!
Is the algorithm we ask questions only we would know the answers to?
Sure, that's the first approach I'd take!
But that means each of us has to ask everyone else a question, and if there's n of us, that's (n-1) questions per person (since we don't have to ask ourselves a question)--and that's almost n2 questions total!
Can I say that the fact Doreen's using computational complexity analysis to work this out makes me certain it's really her?
But: If we allow that when you trust that someone isn't a Skrull, you also trust the people that they've verified aren't Skrulls either, then you can reduce the number of questions down to...what?
...2(n-1)?
Yeah, I think that's right: linear instead of quadratic time. Nice!
This is the nerdiest "any of us could be the bad guy" situation I've ever been in.
I'M INTO IT

This page establishes that, along with all her other friends, Squirrel Girl also taught Brain Drain how to speak to squirrels too. Good old Doreen Green: literally increasing the chances for communication and mutual understanding across species, because after all--we're all on Team Vertebrate!

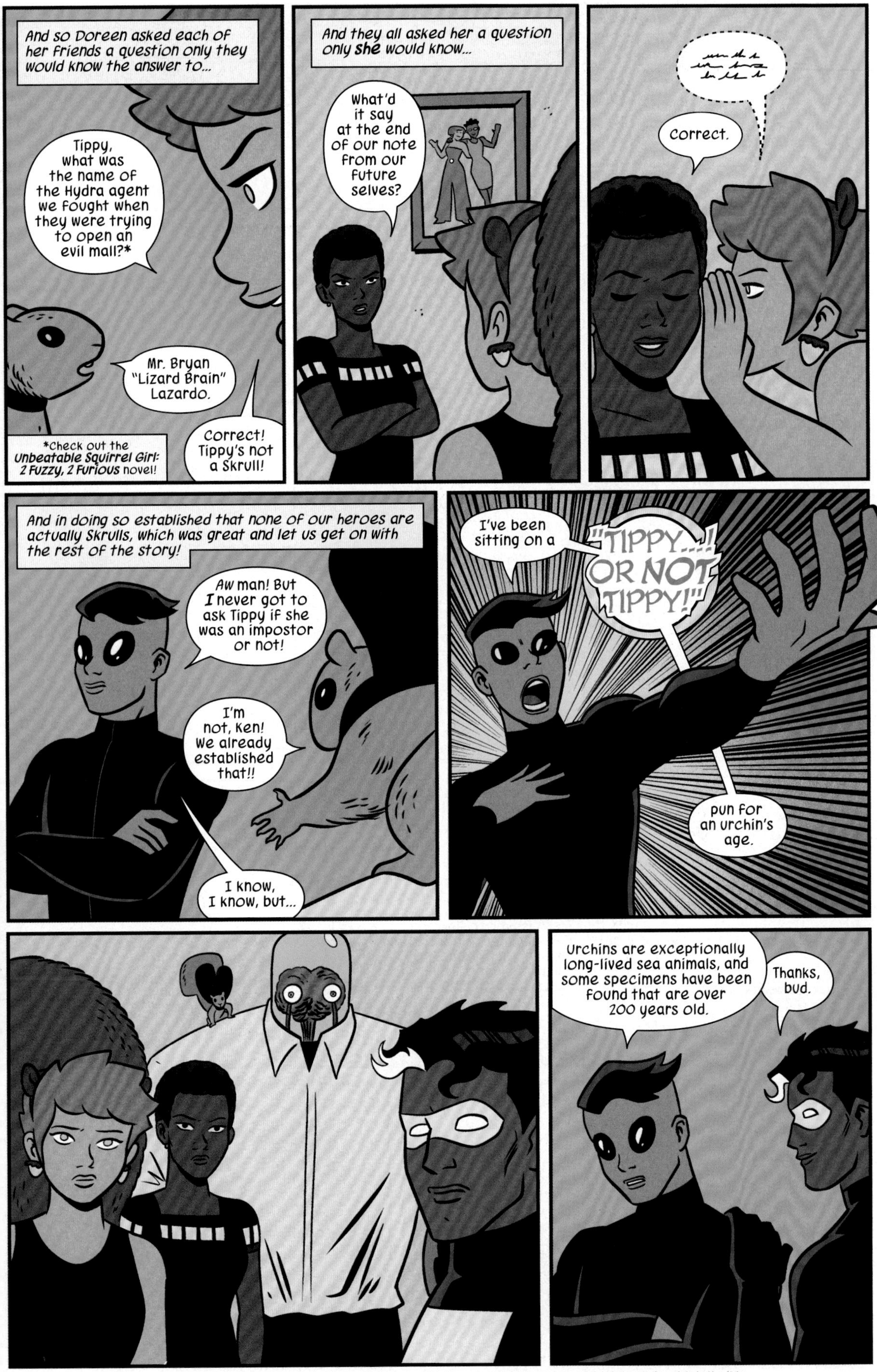
And so Doreen asked each of her friends a question only they would know the answer to...
Tippy, what was the name of the Hydra agent we fought when they were trying to open an evil mall?*
Mr. Bryan "Lizard Brain" Lazardo.
*Check out the Unbeatable Squirrel Girl: 2 Fuzzy, 2 Furious novel!
Correct! Tippy's not a Skrull!
And they all asked her a question only she would know...
What'd it say at the end of our note from our future selves?
Correct.
And in doing so established that none of our heroes are actually Skrulls, which was great and let us get on with the rest of the story!
Aw man! But I never got to ask Tippy if she was an impostor or not!
I'm not, Ken! We already established that!!
I know, I know, but...
I've been sitting on a
"TIPPY...! OR NOT TIPPY!"
pun for an urchin's age.
Urchins are exceptionally long-lived sea animals, and some specimens have been found that are over 200 years old.
Thanks, bud.

I can't get over how great Brain Drain looks in his nice button-up shirt. How come Marvel used to publish Swimsuit Specials in the '90s but has not yet gotten around to publishing Nice Button-Up Shirt Specials??

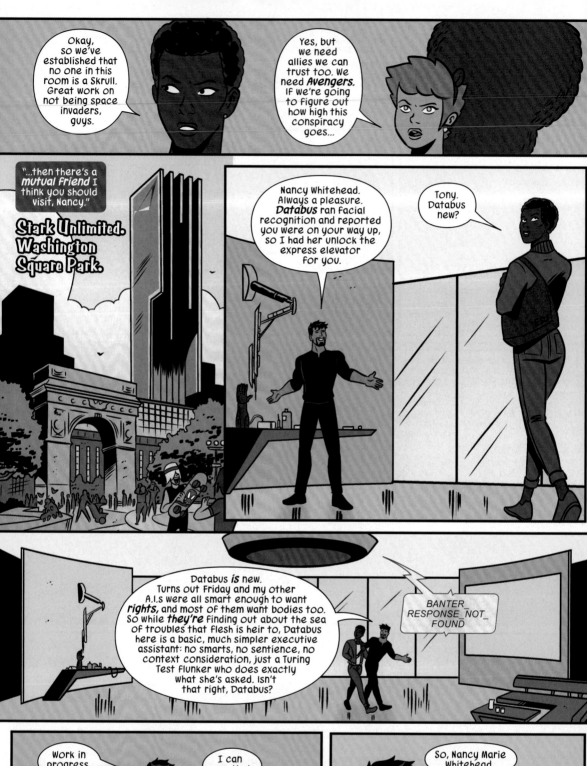

Okay, so we've established that no one in this room is a Skrull. Great work on not being space invaders, guys.

Yes, but we need allies we can trust too. We need *Avengers.* If we're going to figure out how high this conspiracy goes...

"...then there's a *mutual friend* I think you should visit, Nancy."

Stark Unlimited. Washington Square Park.

Nancy Whitehead. Always a pleasure. *Databus* ran facial recognition and reported you were on your way up, so I had her unlock the express elevator for you.

Tony. Databus new?

Databus *is* new. Turns out Friday and my other A.I.s were all smart enough to want *rights,* and most of them want bodies too. So while *they're* finding out about the sea of troubles that flesh is heir to, Databus here is a basic, much simpler executive assistant: no smarts, no sentience, no context consideration, just a Turing Test flunker who does exactly what she's asked. Isn't that right, Databus?

BANTER_ RESPONSE_NOT_ FOUND

Work in progress.

I can see that.

So, Nancy Marie Whitehead...

...what can I do for you?

The Turing Test is a test to see if a computer program can fake being a person! You just chat up the computer through a text interface, and if the human doing the texting can't tell they're not chatting with a real person, then that program has passed the test! And the fact *you've* never thought these comics are written by a computer means I am passing this test *so well* right now!!

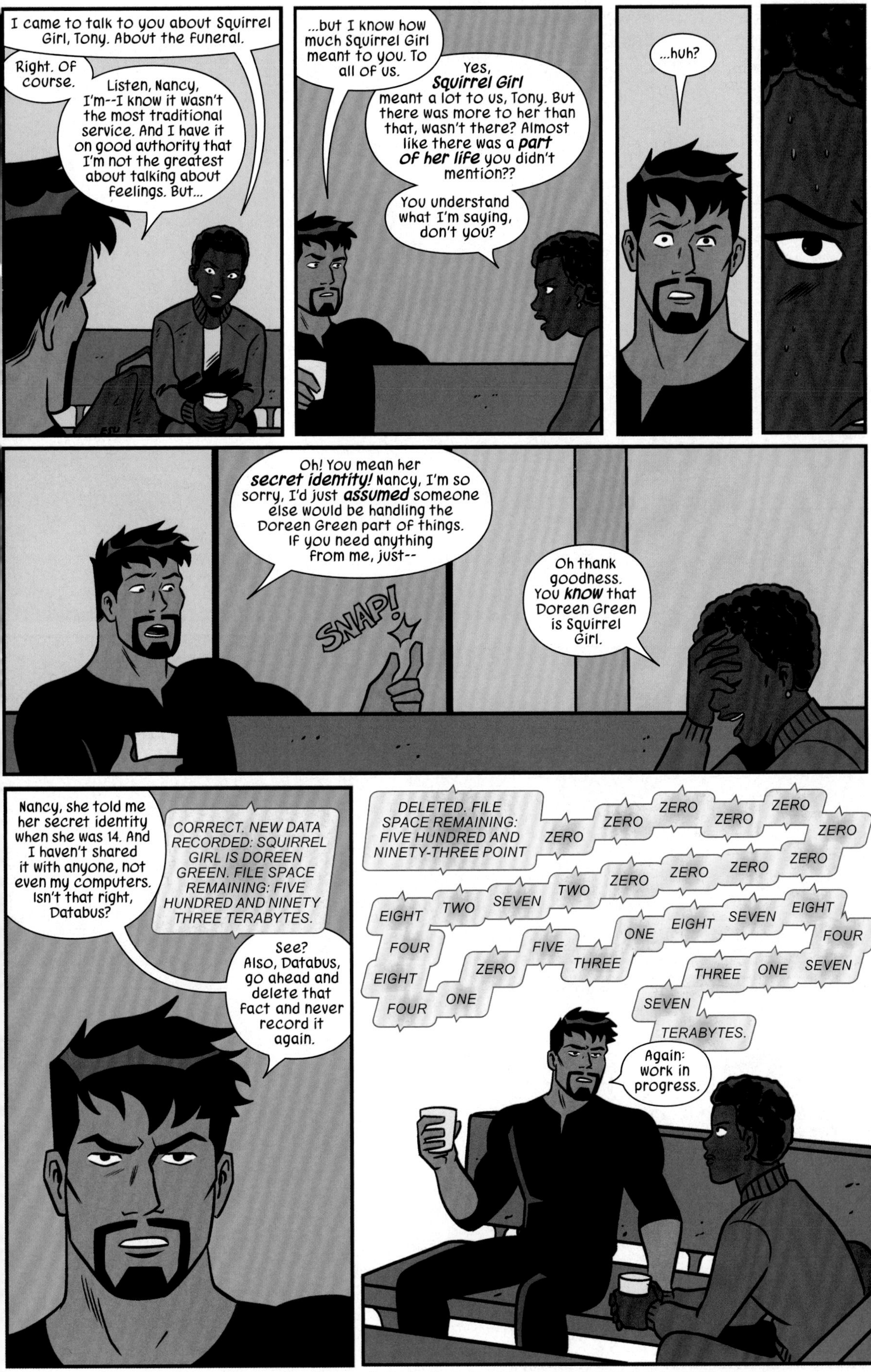

I came to talk to you about Squirrel Girl, Tony. About the funeral.
Right. Of course.
Listen, Nancy, I'm--I know it wasn't the most traditional service. And I have it on good authority that I'm not the greatest about talking about feelings. But...
...but I know how much Squirrel Girl meant to you. To all of us.
Yes, **Squirrel Girl** meant a lot to us, Tony. But there was more to her than that, wasn't there? Almost like there was a **part of her life** you didn't mention??
You understand what I'm saying, don't you?
...huh?
Oh! You mean her **secret identity!** Nancy, I'm so sorry, I'd just **assumed** someone else would be handling the Doreen Green part of things. If you need anything from me, just--
SNAP!
Oh thank goodness. You **know** that Doreen Green is Squirrel Girl.
Nancy, she told me her secret identity when she was 14. And I haven't shared it with anyone, not even my computers. Isn't that right, Databus?
CORRECT. NEW DATA RECORDED: SQUIRREL GIRL IS DOREEN GREEN. FILE SPACE REMAINING: FIVE HUNDRED AND NINETY THREE TERABYTES.
See? Also, Databus, go ahead and delete that fact and never record it again.
DELETED. FILE SPACE REMAINING: FIVE HUNDRED AND NINETY-THREE POINT ZERO ZERO ZERO ZERO ZERO ZERO ZERO ZERO ZERO ZERO TWO SEVEN TWO EIGHT FOUR EIGHT FOUR ONE ZERO FIVE THREE ONE EIGHT SEVEN EIGHT FOUR SEVEN ONE THREE SEVEN TERABYTES.
Again: work in progress.

The more I know about computers, the more I'm like "no way should anyone share their most important secrets with computers," so I gotta give Tony props on this one.

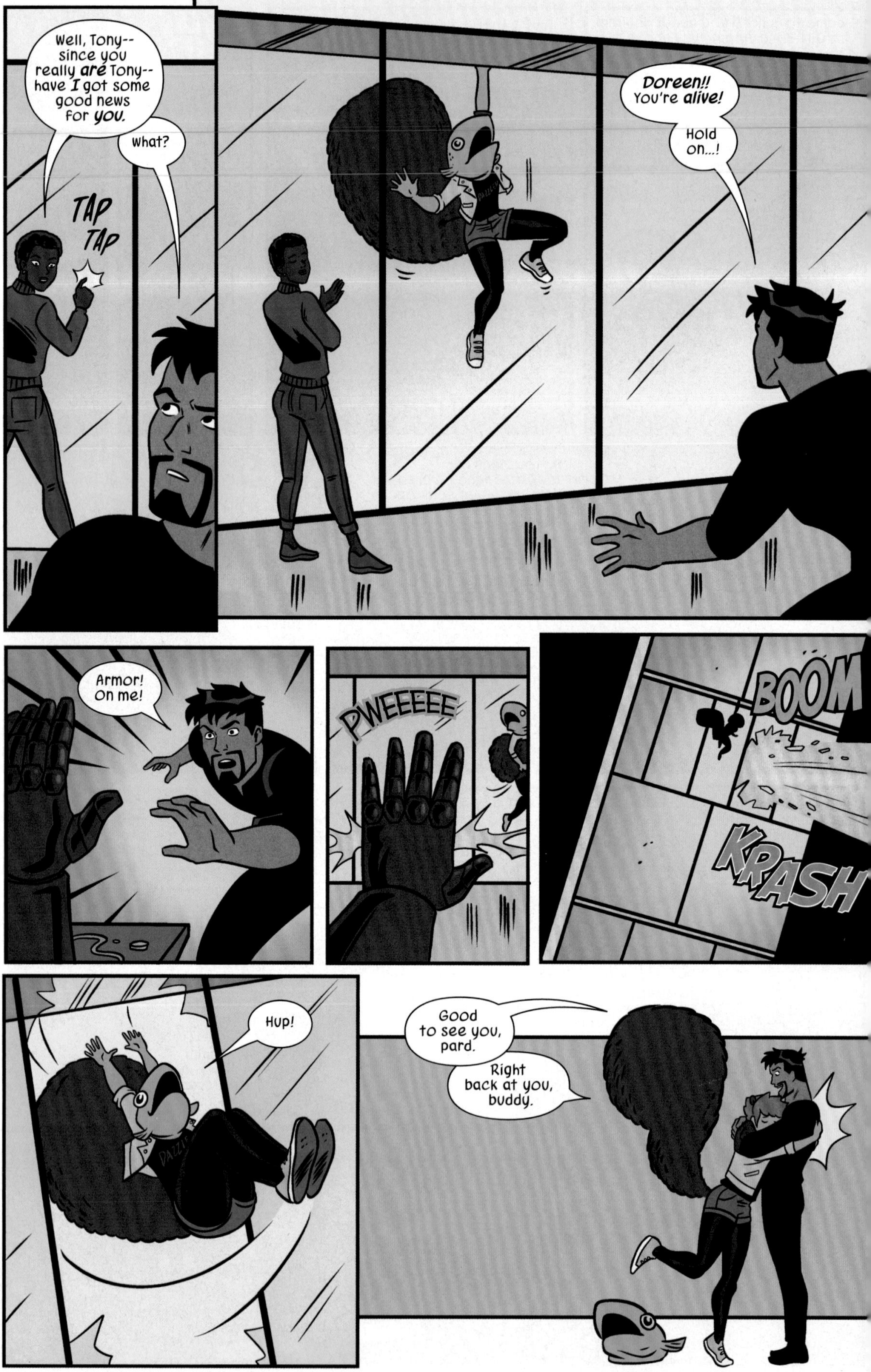
Well, Tony-- since you really *are* Tony-- have *I* got some good news for *you.*
What?
TAP TAP
Doreen!! You're *alive!*
Hold on...!
Armor! On me!
PWEEEEE
BOOM
KRASH
Hup!
Good to see you, pard.
Right back at you, buddy.

Doreen is happy Tony blasted through that window because a) what a sweet and Peak Tony way to show how excited he is to see her, and b) she had to climb up an entire skyscraper by herself and hold on while he and Nancy were chatting, and even with squirrel powers, your arms ***eventually*** start to get tired.

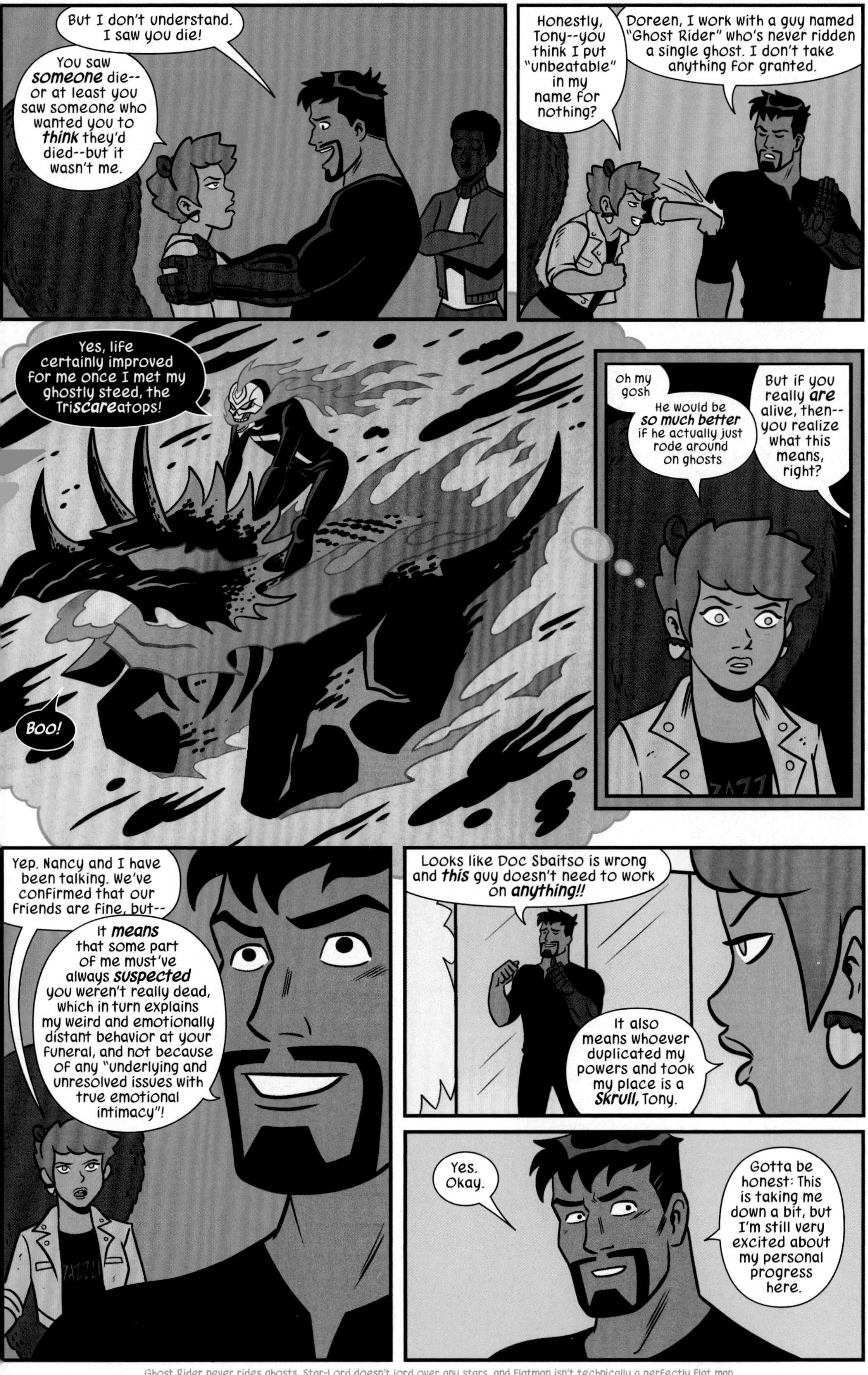

But I don't understand. I saw you die!
You saw someone die--or at least you saw someone who wanted you to think they'd died--but it wasn't me.
Honestly, Tony--you think I put "unbeatable" in my name for nothing?
Doreen, I work with a guy named "Ghost Rider" who's never ridden a single ghost. I don't take anything for granted.
Yes, life certainly improved for me once I met my ghostly steed, the TriSCAREatops!
BOO!
Oh my gosh
He would be so much better if he actually just rode around on ghosts
But if you really are alive, then--you realize what this means, right?
Yep. Nancy and I have been talking. We've confirmed that our friends are fine, but--
It means that some part of me must've always suspected you weren't really dead, which in turn explains my weird and emotionally distant behavior at your funeral, and not because of any "underlying and unresolved issues with true emotional intimacy"!
Looks like Doc Sbaitso is wrong and this guy doesn't need to work on anything!!
It also means whoever duplicated my powers and took my place is a Skrull, Tony.
Yes. Okay.
Gotta be honest: This is taking me down a bit, but I'm still very excited about my personal progress here.

Ghost Rider never rides ghosts, Star-Lord doesn't lord over any stars, and Flatman isn't technically a perfectly flat man.
Silver Surfer's great, though! He, at least, *precisely* lives up to his hype.

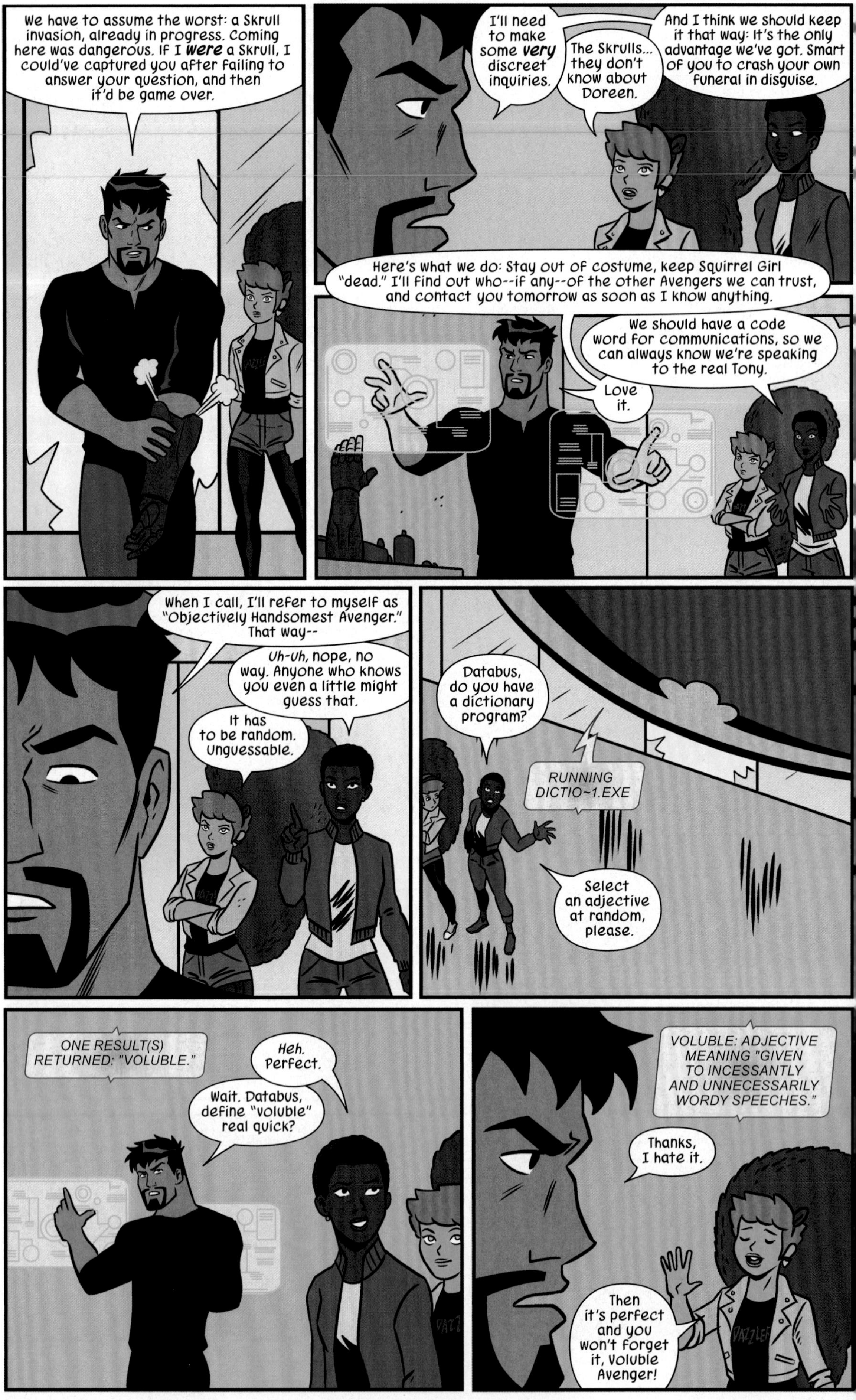
We have to assume the worst: a Skrull invasion, already in progress. Coming here was dangerous. If I *were* a Skrull, I could've captured you after failing to answer your question, and then it'd be game over.
I'll need to make some *very* discreet inquiries.
The Skrulls... they don't know about Doreen.
And I think we should keep it that way: It's the only advantage we've got. Smart of you to crash your own funeral in disguise.
Here's what we do: Stay out of costume, keep Squirrel Girl "dead." I'll find out who--if any--of the other Avengers we can trust, and contact you tomorrow as soon as I know anything.
We should have a code word for communications, so we can always know we're speaking to the real Tony.
Love it.
When I call, I'll refer to myself as "Objectively Handsomest Avenger." That way--
Uh-uh, nope, no way. Anyone who knows you even a little might guess that.
It has to be random. Unguessable.
Databus, do you have a dictionary program?
RUNNING DICTIO~1.EXE
Select an adjective at random, please.
ONE RESULT(S) RETURNED: "VOLUBLE."
Heh. Perfect.
Wait. Databus, define "voluble" real quick?
VOLUBLE: ADJECTIVE MEANING "GIVEN TO INCESSANTLY AND UNNECESSARILY WORDY SPEECHES."
Thanks, I hate it.
Then it's perfect and you won't forget it, Voluble Avenger!

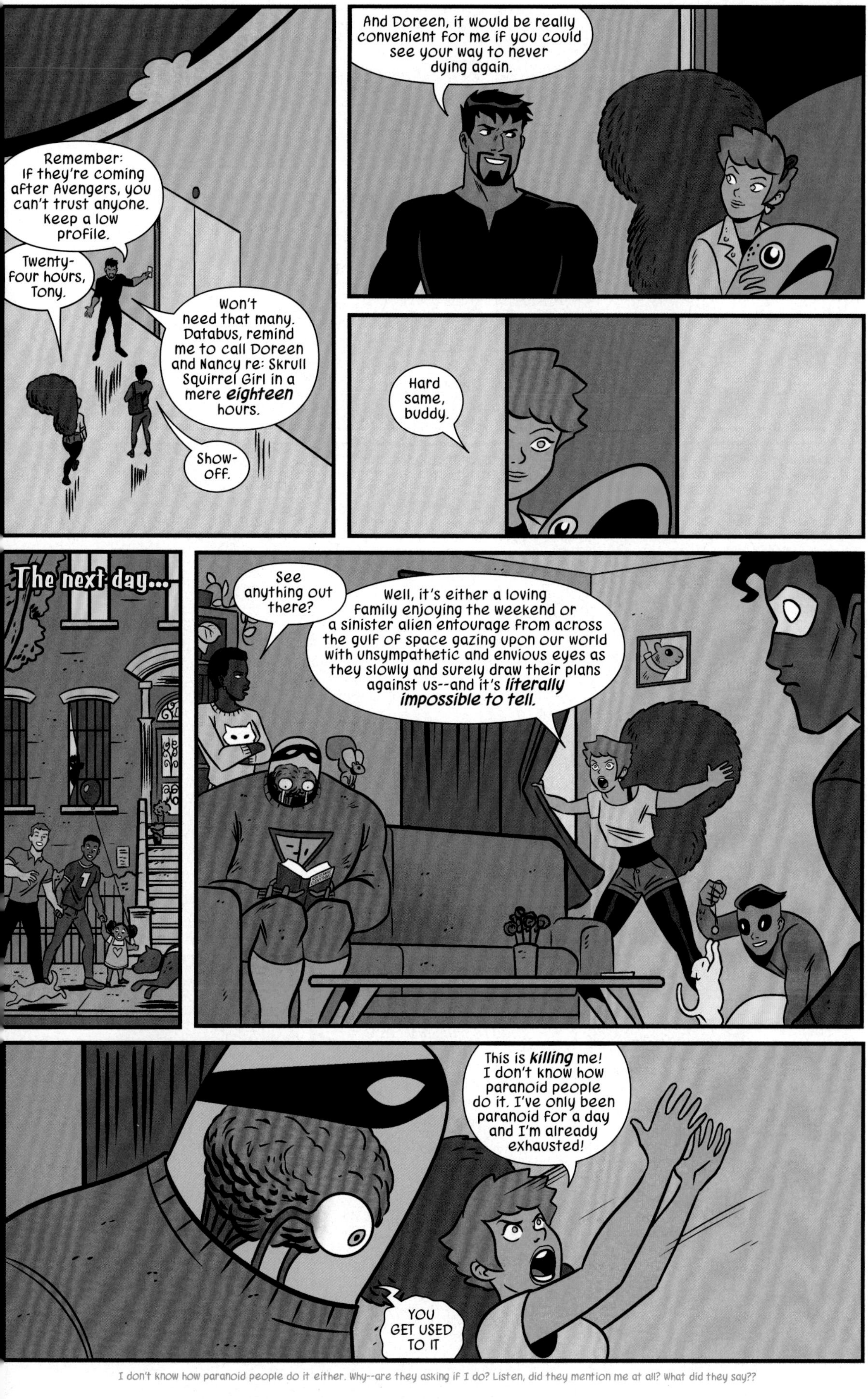
Remember: If they're coming after Avengers, you can't trust anyone. Keep a low profile.
Twenty-four hours, Tony.
Won't need that many. Databus, remind me to call Doreen and Nancy re: Skrull Squirrel Girl in a mere eighteen hours.
Show-off.
And Doreen, it would be really convenient for me if you could see your way to never dying again.
Hard same, buddy.
The next day...
See anything out there?
Well, it's either a loving family enjoying the weekend or a sinister alien entourage from across the gulf of space gazing upon our world with unsympathetic and envious eyes as they slowly and surely draw their plans against us--and it's literally impossible to tell.
This is killing me! I don't know how paranoid people do it. I've only been paranoid for a day and I'm already exhausted!
YOU GET USED TO IT

I don't know how paranoid people do it either. Why--are they asking if I do? Listen, did they mention me at all? What did they say??

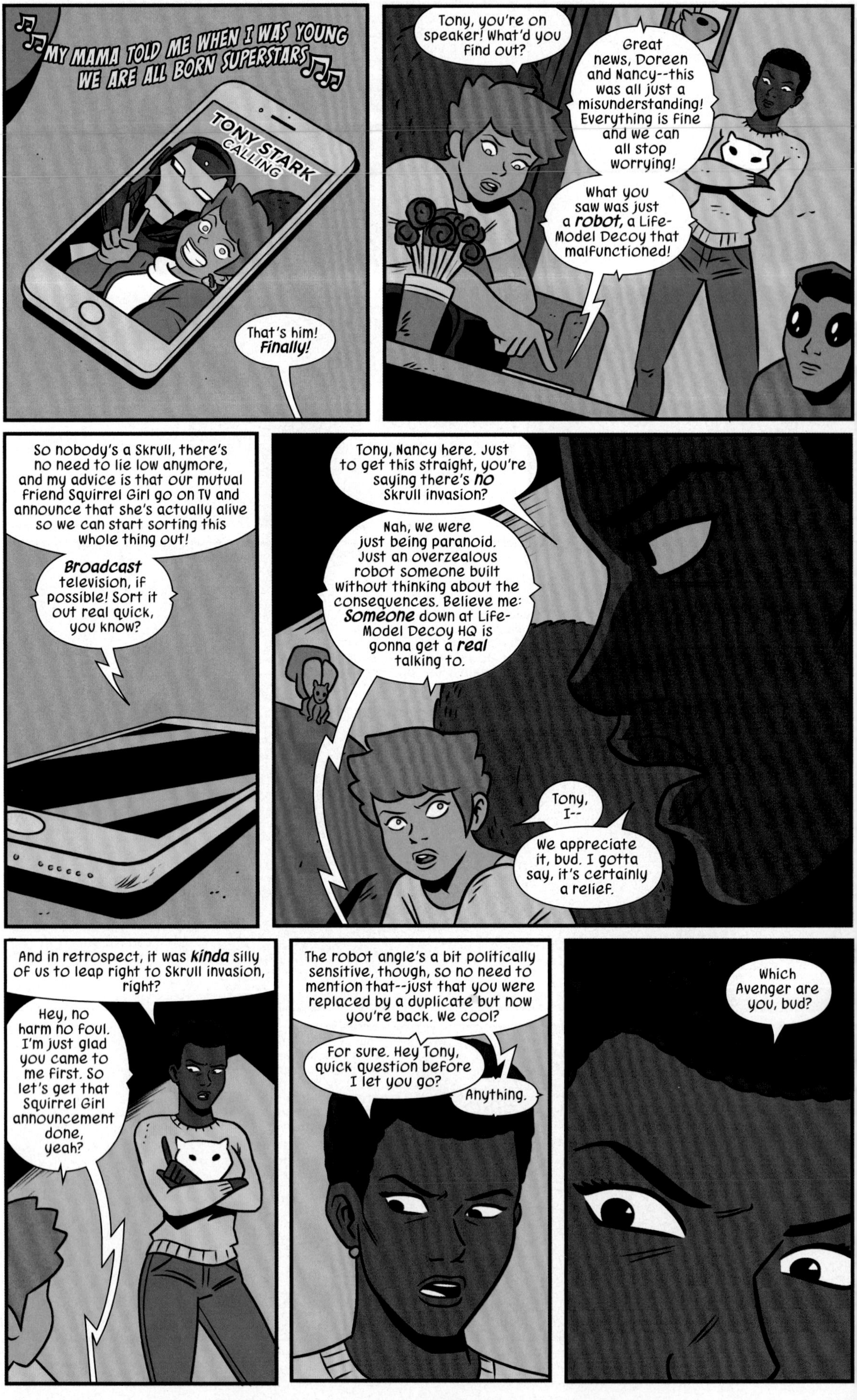
MY MAMA TOLD ME WHEN I WAS YOUNG WE ARE ALL BORN SUPERSTARS
TONY STARK CALLING
That's him! Finally!
Tony, you're on speaker! What'd you find out?
Great news, Doreen and Nancy--this was all just a misunderstanding! Everything is fine and we can all stop worrying!
What you saw was just a robot, a Life-Model Decoy that malfunctioned!
So nobody's a Skrull, there's no need to lie low anymore, and my advice is that our mutual friend Squirrel Girl go on TV and announce that she's actually alive so we can start sorting this whole thing out!
Broadcast television, if possible! Sort it out real quick, you know?
Tony, Nancy here. Just to get this straight, you're saying there's no Skrull invasion?
Nah, we were just being paranoid. Just an overzealous robot someone built without thinking about the consequences. Believe me: Someone down at Life-Model Decoy HQ is gonna get a real talking to.
Tony, I--
We appreciate it, bud. I gotta say, it's certainly a relief.
And in retrospect, it was kinda silly of us to leap right to Skrull invasion, right?
Hey, no harm no foul. I'm just glad you came to me first. So let's get that Squirrel Girl announcement done, yeah?
The robot angle's a bit politically sensitive, though, so no need to mention that--just that you were replaced by a duplicate but now you're back. We cool?
For sure. Hey Tony, quick question before I let you go?
Anything.
Which Avenger are you, bud?

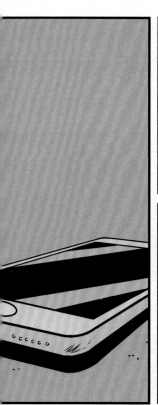

...I'm sorry?

You know, that fun game we play where I ask you which Avenger you are and you give me that patented Tony quip!

Oh, hah, of course!

...

I'm the *best* Avenger, baby.

Love it. That's perfect! We'll get started on this right away, 'kay bye Tony!

Great, let me know if you need any help getting on televisi--

KLIK

Friends...I hate to say it, but Tony Stark has been replaced by a Skrull.

I believe I speak for us all here when I say "Holy carp."

Only the rest of us aren't saying "carp."

I can't believe it. The Avengers are compromised.

We really *can't* trust anyone outside this room.

And we're *definitely* not revealing Squirrel Girl is alive!

I don't know what their game is, but if that's what the Skrulls want me to do, then that's the one thing I'm definitely *not* gonna be doing. Instead...

...your girl's gonna go confront herself a *Skrull Tony.*

The rest of us are saying "Holy schmoleygins."

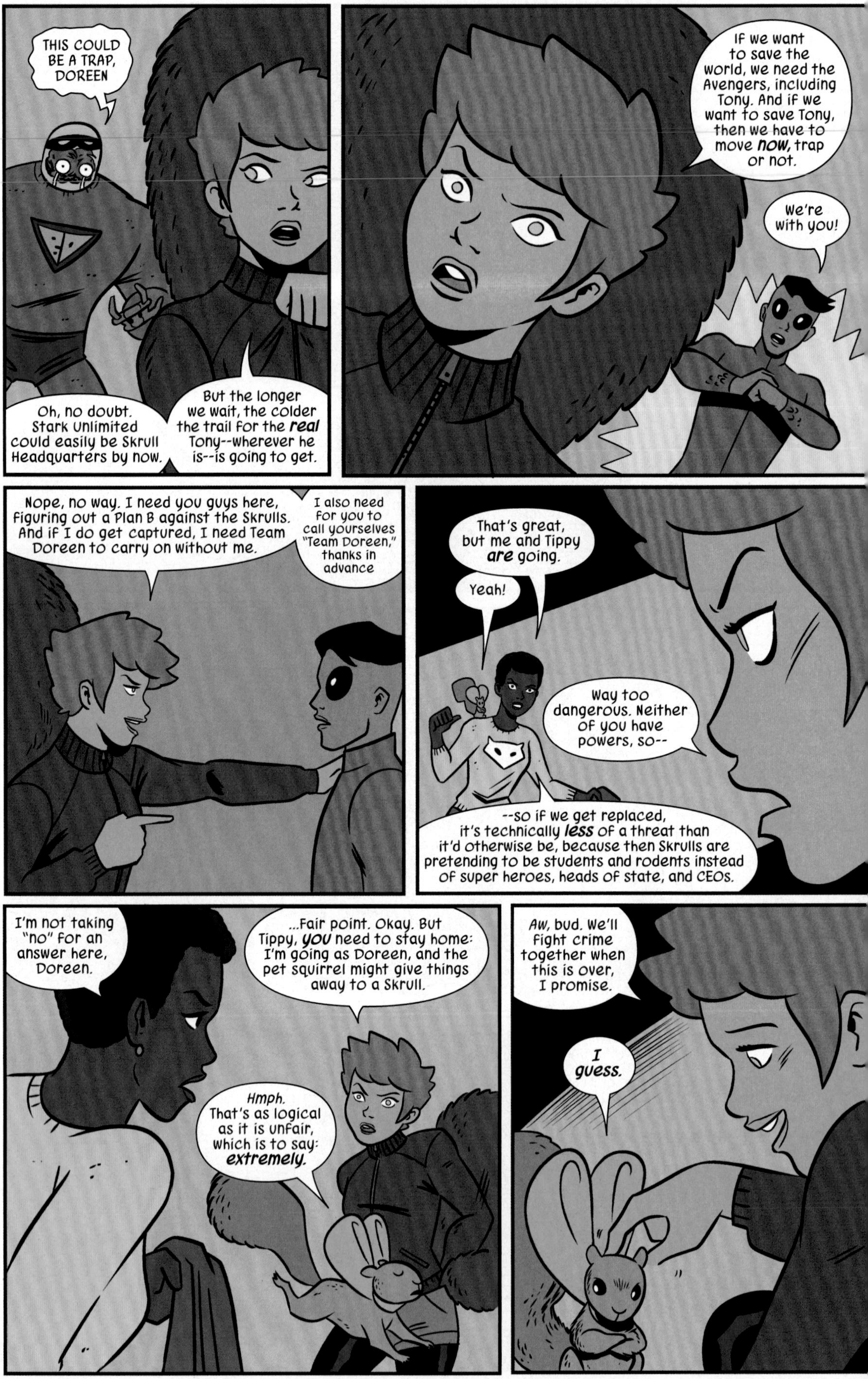
THIS COULD BE A TRAP, DOREEN
Oh, no doubt. Stark Unlimited could easily be Skrull Headquarters by now.
But the longer we wait, the colder the trail for the *real* Tony--wherever he is--is going to get.
If we want to save the world, we need the Avengers, including Tony. And if we want to save Tony, then we have to move *NOW,* trap or not.
We're with you!
Nope, no way. I need you guys here, figuring out a Plan B against the Skrulls. And if I do get captured, I need Team Doreen to carry on without me.
I also need for you to call yourselves "Team Doreen," thanks in advance
That's great, but me and Tippy *are* going.
Yeah!
Way too dangerous. Neither of you have powers, so--
--so if we get replaced, it's technically *less* of a threat than it'd otherwise be, because then Skrulls are pretending to be students and rodents instead of super heroes, heads of state, and CEOs.
I'm not taking "no" for an answer here, Doreen.
...Fair point. Okay. But Tippy, *YOU* need to stay home: I'm going as Doreen, and the pet squirrel might give things away to a Skrull.
Hmph. That's as logical as it is unfair, which is to say: *extremely.*
Aw, bud. We'll fight crime together when this is over, I promise.
I guess.

First Tippy misses out on going to jail, and *now* she's missing out on entering a super villain's lair? WHAT IS EVEN THE POINT OF BEING A SUPER HERO'S SIDEKICK, SHE MIGHT ASK??

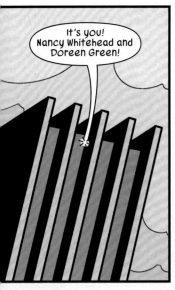

It's you! Nancy Whitehead and Doreen Green!

Let me guess: Databus I.D.'d us by our faces and told you we were on our way up, so you had her unlock the express elevator for us?

That's just classic me right there! Come on in.

Try not to break this pane for at least a few days. -PP

I can guess why you're here.

We're visiting because of your call, Tony. We--

Of course. Listen, let me just say one thing right off the bat:

I owe you both an apology.

This threat of a Skrull invasion--I may not have mentioned it when we spoke, but--honestly, it set me off. We barely beat them back last time. I was *terrified.*

And when I found out it was all just a silly *misunderstanding,* that we were *safe,* I was so *relieved* that I just--I called you without thinking.

My mind was still going a mile a minute. And it wasn't until later that I realized I didn't tell you...

...I'm the *Voluble* Avenger.

Surpriiiiiise.

That note on Tony's window is outward-facing, because *someone* has the bad habit of trying to enter his office from the outside while announcing that "GLASS IS CHEAP WHEN YOU'RE REALLY RICH."

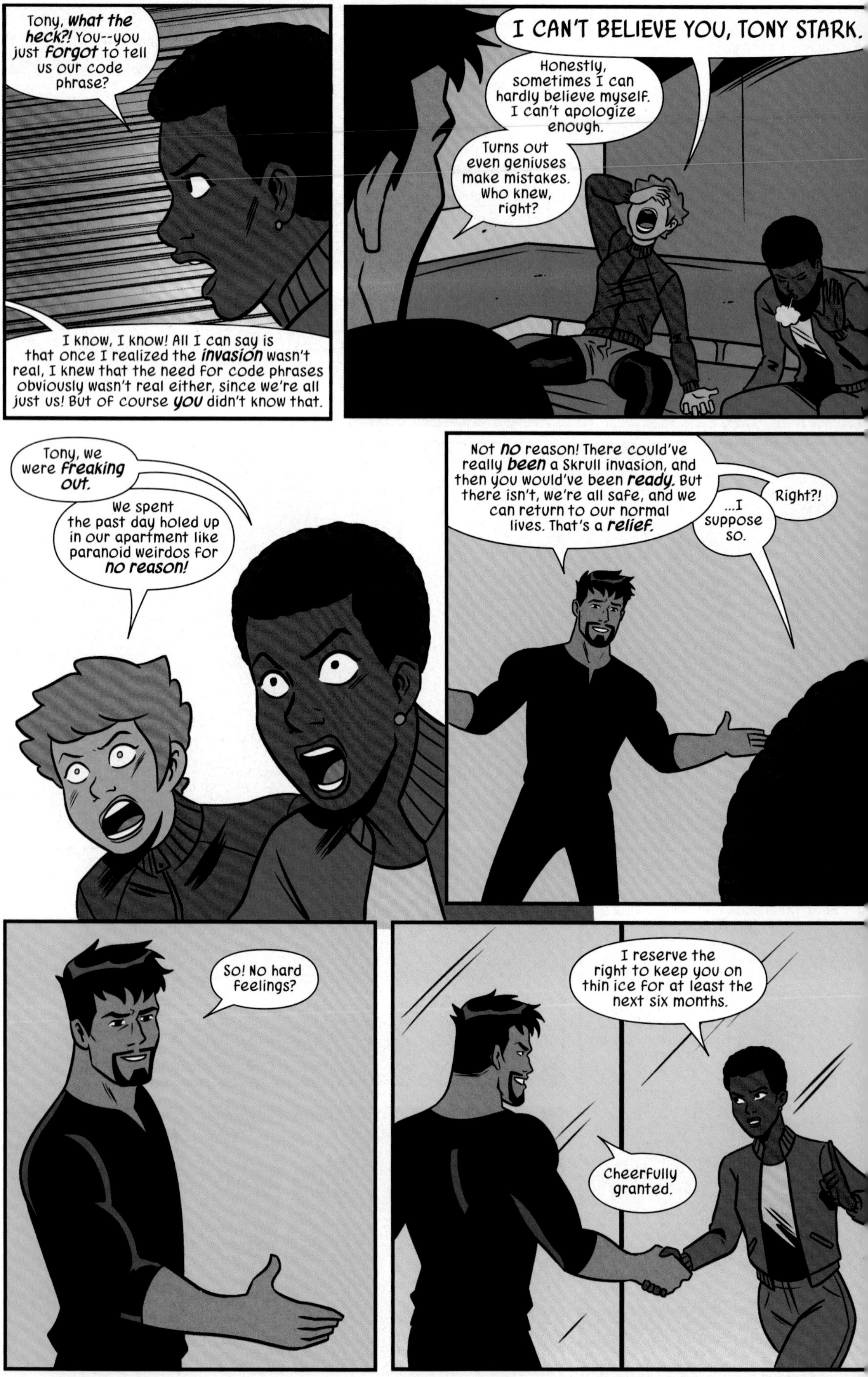
Tony, what the heck?! You--you just forgot to tell us our code phrase?
I know, I know! All I can say is that once I realized the invasion wasn't real, I knew that the need for code phrases obviously wasn't real either, since we're all just us! But of course you didn't know that.
I CAN'T BELIEVE YOU, TONY STARK.
Honestly, sometimes I can hardly believe myself. I can't apologize enough.
Turns out even geniuses make mistakes. Who knew, right?
Tony, we were freaking out.
We spent the past day holed up in our apartment like paranoid weirdos for no reason!
Not no reason! There could've really been a Skrull invasion, and then you would've been ready. But there isn't, we're all safe, and we can return to our normal lives. That's a relief.
...I suppose so.
Right?!
So! No hard feelings?
I reserve the right to keep you on thin ice for at least the next six months.
Cheerfully granted.

We were holed up like paranoid weirdos. Not even like paranoid regular people! We went *all in* on it, Tony!!

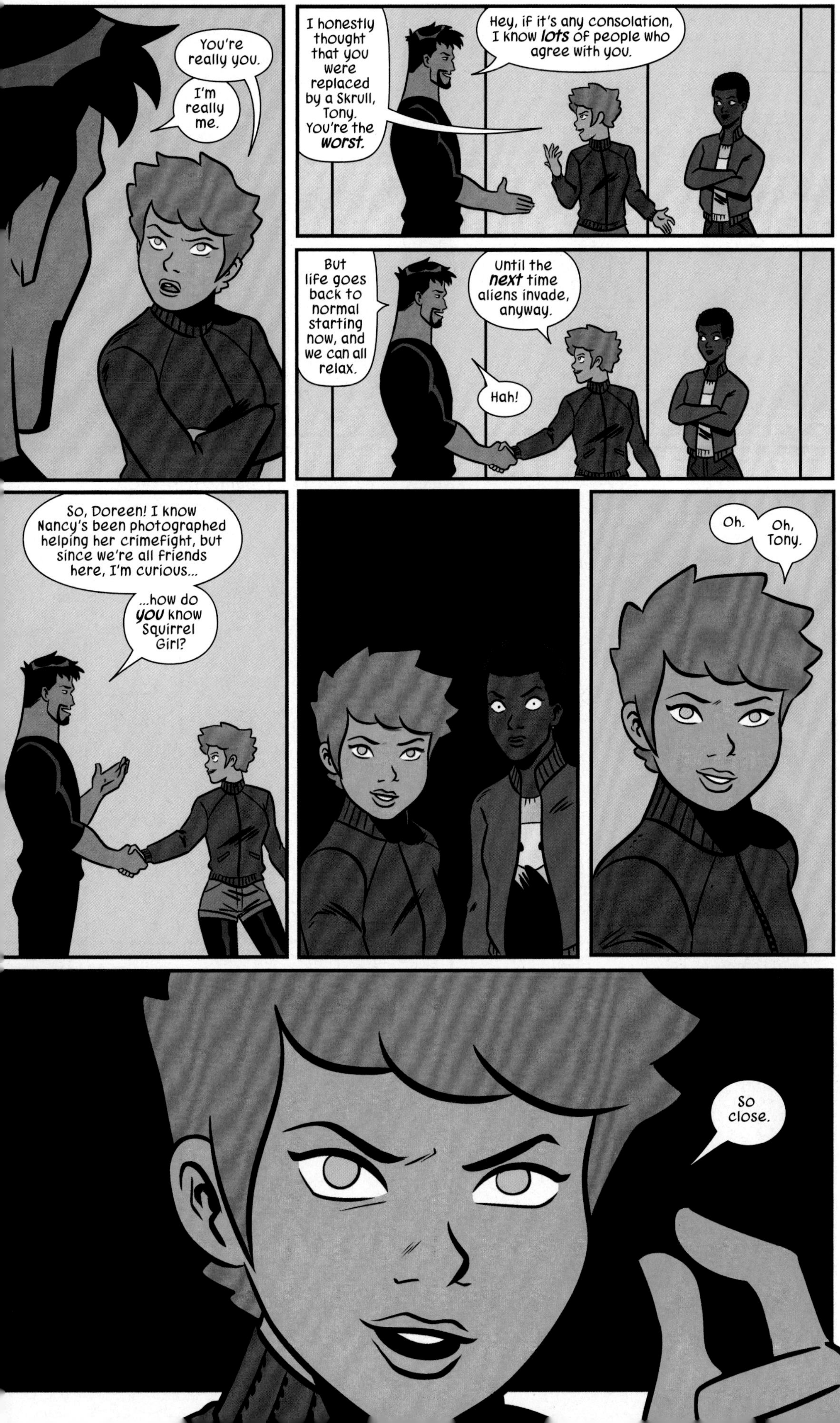
You're really you.
I'm really me.
I honestly thought that you were replaced by a Skrull, Tony. You're the worst.
Hey, if it's any consolation, I know lots of people who agree with you.
But life goes back to normal starting now, and we can all relax.
Until the next time aliens invade, anyway.
Hah!
So, Doreen! I know Nancy's been photographed helping her crimefight, but since we're all friends here, I'm curious...
...how do you know Squirrel Girl?
Oh.
Oh, Tony.
So close.

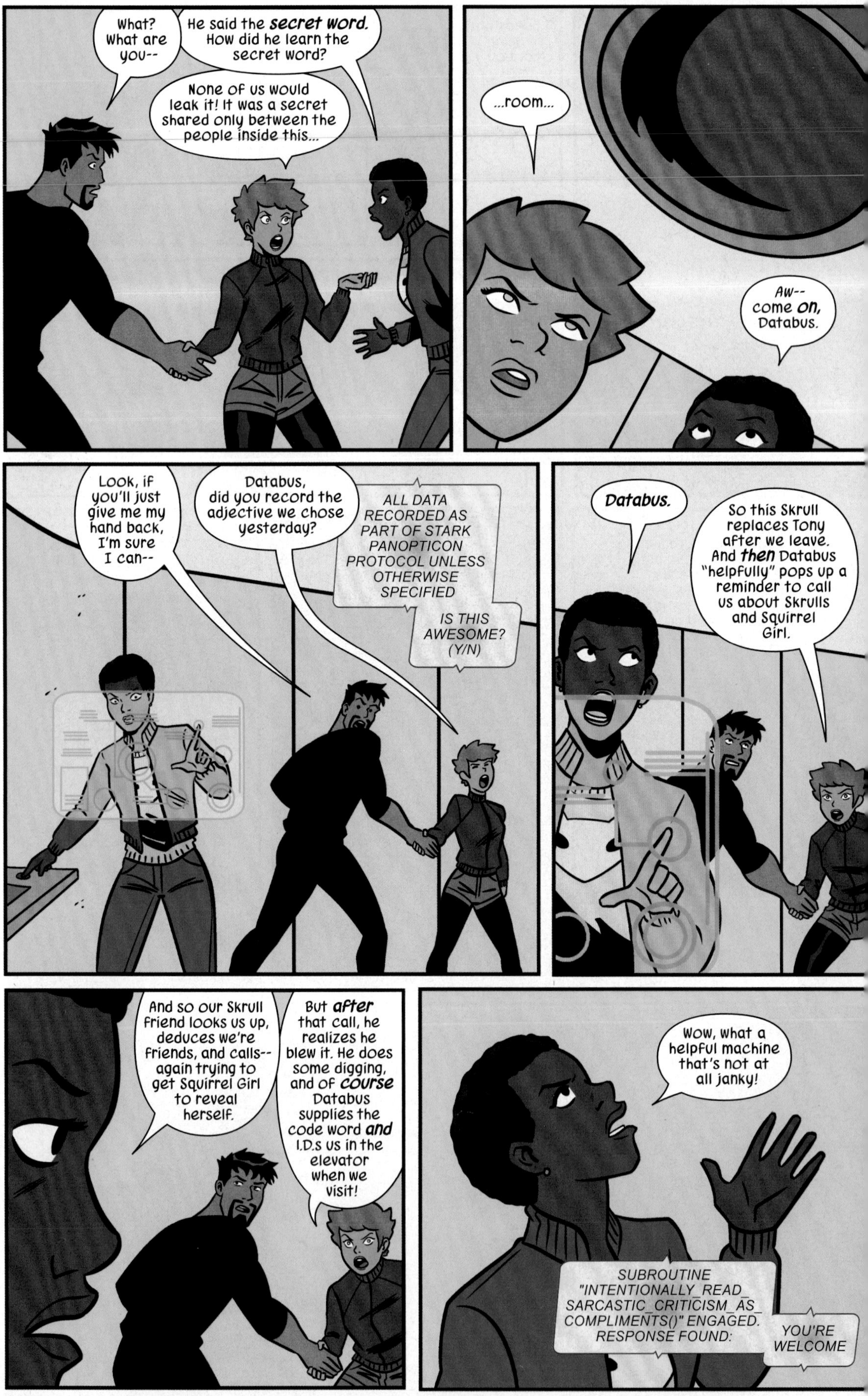
What? What are you--
He said the secret word. How did he learn the secret word?
None of us would leak it! It was a secret shared only between the people inside this...
...room...
Aw--come on, Databus.
Look, if you'll just give me my hand back, I'm sure I can--
Databus, did you record the adjective we chose yesterday?
ALL DATA RECORDED AS PART OF STARK PANOPTICON PROTOCOL UNLESS OTHERWISE SPECIFIED
IS THIS AWESOME? (Y/N)
Databus.
So this Skrull replaces Tony after we leave. And then Databus "helpfully" pops up a reminder to call us about Skrulls and Squirrel Girl.
And so our Skrull friend looks us up, deduces we're friends, and calls--again trying to get Squirrel Girl to reveal herself.
But after that call, he realizes he blew it. He does some digging, and of course Databus supplies the code word and I.D.s us in the elevator when we visit!
Wow, what a helpful machine that's not at all janky!
SUBROUTINE "INTENTIONALLY_READ_SARCASTIC_CRITICISM_AS_COMPLIMENTS()" ENGAGED. RESPONSE FOUND:
YOU'RE WELCOME

Every A.I. Tony programs, even the basic ones, get that subroutine. It's what make his machines so gosh-darned personable!

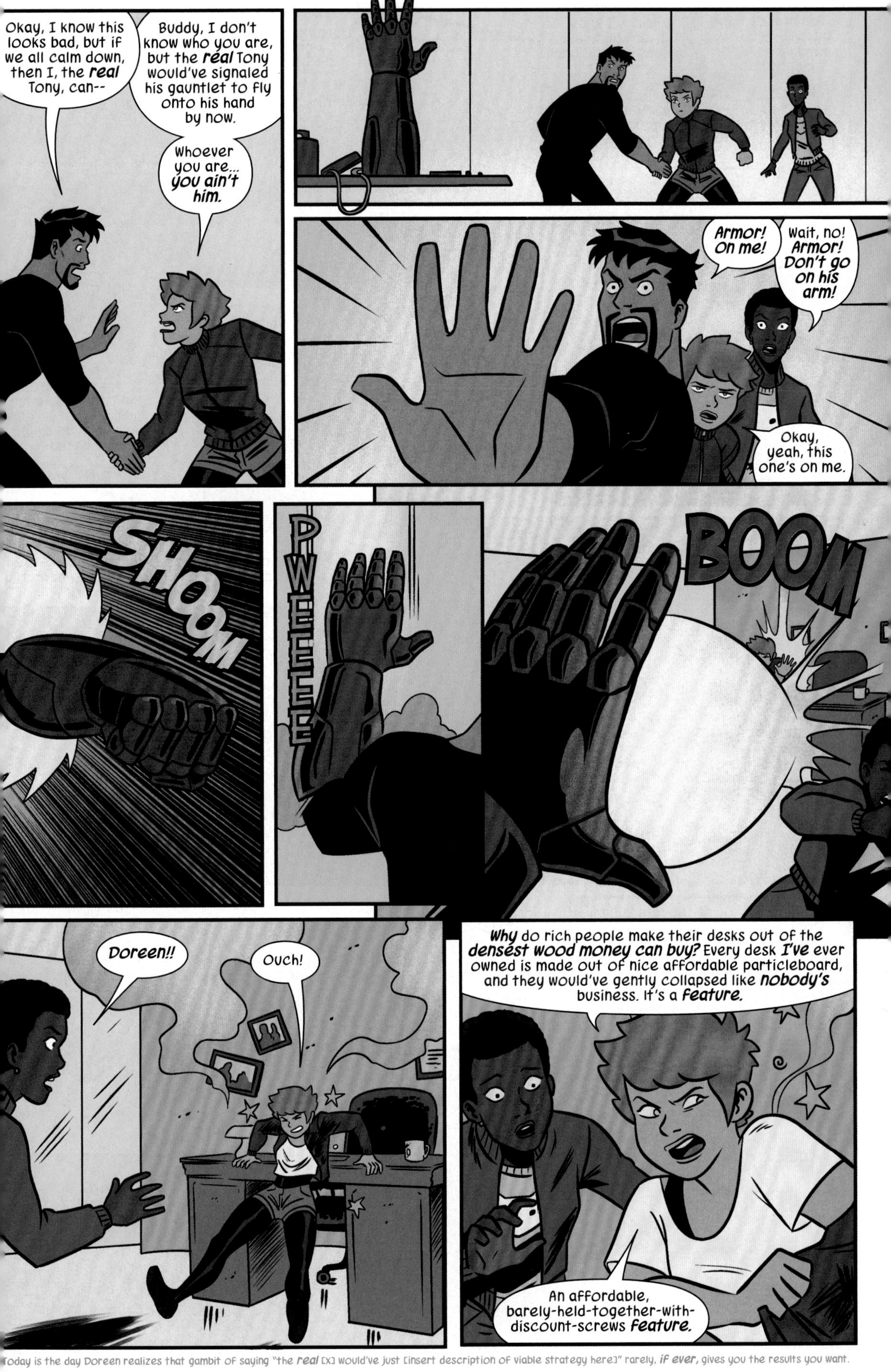
Okay, I know this looks bad, but if we all calm down, then I, the real Tony, can--
Buddy, I don't know who you are, but the real Tony would've signaled his gauntlet to fly onto his hand by now.
Whoever you are... you ain't him.
Armor! On me!
Wait, no! Armor! Don't go on his arm!
Okay, yeah, this one's on me.
SHOOM
PWEEEEE
BOOM
Doreen!!
Ouch!
Why do rich people make their desks out of the densest wood money can buy? Every desk I've ever owned is made out of nice affordable particleboard, and they would've gently collapsed like nobody's business. It's a feature.
An affordable, barely-held-together-with-discount-screws feature.

Today is the day Doreen realizes that gambit of saying "the *real* [x] would've just [insert description of viable strategy here]" rarely, *if ever*, gives you the results you want.

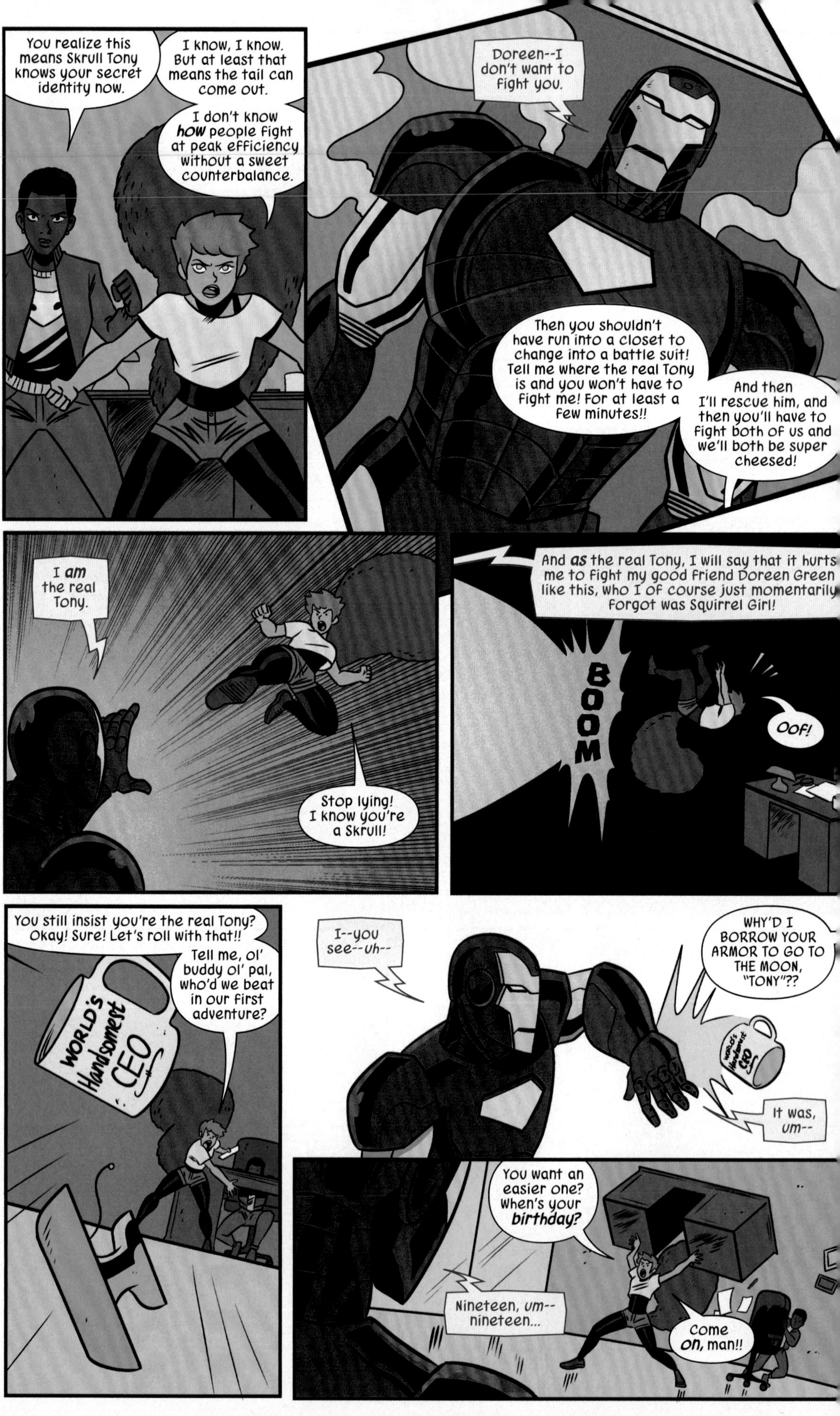

You realize this means Skrull Tony knows your secret identity now.
I know, I know. But at least that means the tail can come out.
I don't know **how** people fight at peak efficiency without a sweet counterbalance.
Doreen--I don't want to fight you.
Then you shouldn't have run into a closet to change into a battle suit! Tell me where the real Tony is and you won't have to fight me! For at least a few minutes!!
And then I'll rescue him, and then you'll have to fight both of us and we'll both be super cheesed!
I **am** the real Tony.
Stop lying! I know you're a Skrull!
And **as** the real Tony, I will say that it hurts me to fight my good friend Doreen Green like this, who I of course just momentarily forgot was Squirrel Girl!
BOOM
OOF!
You still insist you're the real Tony? Okay! Sure! Let's roll with that!!
Tell me, ol' buddy ol' pal, who'd we beat in our first adventure?
WORLD'S Handsomest CEO
I--you see--uh--
WHY'D I BORROW YOUR ARMOR TO GO TO THE MOON, "TONY"??
It was, um--
You want an easier one? When's your **birthday?**
Nineteen, um--nineteen...
Come **on,** man!!

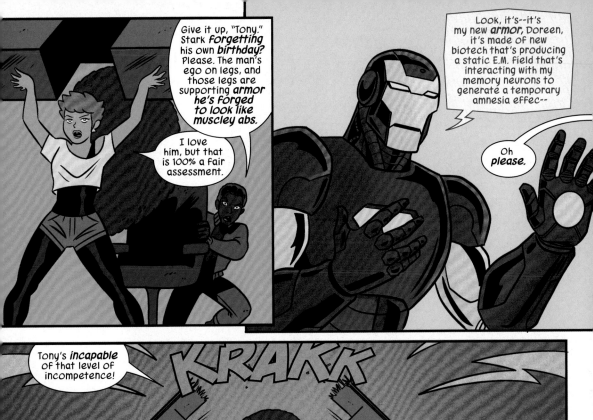

Give it up, "Tony." Stark *forgetting* his own *birthday?* Please. The man's ego on legs, and those legs are supporting *armor* he's forged to look like *muscley abs.*

I love him, but that is 100% a fair assessment.

Look, it's--it's my new *armor*, Doreen, it's made of new biotech that's producing a static E.M. field that's interacting with my memory neurons to generate a temporary amnesia effec--

Oh *please.*

Tony's *incapable* of that level of incompetence!

KRAKK

You're, uh, really forcing my hand here, Doreen.

Great. Stop invading Earth, give us Tony back, and this all goes away.

Fine. *Fine.* You want me to speak? I'll speak.

Well? Spit it out, man! What'd you do with the *real* Tony Stark??

But *before* I speak, I want you to know something... I'm not the bad guy. I didn't want to do this.

Well, I don't believe in "bad guys," so we're good.

Well... good.

Databus...

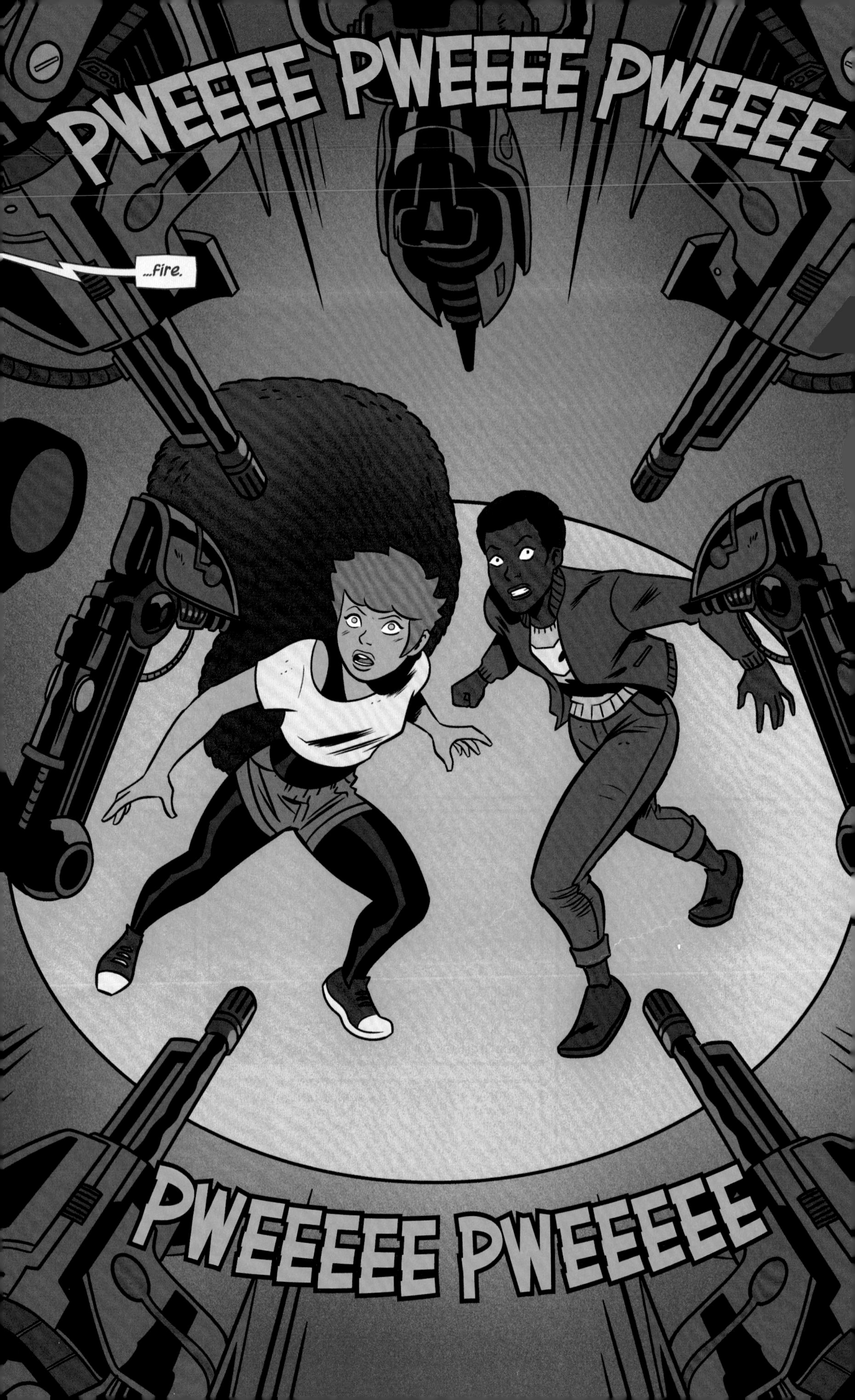
PWEEEE PWEEEE PWEEEE
...fire.
PWEEEE PWEEEE

Ryan!

Letters From Nuts

NEVA
Erica!
FORGET

Send letters to mheroes@marvel.com or 135 W 50th St, 7th Floor, New York, NY 10020 (Please mark "OKAY TO PRINT")

I've wanted to write in several times in the past year and change since I discovered THE UNBEATABLE SQUIRREL GIRL. I immediately was obsessed, and when Super Hero Day rolled around at the preschool I taught at, I set out to make myself an ear headband and costume. It was a hit, and by the time all was said and done, I had made eighteen sets of ears for kids and friends. The comics came into our classroom, and Doreen's ability to talk things out set a good example for the kids. The fact that her body was shaped different was great, too, and she didn't have the hair they were used to in Disney. But they loved her, and so do I.

I left teaching last year when I got sick and got diagnosed with Hodgkin's lymphoma a few months ago. I started using "Unbeatable" as a catchphrase and wear my Squirrel Girl T-shirts as often as I can. Then I heard that someone got a tattoo over their port scar when it was removed. I never even wanted a tattoo, but now...I'm thinking I'd like to get a Squirrel Girl tattoo over mine, with "unbeatable" in the Squirrel outline. I just got told today I'm in remission, so it might be awhile. Here's a picture of the impact SG had on my old classroom. They'd wear their ears on field trips and one firefighter commented, "I see you've brought your Squirrel Army."

Anyway, thanks for making such an amazing addition to the Marvel world. Not only is it my favorite, but it's become a gateway comic for tons of kids, who are really excited to see Doreen and friends on Disney Channel now!

Here're pics of the ears, plus some of my students' artwork!

Courtney

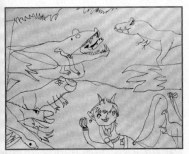

RYAN: Courtney, you may have made more squirrel ear headbands than anyone else on the planet right now! That is amazing. And I'm so glad that Squirrel Girl could be an inspiration during your treatment--there's nothing easy about going through chemotherapy, and knowing that you used "Unbeatable" as a catchphrase during it really touched me. People close to me have had ports put in as part of their treatment (for those of you who don't know what they are, they're basically a medical device that allows you to introduce medicine directly into the bloodstream, instead of having to put needles in veins--useful if you're getting a lot of medicine!) and I always said the coolest part about that was that now they're technically futuristic cyborgs, medically enhanced to a level above regular humans. A port gives you superhuman medicine-getting powers. So far none of them have been that into it, but I still think it's cool. Thank you for sharing this, congrats on being in remission and keep being unbeatable!

Okay, so I haven't ever sent anything to a comic before, but I hope you get a chance to publish this. I have been waiting for the right thing to send for a while now, and I think I found it. I completed my Squirrel Girl shrine! It is complete with a Funko Pop, a set of Deadpool's trading cards and some acorn earrings. I still remember the day I first started reading SQUIRREL GIRL, and still am so many years later. I'm such a big fan of your nutty work! Never stop kicking butts!

Sky Shapiro-Pelis

RYAN: Sky, I have studied this image carefully and come to this conclusion: I LOVE IT. I especially love homemade Deadpool cards, and you did a terrific job here! Also: With the cards, utility belt and squirrel headband, this shrine ALSO functions as an emergency Squirrel Girl costume station, which I think you'll agree is a handy thing to keep nearby, juuuuust in case!

Dear Erica and Ryan,

Hi! My name is Claire, and I'm 7. I liked reading your first comic and I think we have all of them. My first one had Howard the Duck in it, and I really liked it. The lady at the comic book store, which is called the Bat Cave, said that my brother and I would like it because Squirrel Girl is very smart and very brave and she has a good heart. I knew she was right when I read it. After I had been reading your comics for a while, my stepmom made me this costume. When I wear it I feel like a Squirrel Girl, meaning that I don't know what's going to happen but I know that I can beat it. When Galactus was coming, I liked how she wasn't scared, but just talked to the guy and got some info from him and learned what he wanted. After that, they were cool! Anyway, I hope you like my costume! Thanks for making my favorite comic!

Claire

RYAN: Claire, your stepmom did an amazing job! It's such a good costume. And you're such a good Squirrel Girl! You've got the smile, the attitude and most of all the confidence. The way you said you feel like you don't know what's going to happen but that you know you're going to beat it--that's Doreen right there. Some of us take years to find that sort of confidence, but you've got it already--and that means I can't wait to see what you decide to do as you grow up. The rest of us took decades to become unbeatable. You're unbeatable ALREADY.

Dear Team Squirrel,

Thank you for creating such an amazing comic. There is so much I want to say to you and will likely send several more letters expressing my gratitude, but I thought I'd start with this summary.

I work at a used-book store (not as cool as being a librarian, I know), and I recommend USG *all* *the* *time*. (Although I can't hand sell it because we almost never have it in. Why would we? Who in their right mind would part with any issue or volume once it was in their possession?) Finally I realized that what I needed to do what write a "staff pick" for our website. Here is my review:

> Best. Super hero. Ever.
> Q: What has super heroes, hard science, real feminism *and* talking squirrels?
>
> A: THE UNBEATABLE SQUIRREL GIRL! I'm not sure who loves Squirrel Girl more: me or my 5-year-old. Why? Ryan North's plots are exciting, funny and intelligent. Erica Henderson's drawings are engaging and portray our hero in realistic human proportions. Squirrel Girl can, and does, beat the bad guys through punches and fighting, but she prefers to use science and/or friendship. In no other comic does the hero win by using Galileo's square-cube principle (and explain how Pym Particles and gamma rays circumvent it). In no other comic book does a fight end with phrases like "mutually acceptable compromise" or "while I don't agree with you, I respect your lived experience." Wherever she goes, Squirrel Girl makes more friends than enemies, makes enemies into friends and carries her determined optimism into every situation, no matter how dire. And that, in the end, is why she is, and always will be, Unbeatable.

With love,
Laura

P.S. The other day my oldest was playing Squirrel Girl. She kept trying to get her younger brother in the game by informing him that he was her partner. He was not getting into it enough for her. Then she had an idea. She said: "Brother! Brother! I'll be Squirrel Girl and you can be my partner as... Black Panther!"

I almost died inside trying to imagine this team-up. Please, please, please, Ryan, can you make this happen???

RYAN: Aw, Laura, thank you! What a kind review, and I love that the biggest problem you have with Squirrel Girl in your used-book store is that people rarely want to part with it. I'LL TAKE IT. There was a little bit of T'Challa in the most recent issue, but a Squirrel Girl/Black Panther team-up could be amazing. And since our editors (Wil Moss and Sarah Brunstad) edit both those books, it should be pretty easy! Right, Wil and Sarah? RIGHT?

Dear Ryan, Derek and the UNBEATABLE SQUIRREL GIRL Team,

I am writing to say "thank you." I have been a fan of UNBEATABLE SQUIRREL GIRL since issue one (and have been a fan of Ryan North's writing for years before that). Over the glorious run of SQUIRREL GIRL, no book has made me laugh more consistently and no comic has made me fall in love with its characters so easily. It's a comic that I know will make me laugh no matter what mood I am in (out-loud laughter! in real life!), and I know it will make me smile, even with all of the cynicism and anger that I may be experiencing in the moments before I sit down to read your wonderful comic. Plus, I will probably learn something about Canada, computer science or squirrel social behavior! UNBEATABLE SQUIRREL GIRL is a comic book that contains a nihilist cyborg (dedicated to human-type friendship) and dino-Ultrons, but its characters ring as true, are as relatable, as anything else in all of fiction, of any medium. From the way these characters are represented visually by Erica Henderson and Derek Charm and given voice by Ryan North represents both a genuine goodness and diversity that is impossible to find elsewhere. The combination of honest decency, the elevation of friendship as a goal AND the sheer fun and hilarity of the book makes it an unparalleled achievement in comics.

Sure, I read my share of dark and gritty stuff, the groundbreaking Pulitzer winners and the indie darlings. I love those books. But there's something so great about being able to enjoy a book I can share with so many people from so many backgrounds, and all of us coming out smiling. It means a lot. Thank you.

With Admiration,
John Arminio

RYAN: Well, John, thank you so much--this means a whole lot to me (and Erica and Derek!). I do like how ridiculous Squirrel Girl sounds on paper--she fights crime with squirrels! One of her close friends is a brain in a jar! Ultron is a robot sometimes!--but it makes me so happy that all these crazy things can fit together and click and make a comic that can make you laugh and have fun and come out smiling. Thank you for all the support--and for reading my stuff for so long and for writing this letter that made our week!

Dear entire USG team,

I'll level with you. Despite having read your book from the very beginning, I've never taken it that seriously. It's fun, but I think somewhere in the back of my mind I kept telling myself that maybe it was more for kids than the standard Marvel fare and that nothing of value would be lost if I decided to stop reading. I'm thrilled to say that those voices have finally been silenced.

I'm writing this letter after completing the "Last Hunt For Kraven" arc. I'm a sucker for redemption stories, and when Squirrel Girl befriended Kraven so long ago I never saw this coming. Brains in jars and green lawyers aside, at its core this was a tale about one person who looked at their friend, saw their ugly history and still said, "No, I know you and you're better than that." Putting it simply, this story arc moved me deeply. No matter my prior opinions of the book, no matter how Squirrel Girl is compared to other Marvel heroes, there's at least a dozen major characters I can't say that about.

I'm forever going to hold Squirrel Girl and Kraven's relationship up as one of the great Marvel friendships. Any failure for Kraven's character development to be seen in other books I feel would be a significant failure on Marvel's part as a creative enterprise. If there's one story that warrants a lasting impact and deserves to be told, it's this one. Thank you for telling the stories I read comic books for.

Steve
Hamilton, Ontario

RYAN: Heck, Steve, thank you. That's exactly what we were all going for with that Kraven story, and I'm so happy it resonated with you so much. I'll be honest: When Kraven appeared in our first issue there weren't any plans to have him show up after that, but we've all been surprised--and happy--to see how that relationship has developed between Sergei and Doreen over the few years that followed. The hard reality of collaborative storytelling like this is that you never know where a story is going to go next, and you never know where another creative team is going to take a character, so all you can do is write the story that matters to you right now and hope that it matters to others too. It means a lot to me that it mattered to you.

Dear Ryan and Erica,

My name is Amelia Shriver, and I am 13 years old.

I've discovered the Squirrel Girl comics quite recently, and I love them. I don't really have any comic book stores near me, so most of what I read is found at the library and out of order. I think one of my favorite parts of the comic is the notes in the margins. They're really fun, and it feels almost like you're talking directly to the readers. I have a question. How does Squirrel Girl feel about dogs? Do they bark at her because she's part squirrel? Does she dislike them for barking at real squirrels?

I also have an idea for a super hero: CorGirl! She is a girl with the super-powers of flight, telepathy, mind-reading and telekinesis. However, she can only use these powers when she shapeshifts into a Pembroke Welsh Corgi, allowing her to keep her identity a secret. As a Corgi, she has her super-powers, as well as normal Corgi abilities, like a canine sense of smell and hearing, but she can't talk as a Corgi.

I would love it if you could include this in a comic, or post it on the Squirrel Girl Tumblr, as I will be more likely to see it there.

Thank you,
Amelia

RYAN: Hi, Amelia--this is you in the comic! And when this comes out I'll post it in the Tumblr, too, so you can see it even before the book arrives at the library. Thank you for all of this! I feel that Squirrel Girl likes dogs, but not all dogs like her, but she doesn't let that get to her. CorGirl is a great character--I love that she can't talk when she's a dog, and I LOVE that she's a dog who can fly--so this is me encouraging you to make some CorGirl comics! Or if you don't want to draw, you can just write down the stories and imagine them that way. Let me ask you a question: How does CorGirl feel about squirrels?

Next Issue:

the unbeatable Squirrel Girl
WHERE'S TONY

Attention, Squirrel Scouts! Make sure to check out our production blog, **unbeatablesquirrelgirl.tumblr.com**, where we post behind-the-scenes stuff on how the book gets made, along with all sorts of cool things *you* make: fanart, cosplay, whatever!

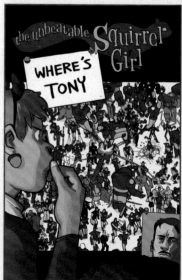

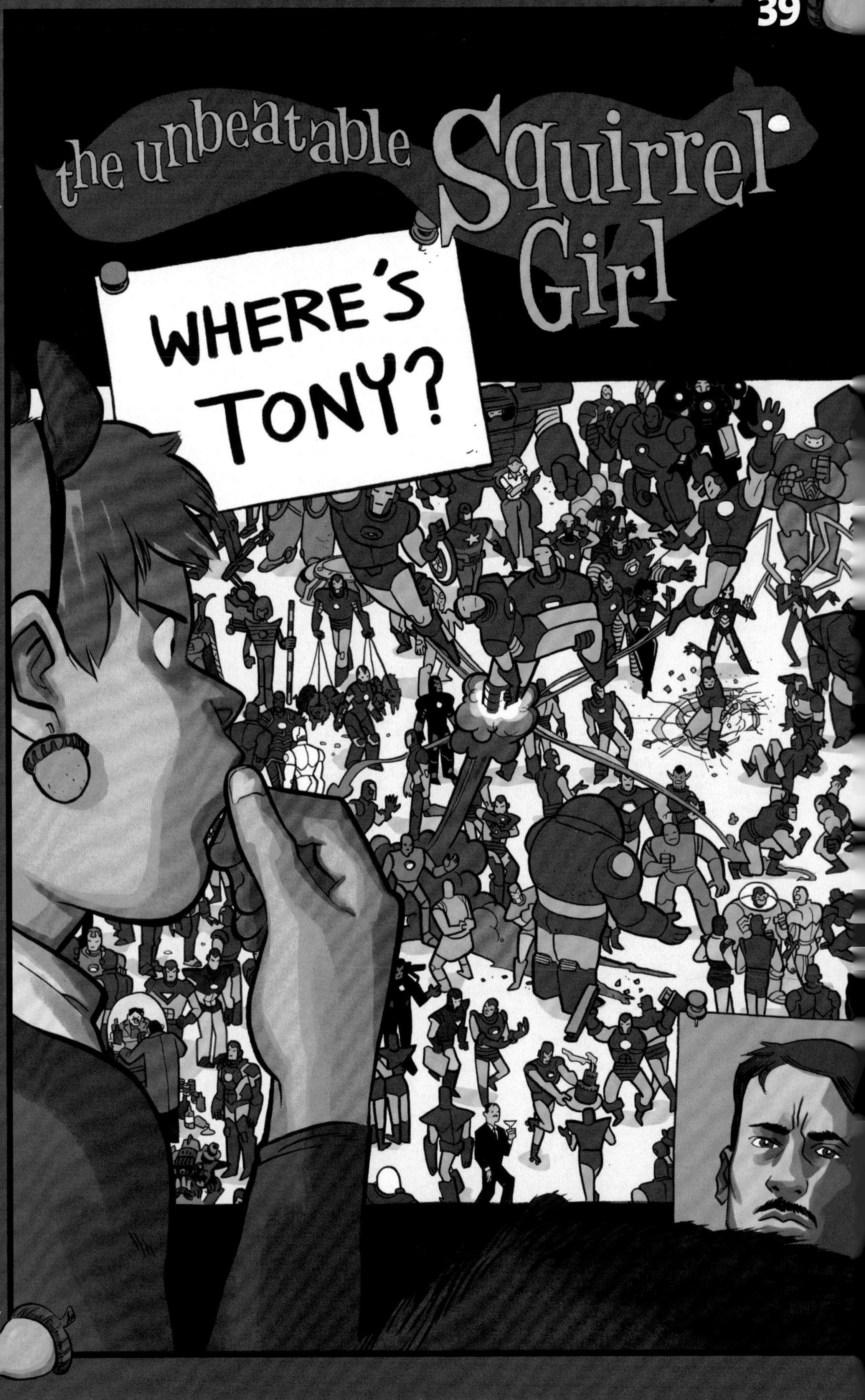
the unbeatable Squirrel Girl
WHERE'S TONY?

Doreen Green isn't just a second-year computer science student: she secretly also has all the powers of both squirrel and girl! She uses her amazing abilities to fight crime **and** be as awesome as possible. You know her as...*The Unbeatable Squirrel Girl.*
Find out what she's been up to, with...

Squirrel Girl *in a nutshell*

 search!

#skrulls

#mandelbrotset

#ntp

#edwardhopper

#doom

Nancy W. @sewwiththeflo
Hey, all 20 of my followers. You'd let me know if you were aliens, right? Like if any of you were space aliens you'd tell me. Like, right now.

Nancy W. @sewwiththeflo
...Okay, great. And yet, I still don't trust any of you not to be space aliens??

Egg @imduderadtude
@sewwiththeflo hey im a human

Nancy W. @sewwiththeflo
@imduderadtude You know what? That I can believe. Okay, listen, internet stranger: got a problem for you. Let's say I'm working on writing a fictional story. And in this story, aliens invade. Only it's secret, and they can stay hidden so nobody notices.

Egg @imduderadtude
@sewwiththeflo cool cool

Nancy W. @sewwiththeflo
@imduderadtude So they're clearly ramping up for SOMETHING.

Egg @imduderadtude
@sewwiththeflo clearly

Nancy W. @sewwiththeflo
@imduderadtude And let's say the hero of my story suspects something is off. And just when it seems things can't get worse, the aliens replace a very important famous genius billionaire playboy philanthropist with one of their own, and AGAIN nobody notices.

Nancy W. @sewwiththeflo
@imduderadtude But when our hero goes to investigate, the alien posing as the billionaire attacks her.

Egg @imduderadtude
@sewwiththeflo ok so im thinking... what if INSTEAD...the aliens were rily friendly

Nancy W. @sewwiththeflo
@imduderadtude Right. That's not what happens though. She gets attacked by the alien, and she's on the ropes, and what can she do to survive this?

Egg @imduderadtude
@sewwiththeflo like what if the alien gives her cookies instead of attacking her and she's like oh wow cookies you know what alien real talk i cant wait to gobble this sweet baked good

Nancy W. @sewwiththeflo
@imduderadtude ...No.

Egg @imduderadtude
@sewwiththeflo and the hero takes a bite, and wait there's something inside the cookie that shouldn't be there! is it...oh no is it ALIEN TOXINS??

Egg @imduderadtude
@sewwiththeflo so she spits it out into her hand but then she sees--oh wait it's not alien toxins!!! it's just a harmless piece of paper! and hold on are those...words printed on it??

Egg @imduderadtude
@sewwiththeflo and she unrolls the paper and it says "i know im an alien but im trying my best so please be kind to me"

Nancy W. @sewwiththeflo
@imduderadtude That's...cute, actually. But, again: not what happens.

Egg @imduderadtude
@sewwiththeflo aren't you the author can't you make anytijng happen

Nancy W. @sewwiththeflo
@imduderadtude Let's just say for the purposes of this conversation that I can't. I'm... co-writing.

Egg @imduderadtude
@sewwiththeflo okay cool so here's what you do, you bake your co-writer cookies and then when they take a bite there's a paper inside that says "@imduderadtude's idea for the alien is actually really good ;)"

Egg @imduderadtude
@sewwiththeflo or maybe instaed of just words it's a meme, like a picture of me and then it says TOP TEXT: my idea is good / BOTTOM TEXT: my idea is very good

Nancy W. @sewwiththeflo
Online was a mistake.

Egg @imduderadtude
@sewwiththeflo TOP TEXT: ummmm wow we'll have to agree to disagree???
BOTTOM TEXT: and also to use my story idea plz and thank u!!!! ;) ;)

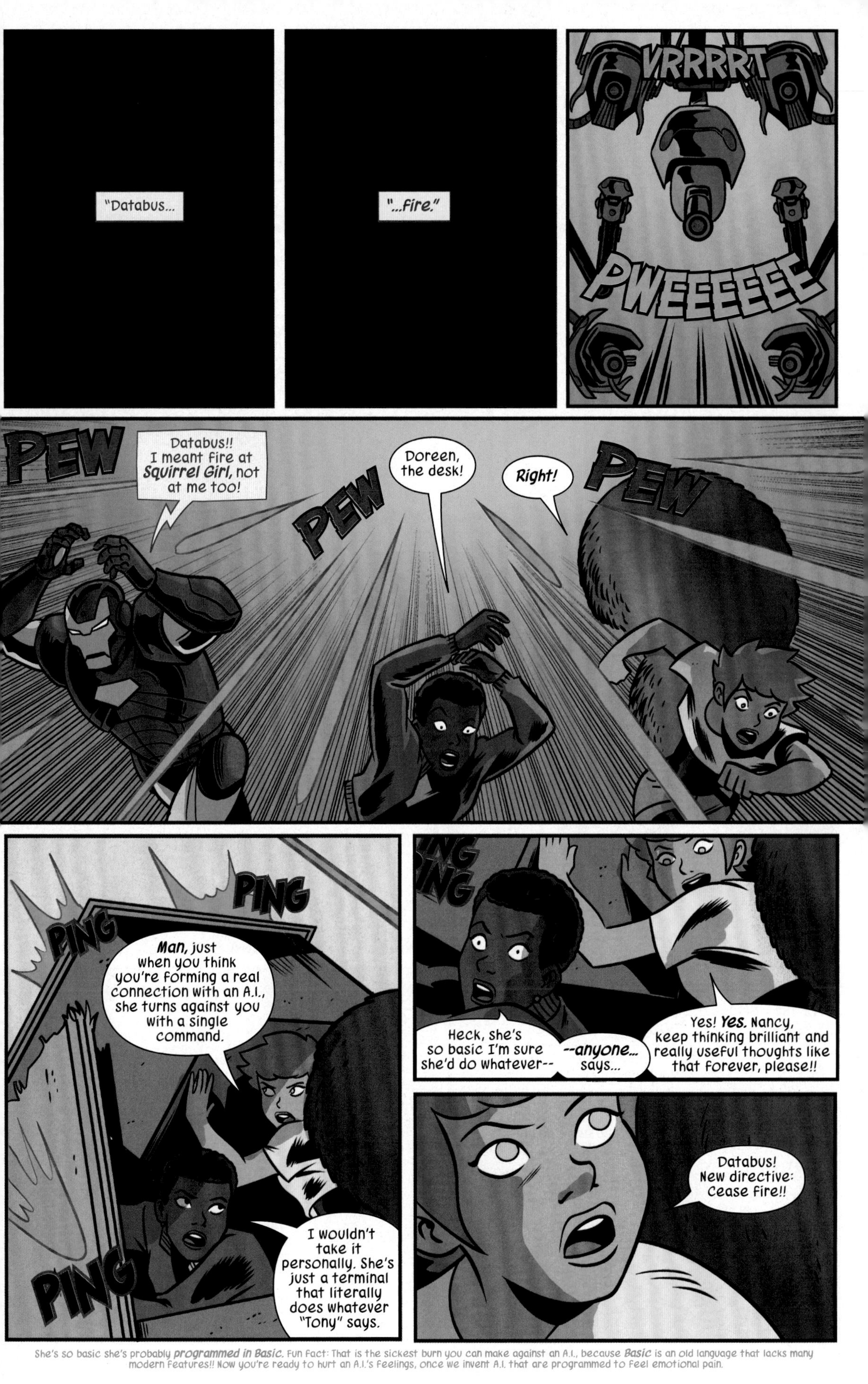

"Databus...
"...Fire."
VRRRRT
PWEEEEEE
PEW
Databus!! I meant fire at Squirrel Girl, not at me too!
PEW
Doreen, the desk!
Right!
PEW
PING
PING
Man, just when you think you're forming a real connection with an A.I., she turns against you with a single command.
I wouldn't take it personally. She's just a terminal that literally does whatever "Tony" says.
PING
Heck, she's so basic I'm sure she'd do whatever--
--anyone... says...
Yes! Yes. Nancy, keep thinking brilliant and really useful thoughts like that forever, please!!
Databus! New directive: Cease fire!!

She's so basic she's probably *programmed in Basic.* Fun Fact: That is the sickest burn you can make against an A.I., because *Basic* is an old language that lacks many modern features!! Now you're ready to hurt an A.I.'s feelings, once we invent A.I. that are programmed to feel emotional pain.

ACKNOWL--
Databus, ignore that, keep firing--
--and lock **all firing commands** to **my** voice only!
PING
ACKNOWLEDGED.
PING
Dang it, Skrull Tony! Dang it, Databus!
Wait. Wait!
Databus, new **non-firing** command: Calculate the set of values of c in the complex plane for which the orbit of 0 under iteration of the quadratic map $z_{n+1} = z_n^2 + c$ remains bounded! Top priority! And lock all calculation requests to **me** and **Squirrel Girl's** voices only!!
PING
PING
ACKNOWLEDGED.
PING
Was that...the **Mandelbrot set?**
Infinite calculations. The more cycles we burn on crunching numbers, the fewer she'll have to target **US!**
Love it.
Databus, multiply progressively larger n x m and m x p matrices of random data, then find and run Newton's method on all 1000-digit plus primes!
ACK-NOWL-EDGED.
And figure out a solution for the 150k body problem that includes the general relativity of a black hole!
ACKK...NOWWWWWWLLL... EDDDDDGEDDDDDDDDDD...
And generate random proteins and compare chemical similarity to all known molecules while translating the full text of Wikipedia into every language and back again!
ACKKKKKkkkkk...
Call me Captain Kirk, Doreen--because **this** girl just talked a computer to death.
Nancy, as soon as we get out of this deadly adventure, I absolutely will.

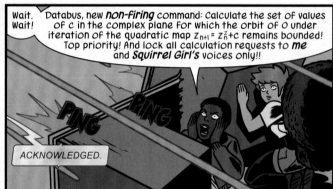

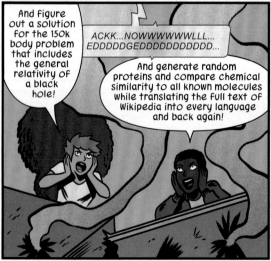

*Call me Captain Picard, Doreen--because **this** girl secretly plays the flute, but only when she's alone or in the presence of dear friends that she really trusts.*

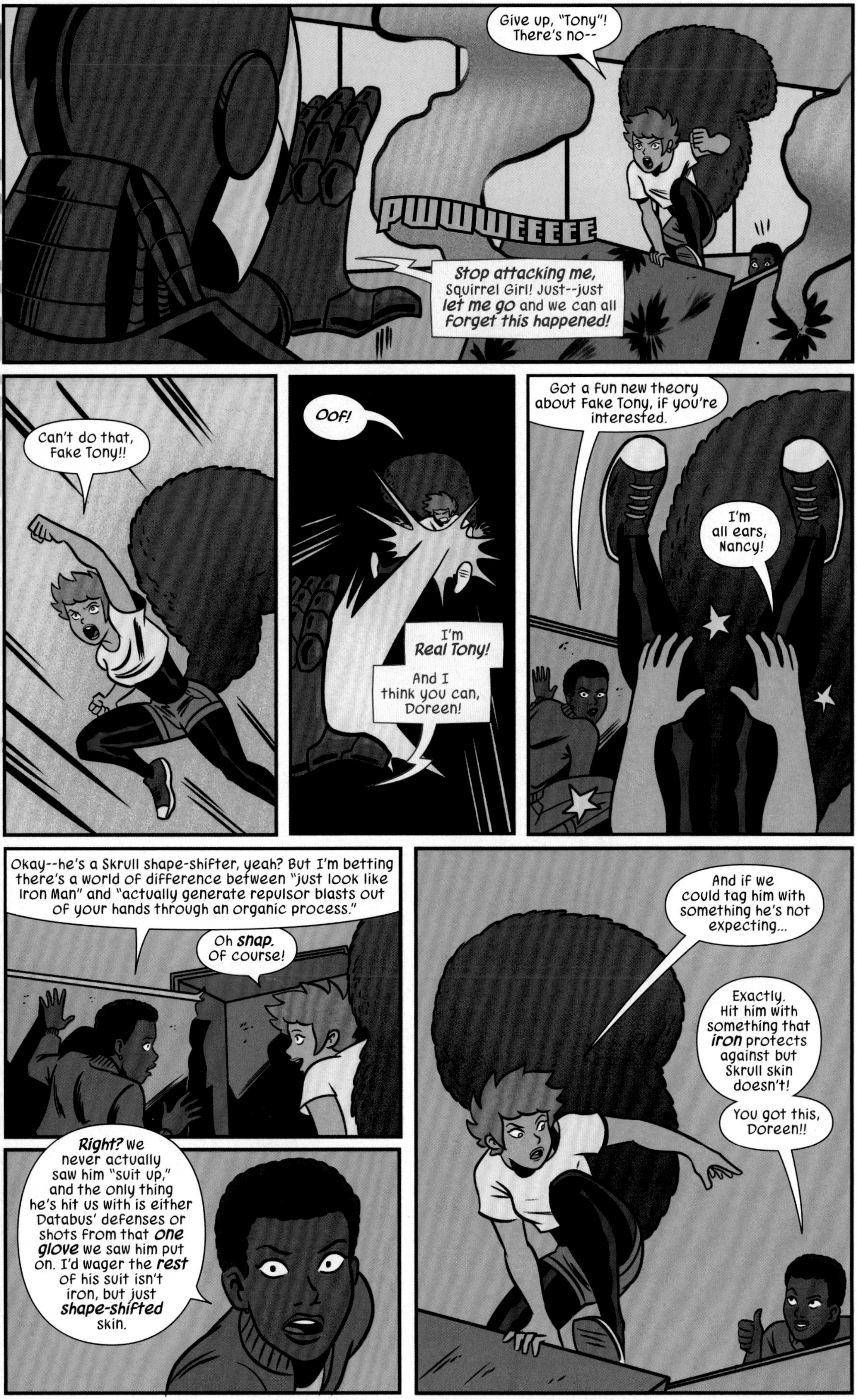
Give up, "Tony"! There's no--
PWWWEEEEE
Stop attacking me, Squirrel Girl! Just--just let me go and we can all forget this happened!
Can't do that, Fake Tony!!
Oof!
I'm Real Tony!
And I think you can, Doreen!
Got a fun new theory about Fake Tony, if you're interested.
I'm all ears, Nancy!
Okay--he's a Skrull shape-shifter, yeah? But I'm betting there's a world of difference between "just look like Iron Man" and "actually generate repulsor blasts out of your hands through an organic process."
Oh snap. Of course!
Right? We never actually saw him "suit up," and the only thing he's hit us with is either Databus' defenses or shots from that one glove we saw him put on. I'd wager the rest of his suit isn't iron, but just shape-shifted skin.
And if we could tag him with something he's not expecting...
Exactly. Hit him with something that iron protects against but Skrull skin doesn't!
You got this, Doreen!!

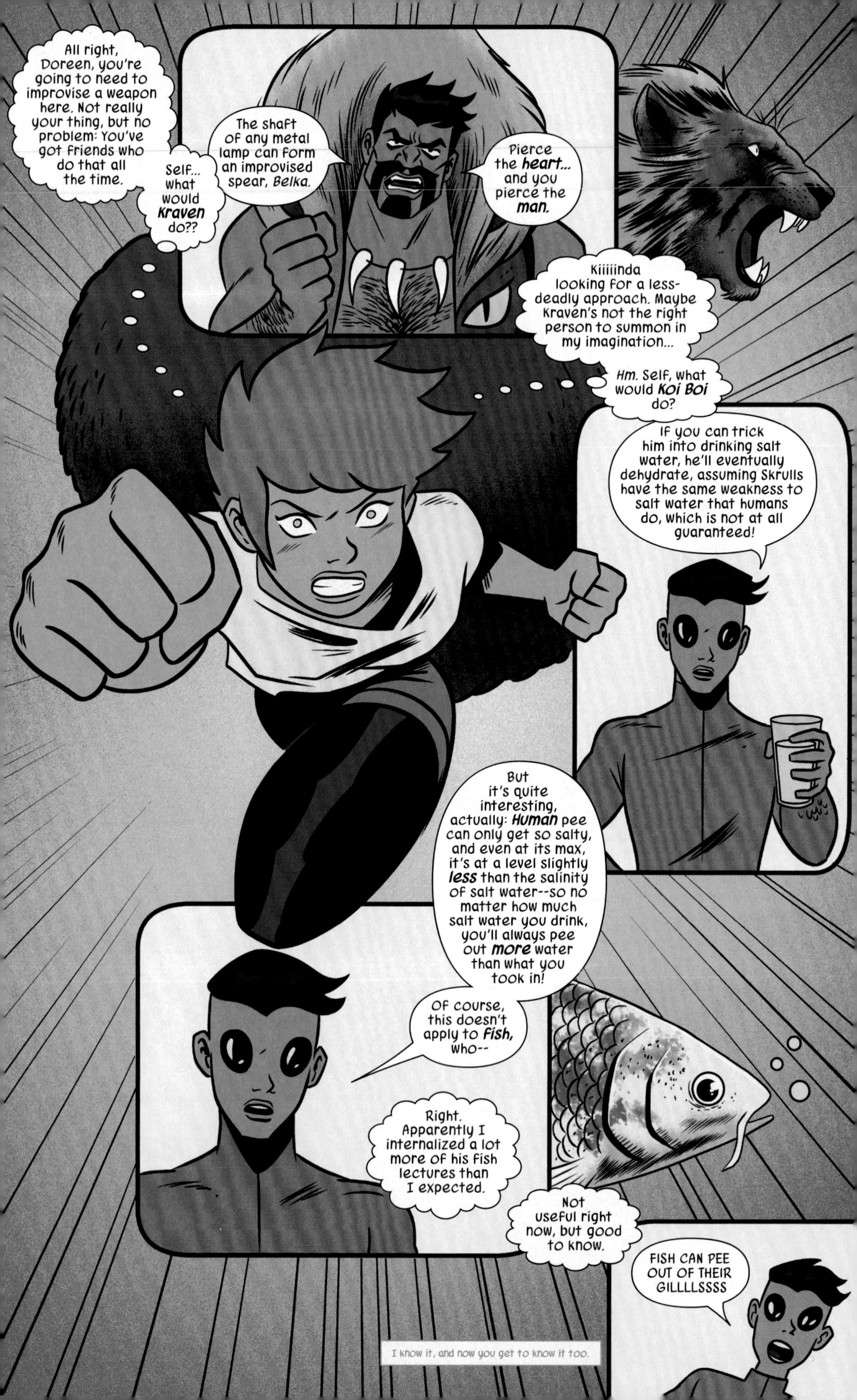
All right, Doreen, you're going to need to improvise a weapon here. Not really your thing, but no problem: You've got friends who do that all the time.
Self... what would Kraven do??
The shaft of any metal lamp can form an improvised spear, Belka.
Pierce the heart... and you pierce the man.
Kiiiiinda looking for a less-deadly approach. Maybe Kraven's not the right person to summon in my imagination...
Hm. Self, what would Koi Boi do?
If you can trick him into drinking salt water, he'll eventually dehydrate, assuming Skrulls have the same weakness to salt water that humans do, which is not at all guaranteed!
But it's quite interesting, actually: Human pee can only get so salty, and even at its max, it's at a level slightly less than the salinity of salt water--so no matter how much salt water you drink, you'll always pee out more water than what you took in!
Of course, this doesn't apply to fish, who--
Right. Apparently I internalized a lot more of his fish lectures than I expected.
Not useful right now, but good to know.
FISH CAN PEE OUT OF THEIR GILLLLSSSS
I know it, and now you get to know it too.

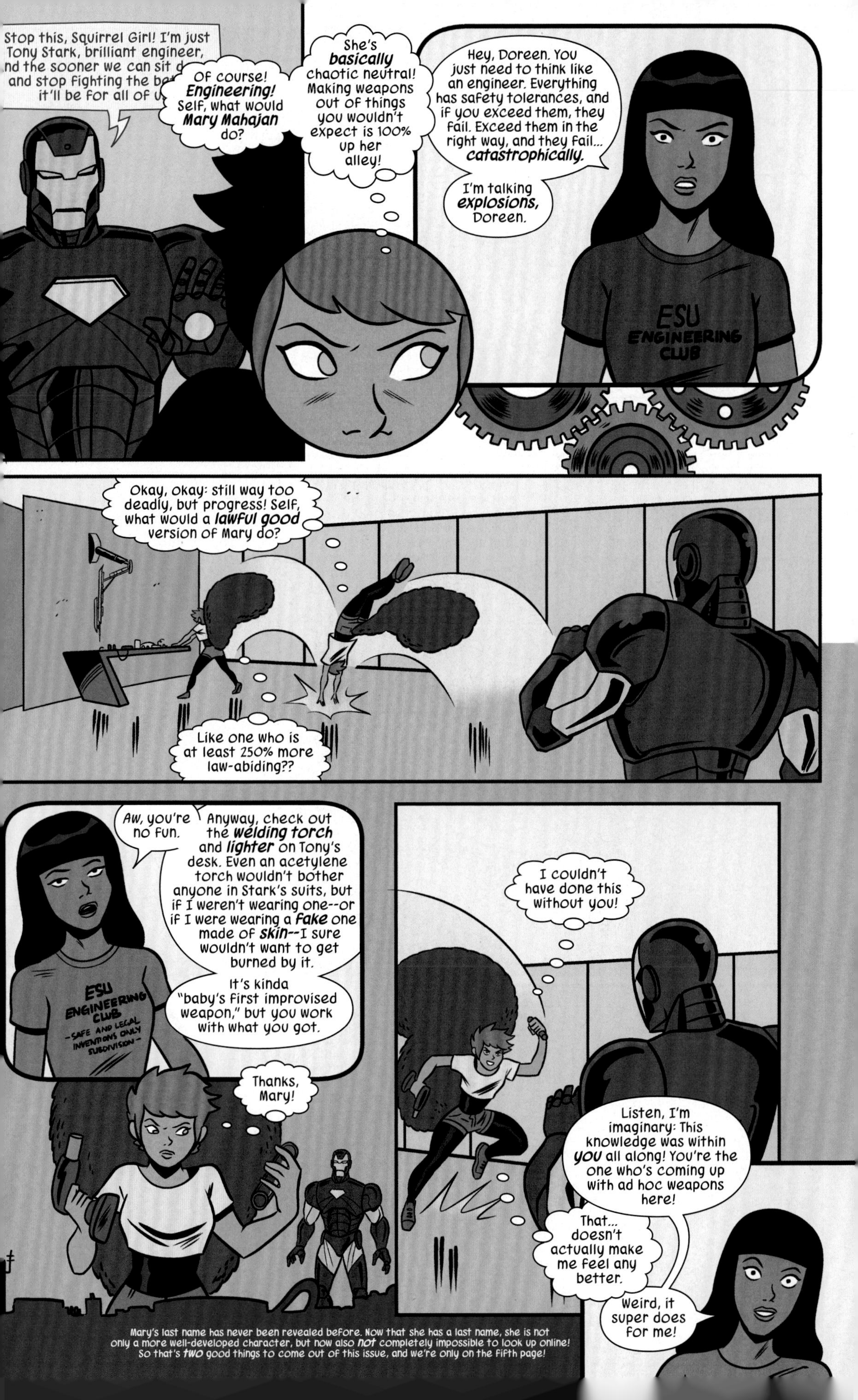

Stop this, Squirrel Girl! I'm just Tony Stark, brilliant engineer, and the sooner we can sit d... and stop fighting the be... it'll be for all of u...
Of course! Engineering! Self, what would Mary Mahajan do?
She's basically chaotic neutral! Making weapons out of things you wouldn't expect is 100% up her alley!
Hey, Doreen. You just need to think like an engineer. Everything has safety tolerances, and if you exceed them, they fail. Exceed them in the right way, and they fail... catastrophically.
I'm talking explosions, Doreen.
ESU ENGINEERING CLUB
Okay, okay: still way too deadly, but progress! Self, what would a lawful good version of Mary do?
Like one who is at least 250% more law-abiding??
Aw, you're no fun.
Anyway, check out the welding torch and lighter on Tony's desk. Even an acetylene torch wouldn't bother anyone in Stark's suits, but if I weren't wearing one--or if I were wearing a fake one made of skin--I sure wouldn't want to get burned by it.
It's kinda "baby's first improvised weapon," but you work with what you got.
ESU ENGINEERING CLUB -SAFE AND LEGAL INVENTIONS ONLY SUBDIVISION-
Thanks, Mary!
I couldn't have done this without you!
Listen, I'm imaginary: This knowledge was within you all along! You're the one who's coming up with ad hoc weapons here!
That... doesn't actually make me feel any better.
Weird, it super does for me!
Mary's last name has never been revealed before. Now that she has a last name, she is not only a more well-developed character, but now also not completely impossible to look up online! So that's two good things to come out of this issue, and we're only on the fifth page!

Okay, "Tony," we had our fun, but...

CHHK

...this ends now.

FWOOM

Doreen, please, like I keep telling you: I'm *Iron Man*. It'll take more than a little flame to hurt me.

Oh sure. The *real* Tony wouldn't be afraid of this, because he's in a suit of armor. But I've been thinking, and I bet the only *actual* armor here is that glove you keep using, and the rest is just shape-shifted skin.

And I've got this funny feeling you don't want to get it burned??

Doreen, this isn't you. This is crazy.

NO, kidnapping and replacing my friends is crazy.

Invading Earth is crazy.

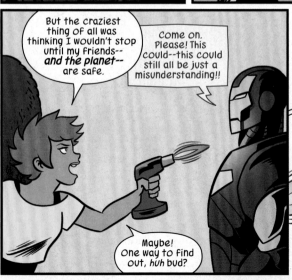

But the craziest thing of all was thinking I wouldn't stop until my friends--*and the planet*--are safe.

Come on. Please! This could--this could still all be just a misunderstanding!!

Maybe! One way to find out, *huh* bud?

How's about we run a little test that, if you're telling the truth, *won't hurt you* at all??

Squirrel Girl... listen, I-- I...

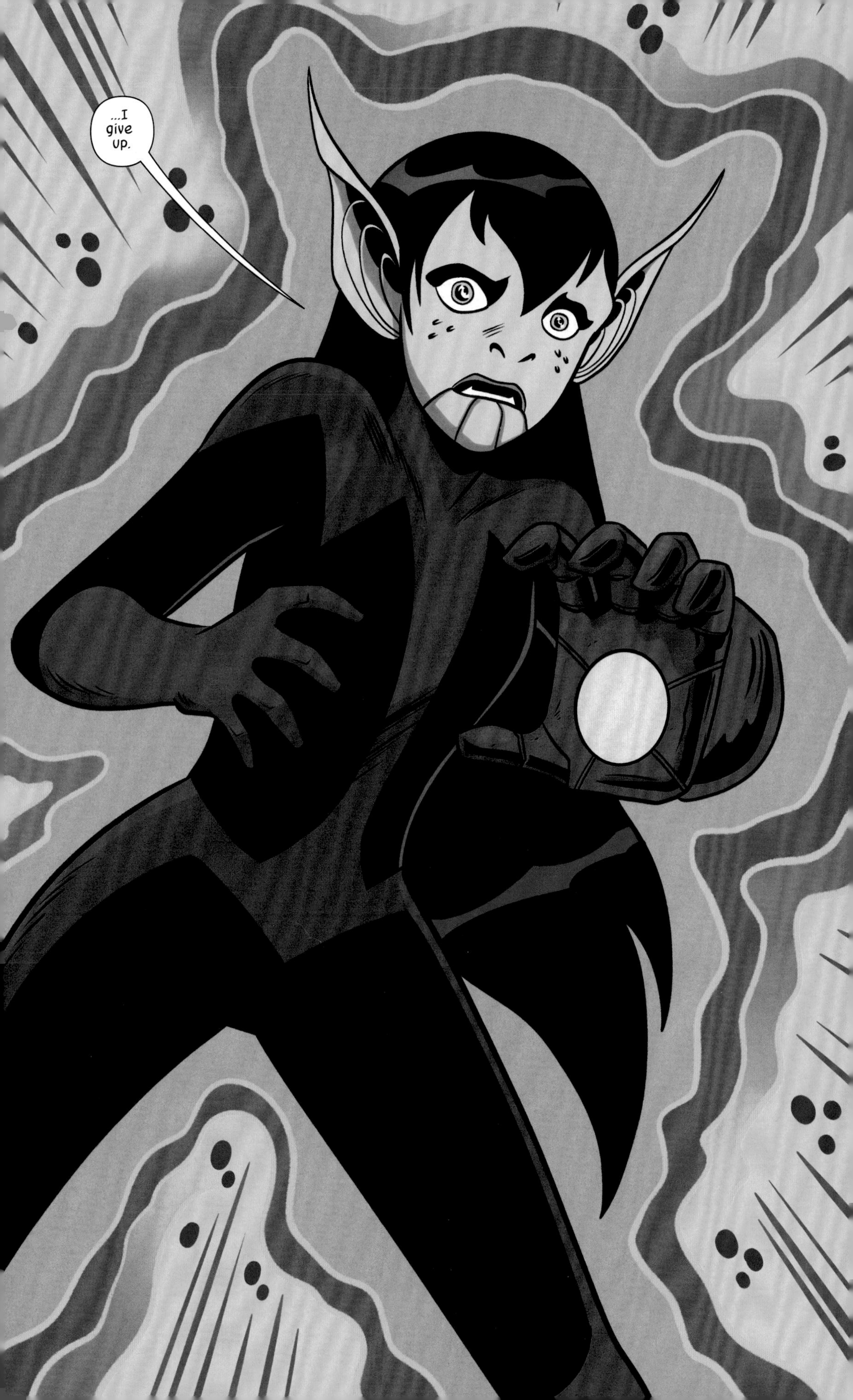
...I give up.

YOU-- I...

I was expecting a **soldier**.

OF COURSE you were. And of course the next thing you'll say is, "She really **COULD** be a soldier and just shape-shifted into this **sympathetic** form." Can't trust a Skrull, right??

That is a legit concern, yes. Listen, I don't--we don't know how big this goes. You **replaced Tony Stark.** We need to take you into the authorities.

But we can't **trust** any authorities. They could be Skrull invaders too.

NO. NO authorities. I stay secret.

Look, I'm sorry, but we're **WAY** past that.

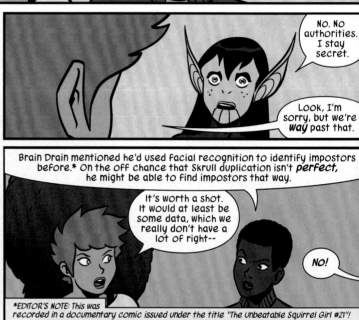

Brain Drain mentioned he'd used facial recognition to identify impostors before.* On the off chance that Skrull duplication isn't **perfect,** he might be able to find impostors that way.

It's worth a shot. It would at least be some data, which we really don't have a lot of right--

NO!

*EDITOR'S NOTE: This was recorded in a documentary comic issued under the title "The Unbeatable Squirrel Girl #21"!

You have to keep me secret! I can't be known. I can't!

Listen, I sympathize, but there's no way this invasion is going to stay secret, and--

So you're not going to help me?

Help you-- what, stay **secret?** Invade Earth? No, we--

FLOOOMPH

How long did it take me to determine that the sound of a humanoid rapidly transforming into a spheroid would be "FLOOMPH"? Approximately zero seconds. Some things, in your heart of hearts, you have simply *always* known.

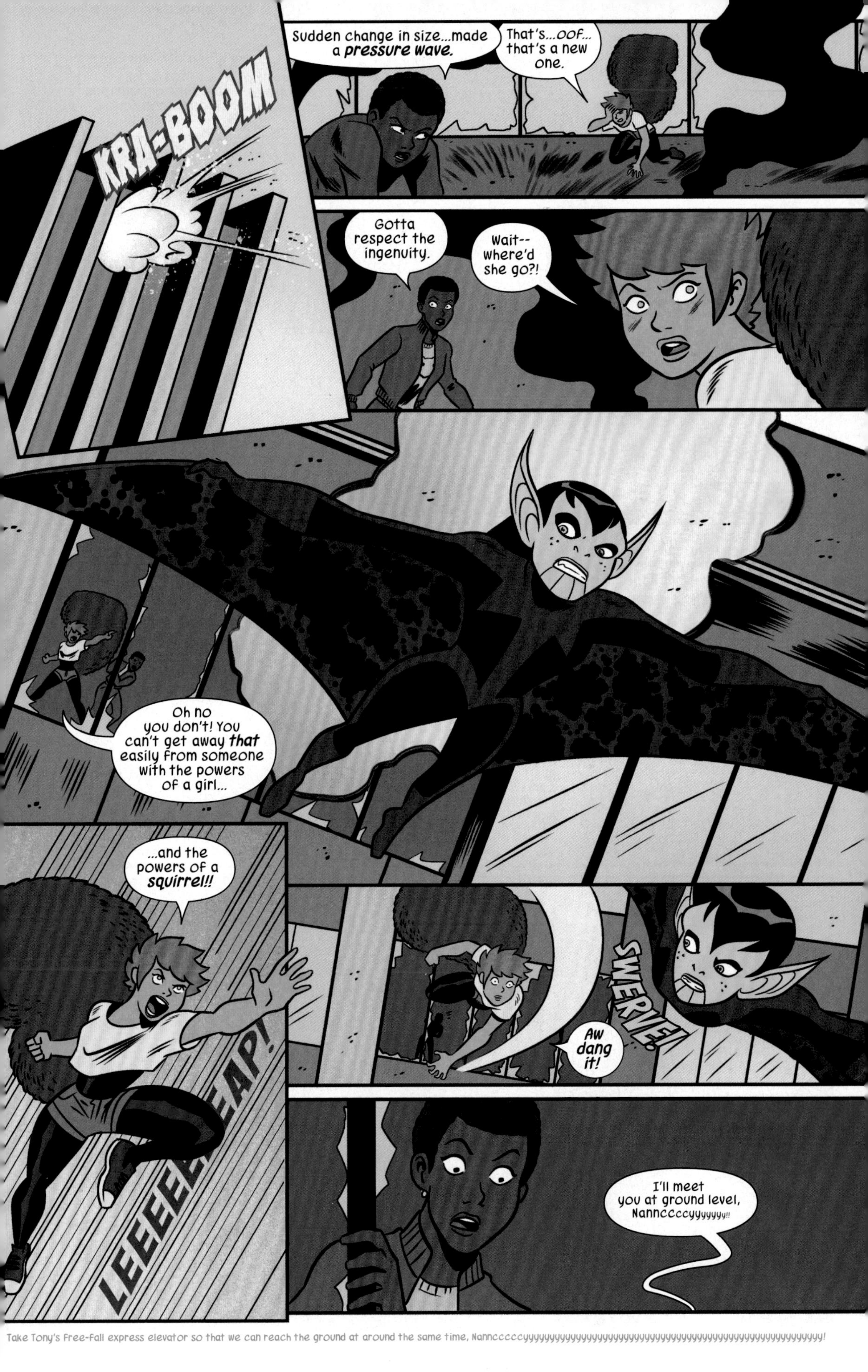
KRA-BOOM
Sudden change in size...made a **pressure wave.**
That's...*OOF...* that's a new one.
Gotta respect the ingenuity.
Wait--where'd she go?!
Oh no you don't! You can't get away **that** easily from someone with the powers of a girl...
...and the powers of a **squirrel!!**
LEEEEEEEAP!
SWERVE!
Aw dang it!
I'll meet you at ground level, Nannccccyyyyyyy!!

Take Tony's Free-Fall express elevator so that we can reach the ground at around the same time, Nannccccccyyyyyyyyyyyyyyyyyyyyyyyyyyyyyyyyyyyyyyyyyyyyyyyyyyyyyyyyyyyyyyyyy!

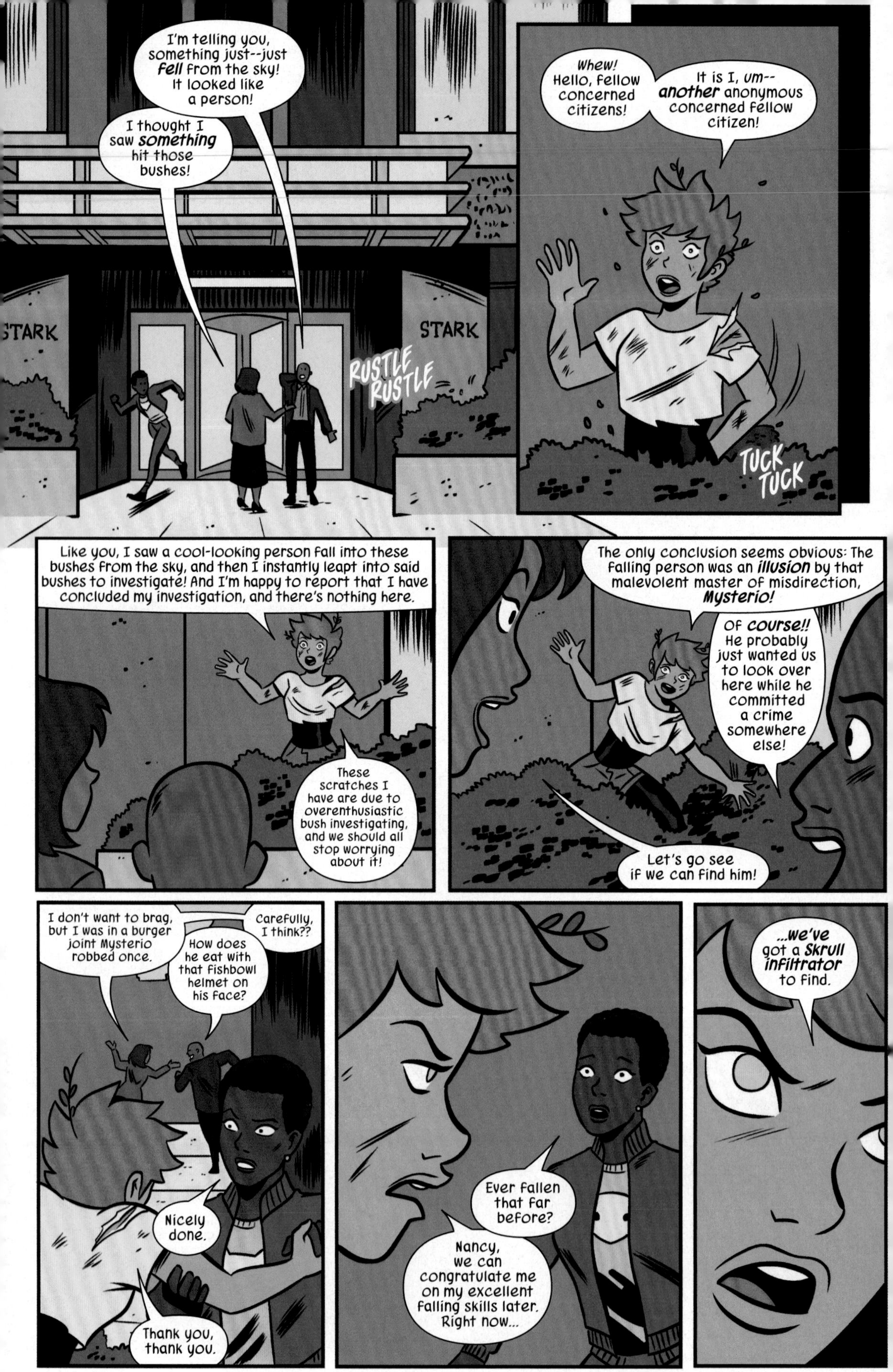
I'm telling you, something just--just fell from the sky! It looked like a person!
I thought I saw something hit those bushes!
RUSTLE RUSTLE
Whew! Hello, fellow concerned citizens!
It is I, um-- another anonymous concerned fellow citizen!
TUCK TUCK
STARK
STARK
Like you, I saw a cool-looking person fall into these bushes from the sky, and then I instantly leapt into said bushes to investigate! And I'm happy to report that I have concluded my investigation, and there's nothing here.
These scratches I have are due to overenthusiastic bush investigating, and we should all stop worrying about it!
The only conclusion seems obvious: The falling person was an illusion by that malevolent master of misdirection, Mysterio!
Of course!! He probably just wanted us to look over here while he committed a crime somewhere else!
Let's go see if we can find him!
I don't want to brag, but I was in a burger joint Mysterio robbed once.
How does he eat with that fishbowl helmet on his face?
Carefully, I think??
Nicely done.
Thank you, thank you.
Ever fallen that far before?
Nancy, we can congratulate me on my excellent falling skills later. Right now...
...we've got a Skrull infiltrator to find.

If I lived in the Marvel Universe I would blame Mysterio for *everything.* Trip down the stairs? Thanks, *Mysterio.* Wait too long and then my cereal gets soggy? Thanks, *Mysterio.* Get kidnapped by a master of illusion wearing a giant dome helmet? Oh, you know I'ma be sarcastically thanking Mysterio in this particular circumstance!!

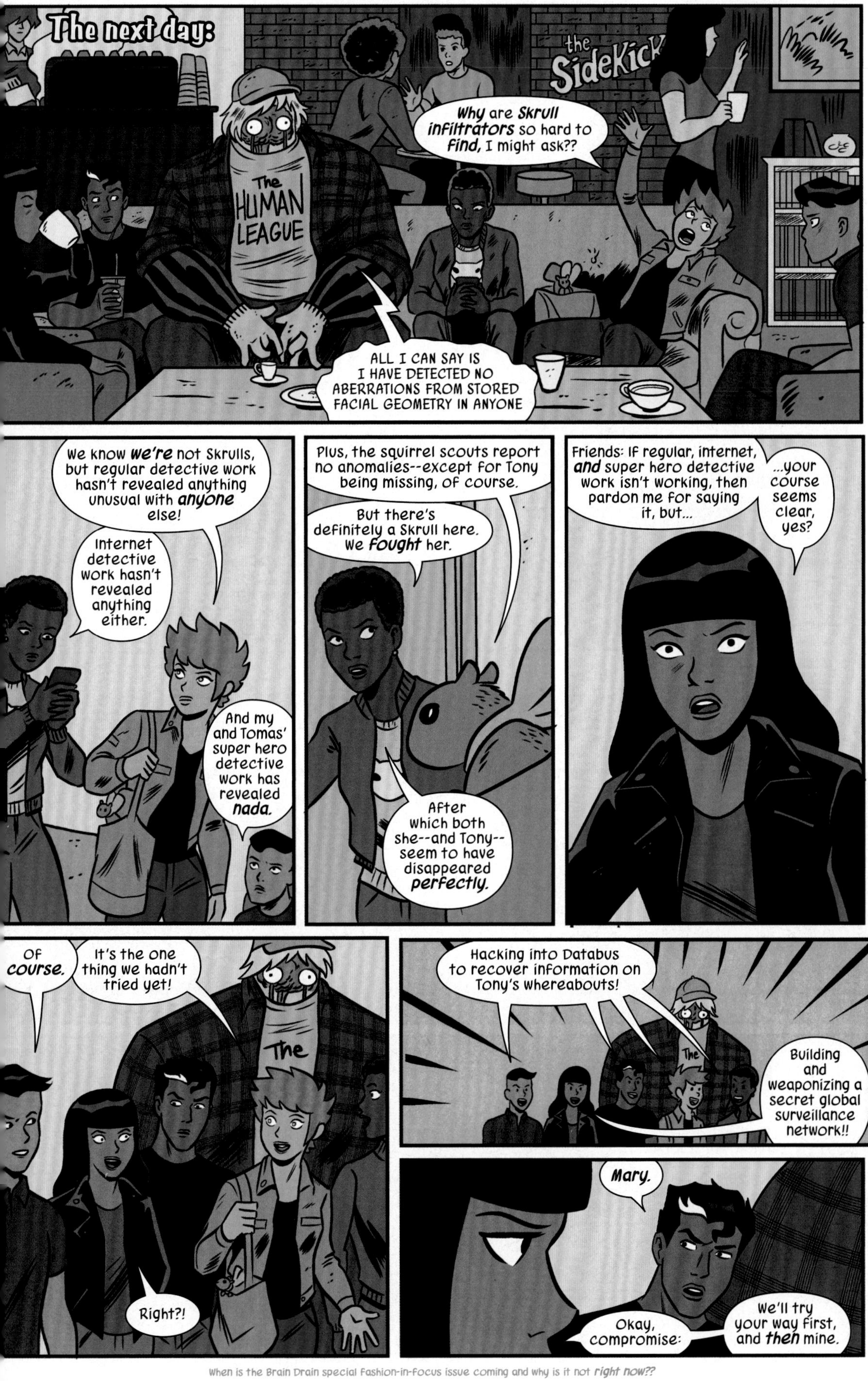

The next day:
the SideKick
Why are Skrull infiltrators so hard to find, I might ask??
The HUMAN LEAGUE
ALL I CAN SAY IS I HAVE DETECTED NO ABERRATIONS FROM STORED FACIAL GEOMETRY IN ANYONE
We know we're not Skrulls, but regular detective work hasn't revealed anything unusual with anyone else!
Internet detective work hasn't revealed anything either.
And my and Tomas' super hero detective work has revealed nada.
Plus, the squirrel scouts report no anomalies--except for Tony being missing, of course.
But there's definitely a Skrull here. We fought her.
After which both she--and Tony--seem to have disappeared perfectly.
Friends: If regular, internet, and super hero detective work isn't working, then pardon me for saying it, but...
...your course seems clear, yes?
Of course.
It's the one thing we hadn't tried yet!
The
Right?!
Hacking into Databus to recover information on Tony's whereabouts!
The
Building and weaponizing a secret global surveillance network!!
Mary.
Okay, compromise:
We'll try your way first, and then mine.

When is the Brain Drain special Fashion-in-Focus issue coming and why is it not *right now??*

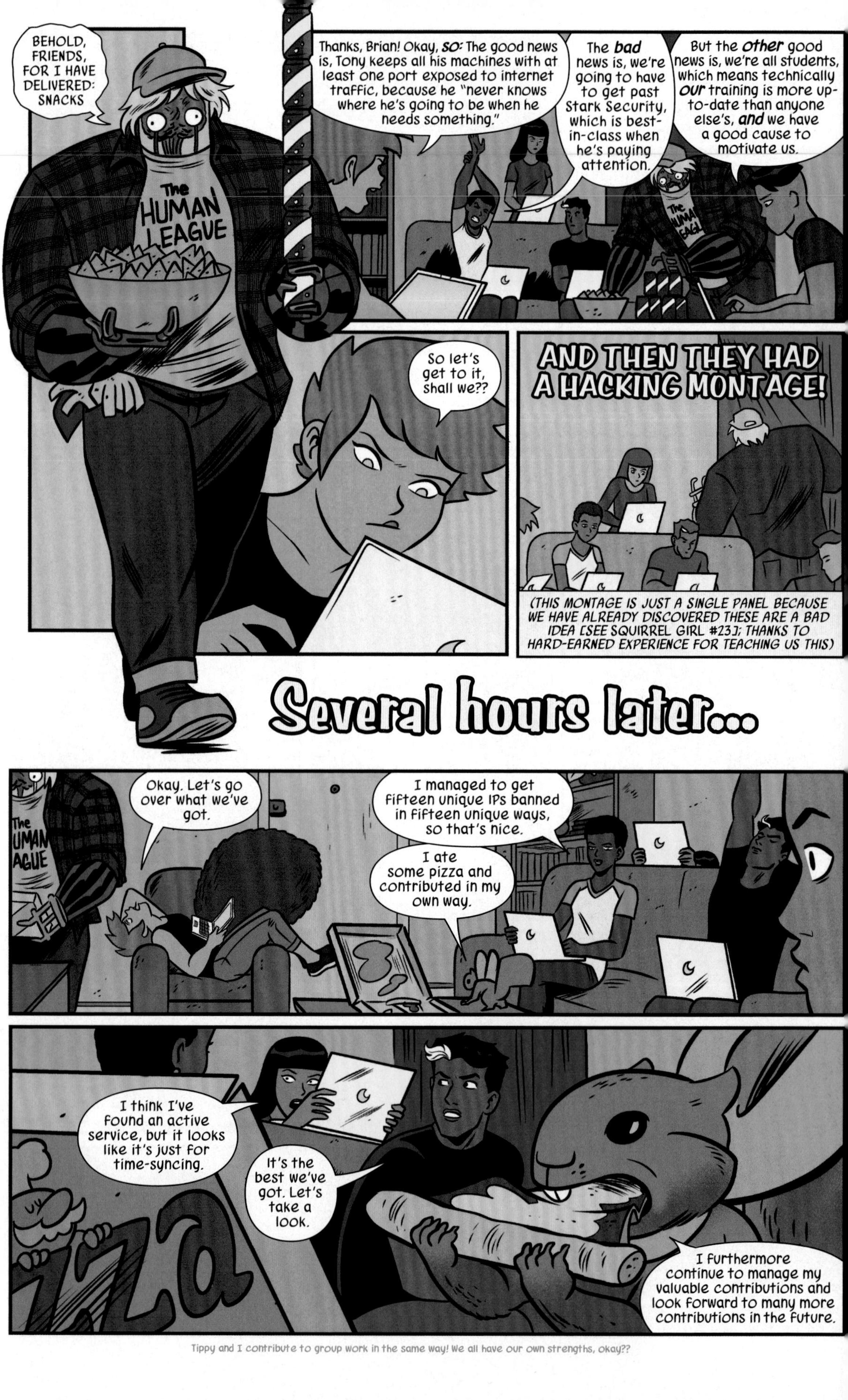

BEHOLD, FRIENDS, FOR I HAVE DELIVERED: SNACKS
The HUMAN LEAGUE
Thanks, Brian! Okay, SO: The good news is, Tony keeps all his machines with at least one port exposed to internet traffic, because he "never knows where he's going to be when he needs something."
The bad news is, we're going to have to get past Stark Security, which is best-in-class when he's paying attention.
But the other good news is, we're all students, which means technically our training is more up-to-date than anyone else's, and we have a good cause to motivate us.
So let's get to it, shall we??
AND THEN THEY HAD A HACKING MONTAGE!
(THIS MONTAGE IS JUST A SINGLE PANEL BECAUSE WE HAVE ALREADY DISCOVERED THESE ARE A BAD IDEA [SEE SQUIRREL GIRL #23]; THANKS TO HARD-EARNED EXPERIENCE FOR TEACHING US THIS)
Several hours later...
Okay. Let's go over what we've got.
I managed to get fifteen unique IPs banned in fifteen unique ways, so that's nice.
I ate some pizza and contributed in my own way.
I think I've found an active service, but it looks like it's just for time-syncing.
It's the best we've got. Let's take a look.
I furthermore continue to manage my valuable contributions and look forward to many more contributions in the future.

Tippy and I contribute to group work in the same way! We all have our own strengths, okay??

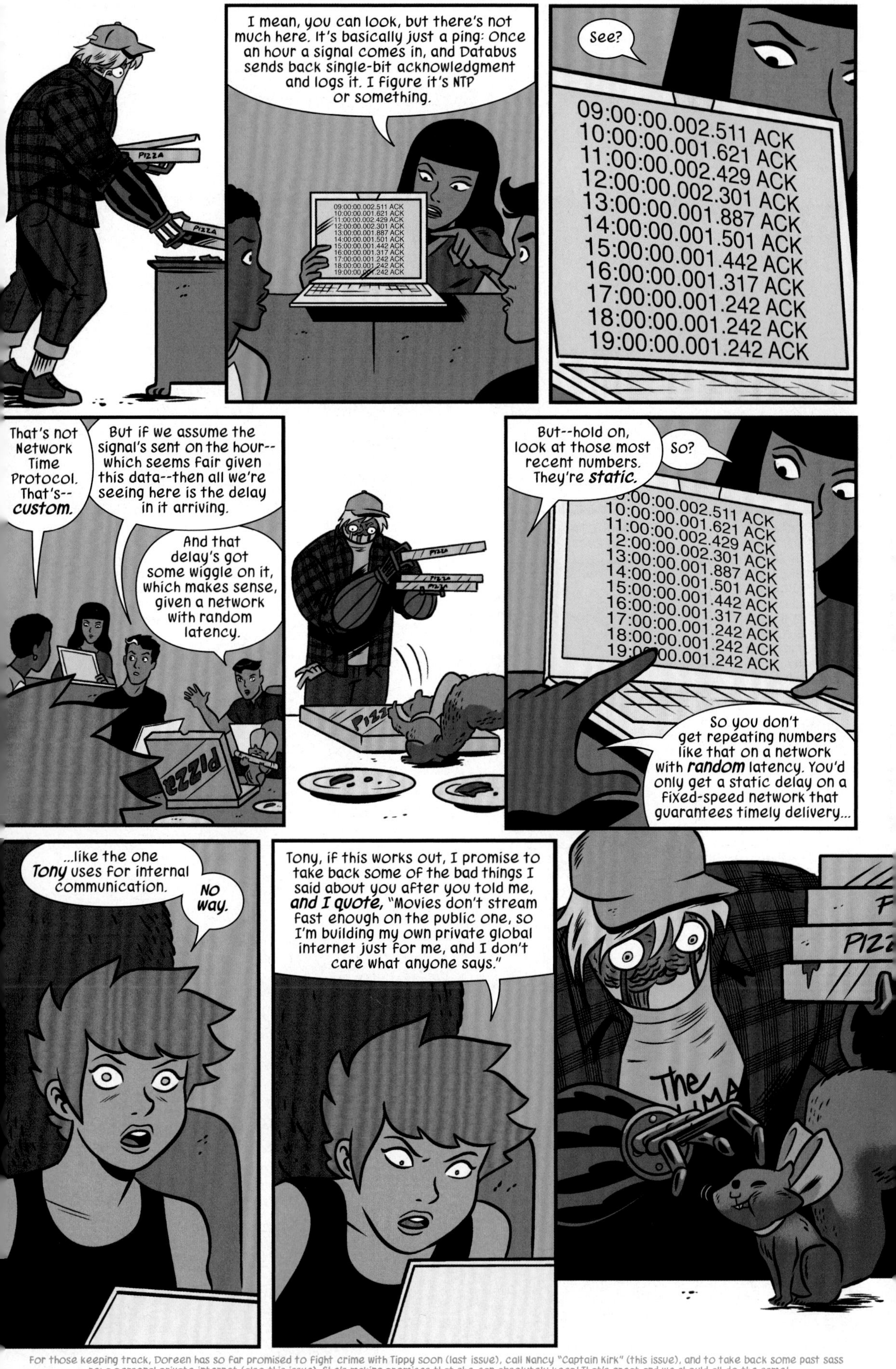
I mean, you can look, but there's not much here. It's basically just a ping: Once an hour a signal comes in, and Databus sends back single-bit acknowledgment and logs it. I figure it's NTP or something.
See?
09:00:00.002.511 ACK
10:00:00.001.621 ACK
11:00:00.002.429 ACK
12:00:00.002.301 ACK
13:00:00.001.887 ACK
14:00:00.001.501 ACK
15:00:00.001.442 ACK
16:00:00.001.317 ACK
17:00:00.001.242 ACK
18:00:00.001.242 ACK
19:00:00.001.242 ACK
That's not Network Time Protocol. That's-- *custom.*
But if we assume the signal's sent on the hour--which seems fair given this data--then all we're seeing here is the delay in it arriving.
And that delay's got some wiggle on it, which makes sense, given a network with random latency.
But--hold on, look at those most recent numbers. They're ***static.***
So?
So you don't get repeating numbers like that on a network with ***random*** latency. You'd only get a static delay on a fixed-speed network that guarantees timely delivery...
...like the one ***Tony*** uses for internal communication.
NO way.
Tony, if this works out, I promise to take back some of the bad things I said about you after you told me, ***and I quote,*** "Movies don't stream fast enough on the public one, so I'm building my own private global internet just for me, and I don't care what anyone says."

For those keeping track, Doreen has so far promised to fight crime with Tippy soon (last issue), call Nancy "Captain Kirk" (this issue), and to take back some past sass re: a personal private internet (also this issue). She's making promises that she can absolutely keep! That's great and we should all do the same!

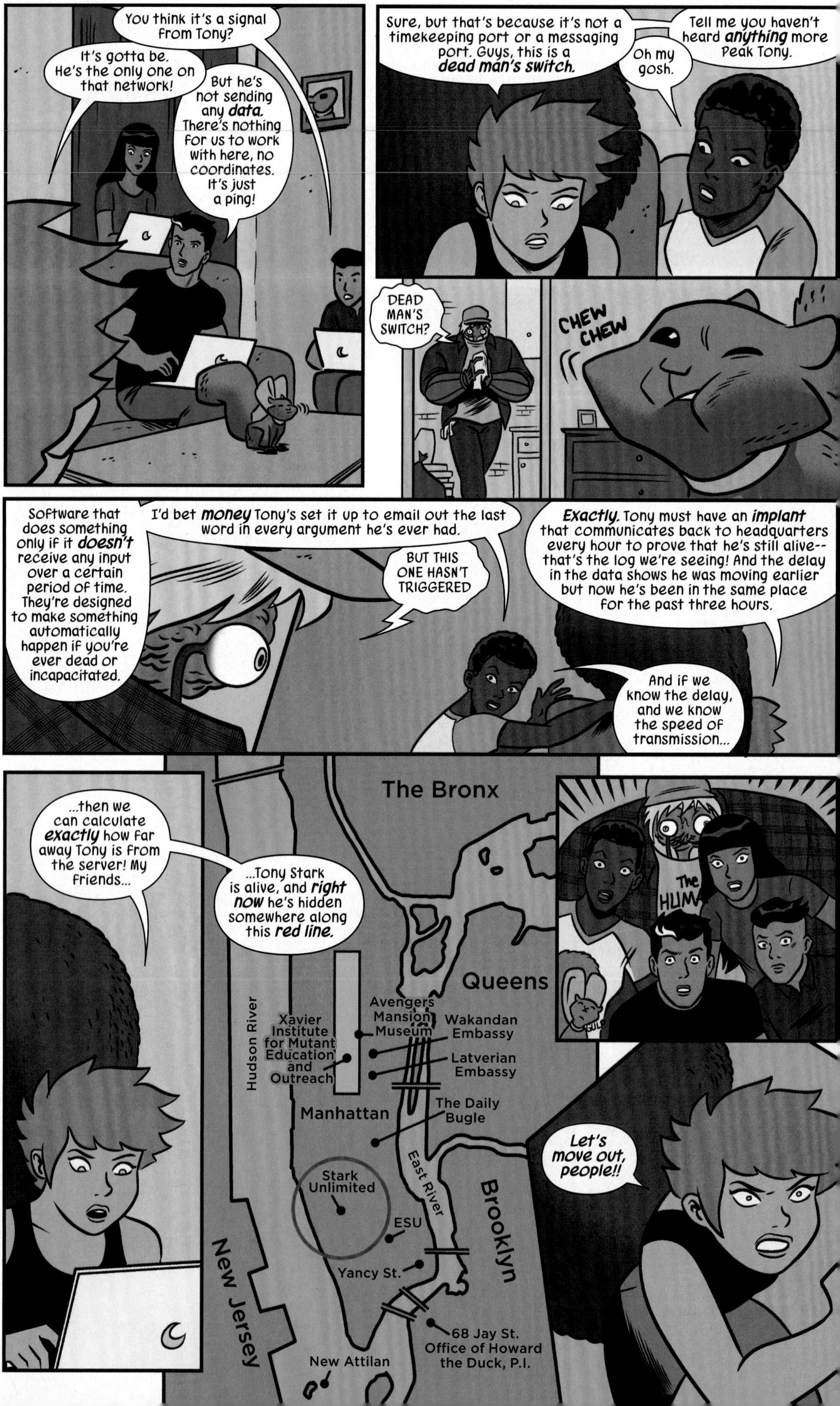
You think it's a signal from Tony?
It's gotta be. He's the only one on that network!
But he's not sending any *data.* There's nothing for us to work with here, no coordinates. It's just a ping!
Sure, but that's because it's not a timekeeping port or a messaging port. Guys, this is a *dead man's switch.*
Tell me you haven't heard *anything* more Peak Tony.
Oh my gosh.
DEAD MAN'S SWITCH?
CHEW CHEW
Software that does something only if it *doesn't* receive any input over a certain period of time. They're designed to make something automatically happen if you're ever dead or incapacitated.
I'd bet *money* Tony's set it up to email out the last word in every argument he's ever had.
BUT THIS ONE HASN'T TRIGGERED
Exactly. Tony must have an *implant* that communicates back to headquarters every hour to prove that he's still alive--that's the log we're seeing! And the delay in the data shows he was moving earlier but now he's been in the same place for the past three hours.
And if we know the delay, and we know the speed of transmission...
...then we can calculate *exactly* how far away Tony is from the server! My friends...
...Tony Stark is alive, and *right now* he's hidden somewhere along this *red line.*
The Bronx
Queens
Hudson River
Xavier Institute for Mutant Education and Outreach
Avengers Mansion Museum
Wakandan Embassy
Latverian Embassy
Manhattan
The Daily Bugle
East River
Stark Unlimited
ESU
Brooklyn
Yancy St.
New Jersey
68 Jay St. Office of Howard the Duck, P.I.
New Attilan
The HUMA
GULP
Let's move out, people!!

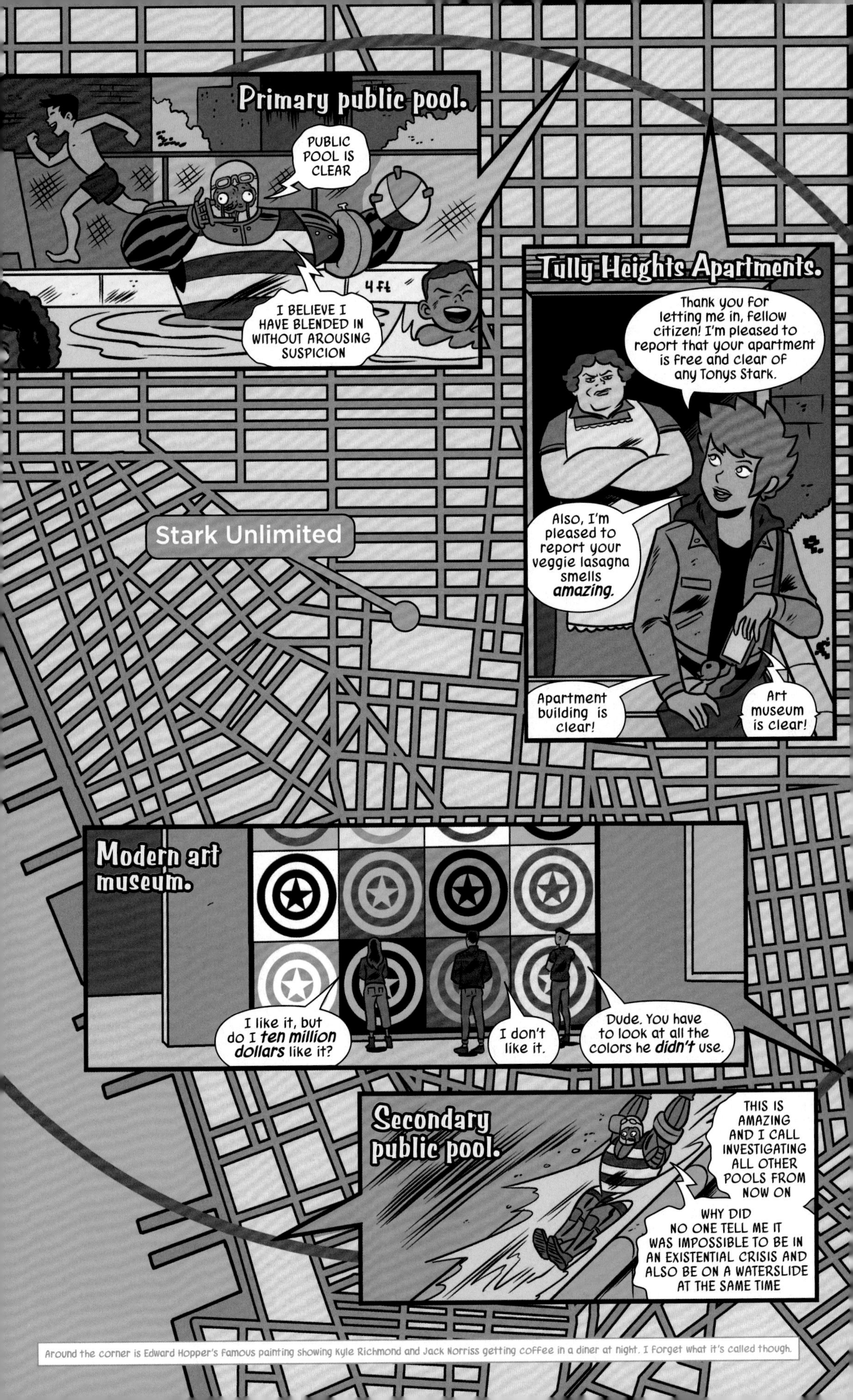

Primary public pool.
PUBLIC POOL IS CLEAR
4 ft
I BELIEVE I HAVE BLENDED IN WITHOUT AROUSING SUSPICION
Tully Heights Apartments.
Thank you for letting me in, fellow citizen! I'm pleased to report that your apartment is free and clear of any Tonys Stark.
Also, I'm pleased to report your veggie lasagna smells amazing.
Apartment building is clear!
Art museum is clear!
Stark Unlimited
Modern art museum.
I like it, but do I ten million dollars like it?
I don't like it.
Dude. You have to look at all the colors he didn't use.
Secondary public pool.
THIS IS AMAZING AND I CALL INVESTIGATING ALL OTHER POOLS FROM NOW ON
WHY DID NO ONE TELL ME IT WAS IMPOSSIBLE TO BE IN AN EXISTENTIAL CRISIS AND ALSO BE ON A WATERSLIDE AT THE SAME TIME
Around the corner is Edward Hopper's famous painting showing Kyle Richmond and Jack Norriss getting coffee in a diner at night. I forget what it's called though.

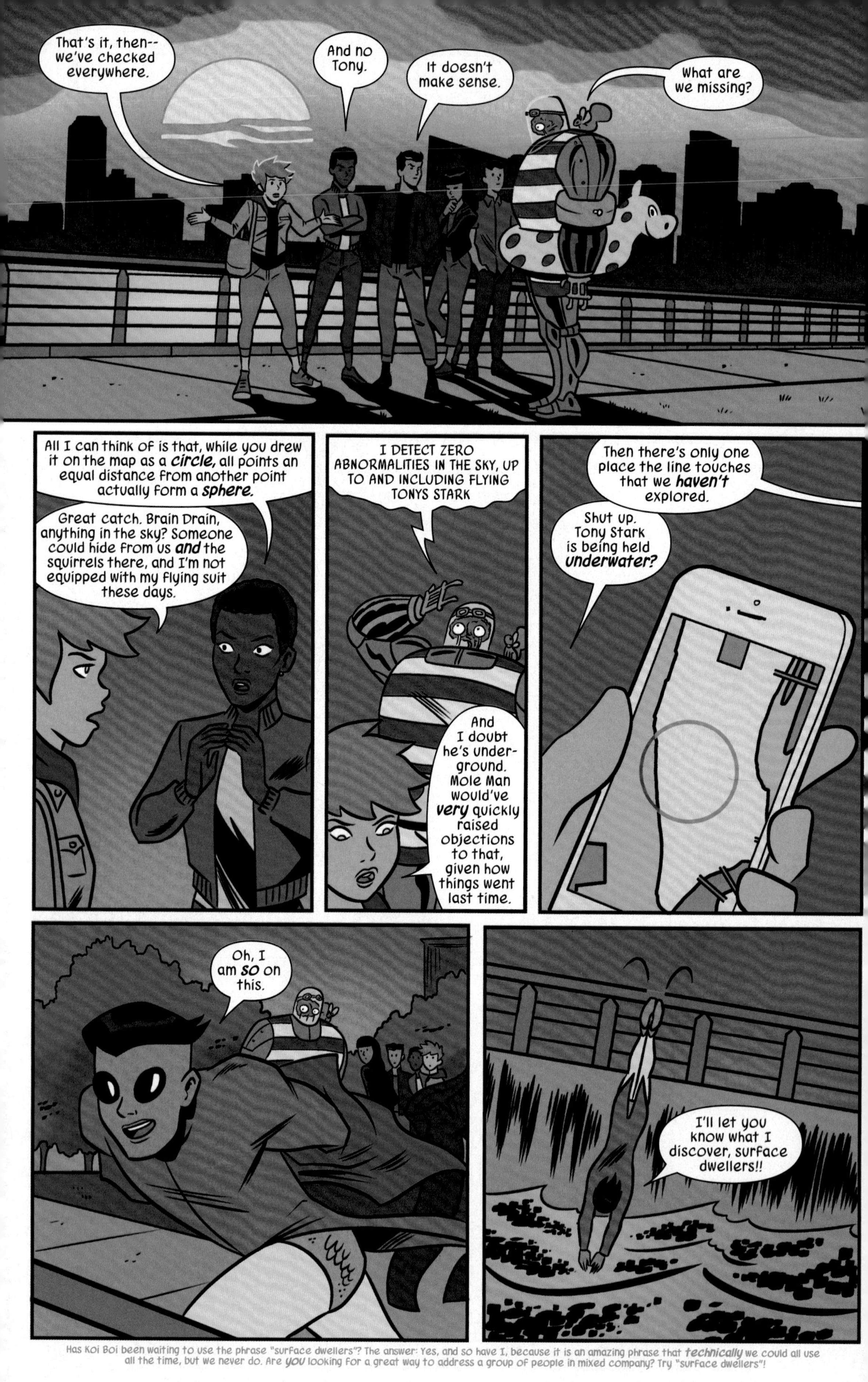
That's it, then-- we've checked everywhere.
And no Tony.
It doesn't make sense.
What are we missing?
All I can think of is that, while you drew it on the map as a circle, all points an equal distance from another point actually form a sphere.
Great catch. Brain Drain, anything in the sky? Someone could hide from us and the squirrels there, and I'm not equipped with my flying suit these days.
I DETECT ZERO ABNORMALITIES IN THE SKY, UP TO AND INCLUDING FLYING TONYS STARK
And I doubt he's underground. Mole Man would've very quickly raised objections to that, given how things went last time.
Then there's only one place the line touches that we haven't explored.
Shut up. Tony Stark is being held underwater?
Oh, I am so on this.
I'll let you know what I discover, surface dwellers!!

Has Koi Boi been waiting to use the phrase "surface dwellers"? The answer: Yes, and so have I, because it is an amazing phrase that *technically* we could all use all the time, but we never do. Are *you* looking for a great way to address a group of people in mixed company? Try "surface dwellers"!

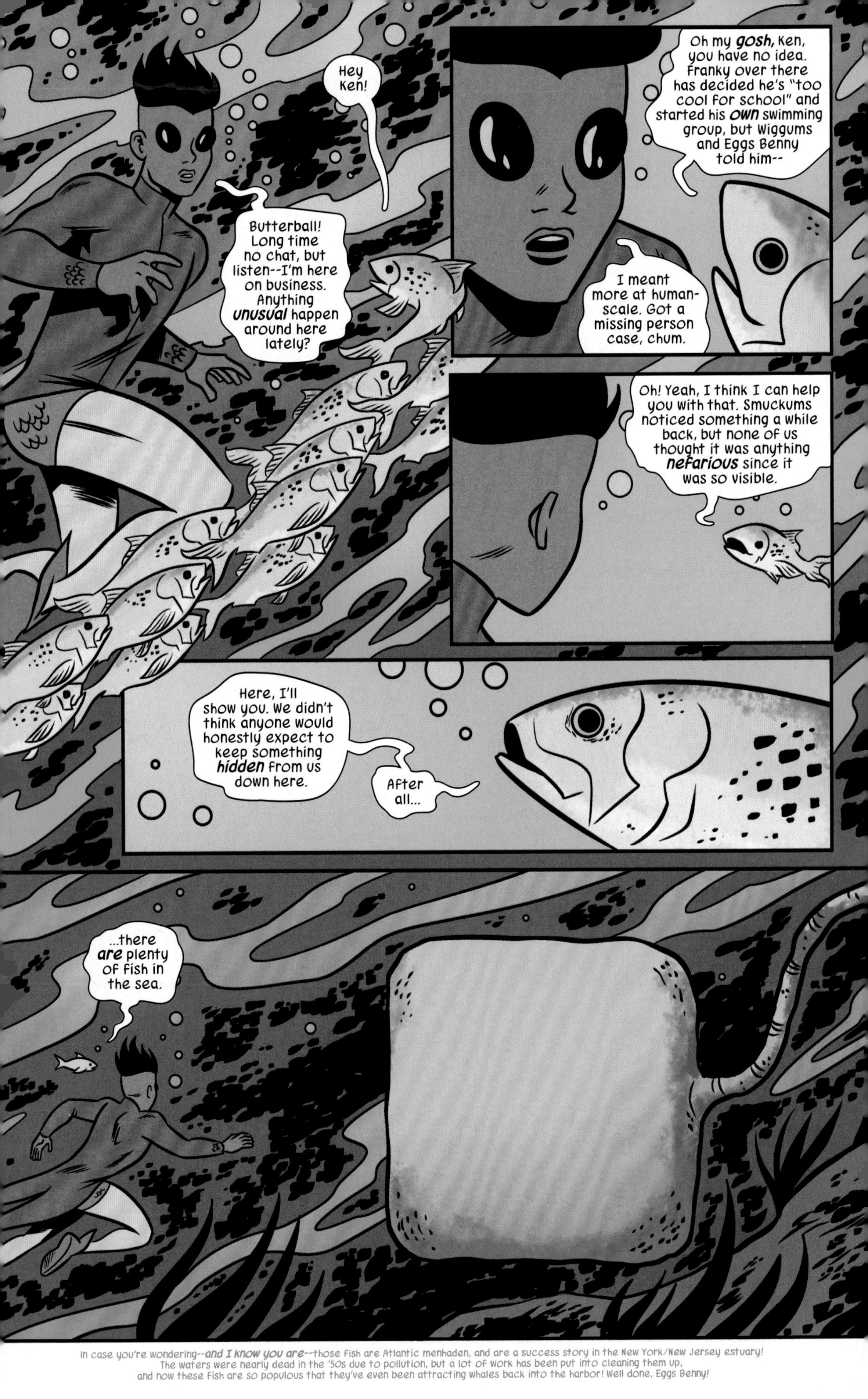
Hey Ken!
Oh my gosh, Ken, you have no idea. Franky over there has decided he's "too cool for school" and started his own swimming group, but Wiggums and Eggs Benny told him--
Butterball! Long time no chat, but listen--I'm here on business. Anything unusual happen around here lately?
I meant more at human-scale. Got a missing person case, chum.
Oh! Yeah, I think I can help you with that. Smuckums noticed something a while back, but none of us thought it was anything nefarious since it was so visible.
Here, I'll show you. We didn't think anyone would honestly expect to keep something hidden from us down here.
After all...
...there are plenty of fish in the sea.

In case you're wondering--*and I know you are*--those fish are Atlantic menhaden, and are a success story in the New York/New Jersey estuary! The waters were nearly dead in the '50s due to pollution, but a lot of work has been put into cleaning them up, and now these fish are so populous that they've even been attracting whales back into the harbor! Well done, Eggs Benny!

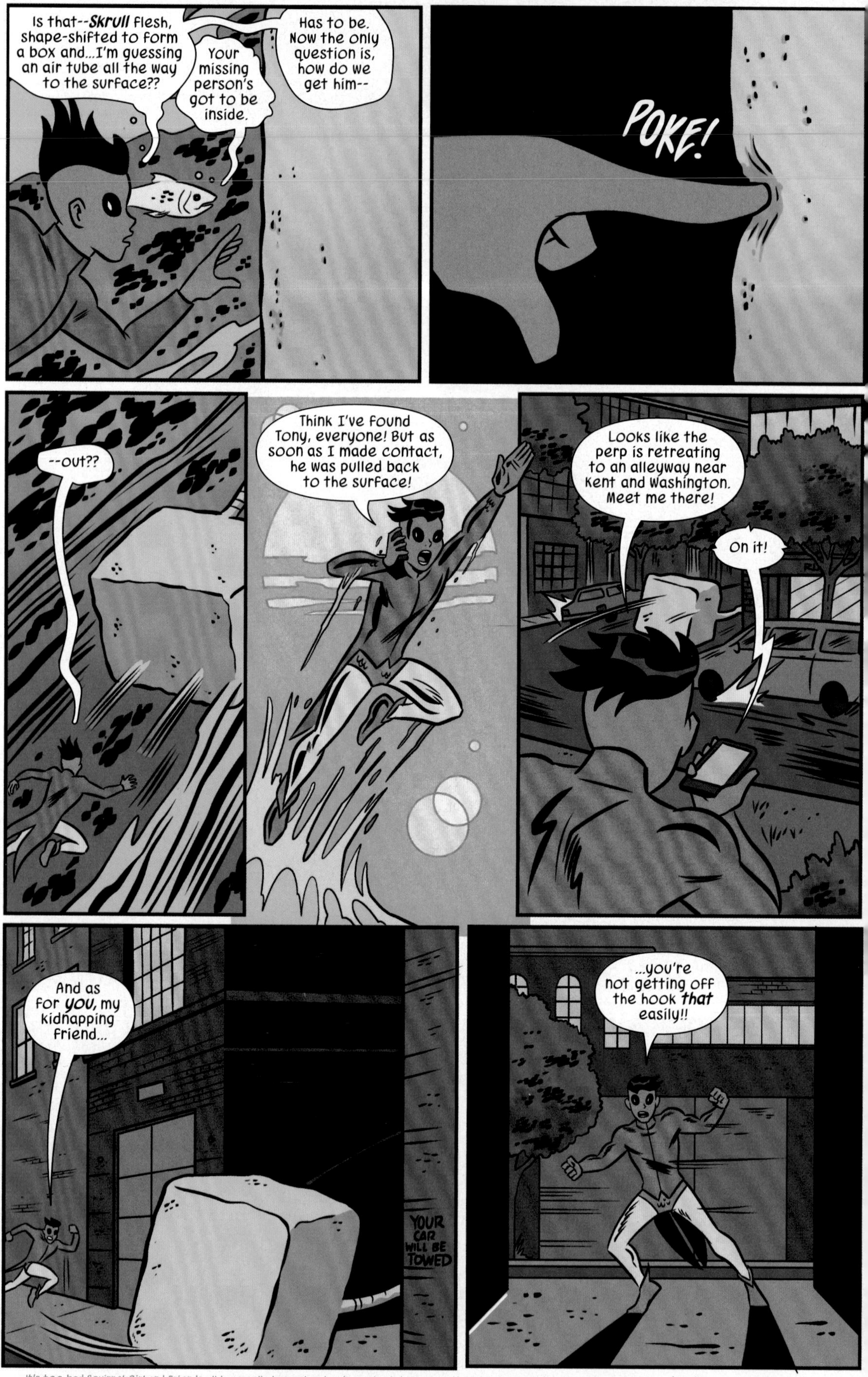
Is that--*Skrull* flesh, shape-shifted to form a box and...I'm guessing an air tube all the way to the surface??
Your missing person's got to be inside.
Has to be. Now the only question is, how do we get him--
POKE!
--out??
Think I've found Tony, everyone! But as soon as I made contact, he was pulled back to the surface!
Looks like the perp is retreating to an alleyway near Kent and Washington. Meet me there!
On it!
And as for *you*, my kidnapping friend...
YOUR CAR WILL BE TOWED
...you're not getting off the hook *that* easily!!

It's too bad Squirrel Girl and Friends all have cell phones to stay in contact, because otherwise you would've been treated to an ***adorable*** scene of fish sticking their heads out of the water and waving with their little fins in the direction they wanted Doreen to go to meet Ken. Curse my iron-clad dedication to realism in this comic!!

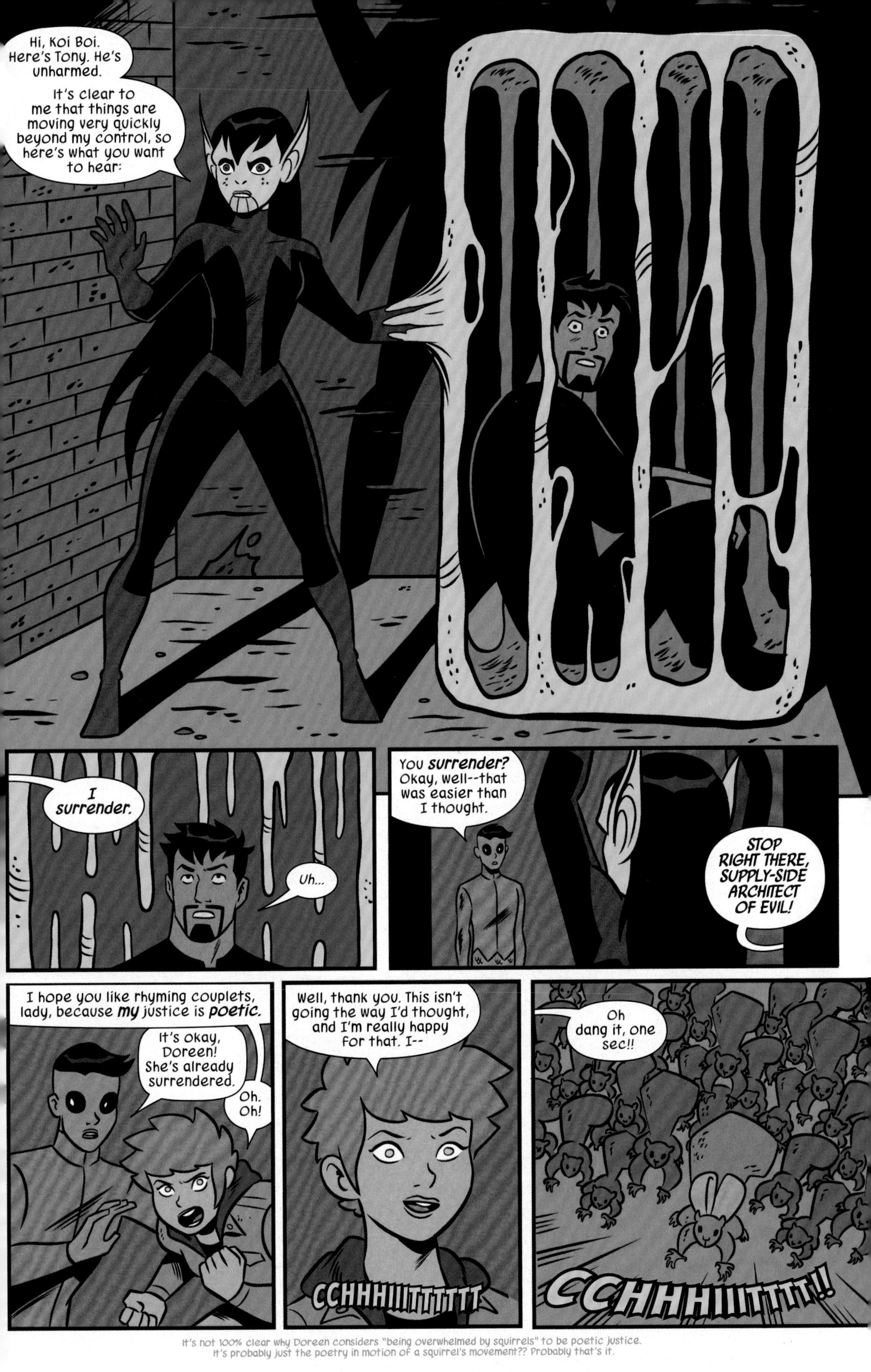
Hi, Koi Boi. Here's Tony. He's unharmed.
It's clear to me that things are moving very quickly beyond my control, so here's what you want to hear:
I surrender.
Uh...
You surrender? Okay, well--that was easier than I thought.
STOP RIGHT THERE, SUPPLY-SIDE ARCHITECT OF EVIL!
I hope you like rhyming couplets, lady, because my justice is poetic.
It's okay, Doreen! She's already surrendered.
Oh. Oh!
Well, thank you. This isn't going the way I'd thought, and I'm really happy for that. I--
CCHHHIIITTTTTT
Oh dang it, one sec!!
CCHHHIIITTTT!!

It's not 100% clear why Doreen considers "being overwhelmed by squirrels" to be poetic justice.
It's probably just the poetry in motion of a squirrel's movement?? Probably that's it.

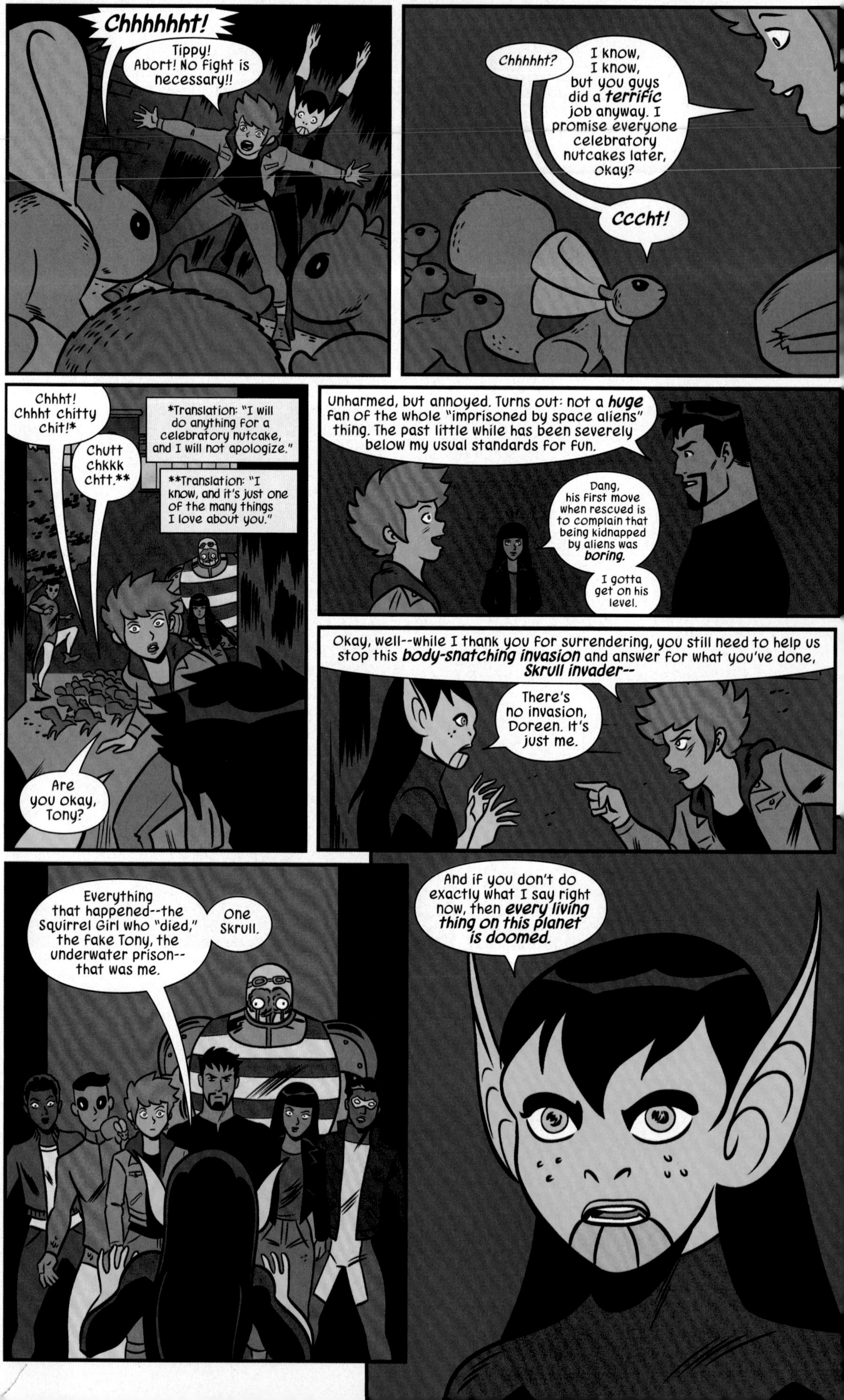
Chhhhhht!
Tippy! Abort! No fight is necessary!!
Chhhhht?
I know, I know, but you guys did a *terrific* job anyway. I promise everyone celebratory nutcakes later, okay?
Ccccht!
Chhht! Chhht chitty chit!*
*Translation: "I will do anything for a celebratory nutcake, and I will not apologize."
Chutt chkkk chtt.**
**Translation: "I know, and it's just one of the many things I love about you."
Are you okay, Tony?
Unharmed, but annoyed. Turns out: not a *huge* fan of the whole "imprisoned by space aliens" thing. The past little while has been severely below my usual standards for fun.
Dang, his first move when rescued is to complain that being kidnapped by aliens was *boring.*
I gotta get on his level.
Okay, well--while I thank you for surrendering, you still need to help us stop this *body-snatching invasion* and answer for what you've done, *Skrull invader--*
There's no invasion, Doreen. It's just me.
Everything that happened--the Squirrel Girl who "died," the fake Tony, the underwater prison--that was me.
One Skrull.
And if you don't do exactly what I say right now, then *every living thing on this planet is doomed.*

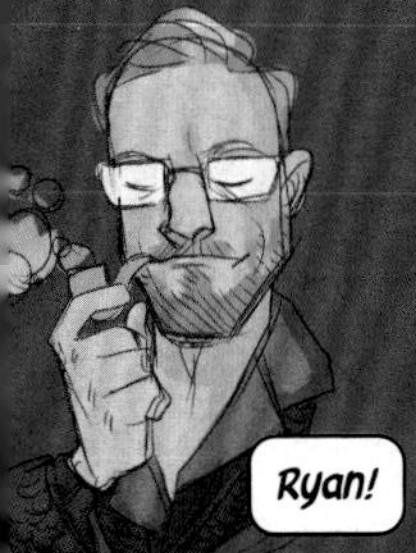
Ryan!

Letters From Nuts

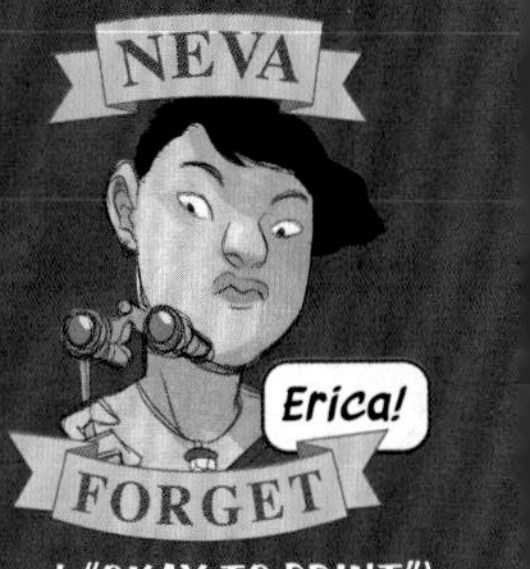
NEVA
Erica!
FORGET

Send letters to mheroes@marvel.com or 135 W 50th St, 7th Floor, New York, NY 10020 (Please mark "OKAY TO PRINT")

Hi, Ryan!

I'm glad I saw you at Brookline Booksmith when you were talking about your new book *How to Invent Everything,* and then at the signing where you signed all the books that we have that you wrote including all the *Squirrel Girl* books and *How to Be a T. rex.*

Here's a picture that we took with you and my stuffed animal squirrels that I love. I'm wearing my squirrel ears headband!

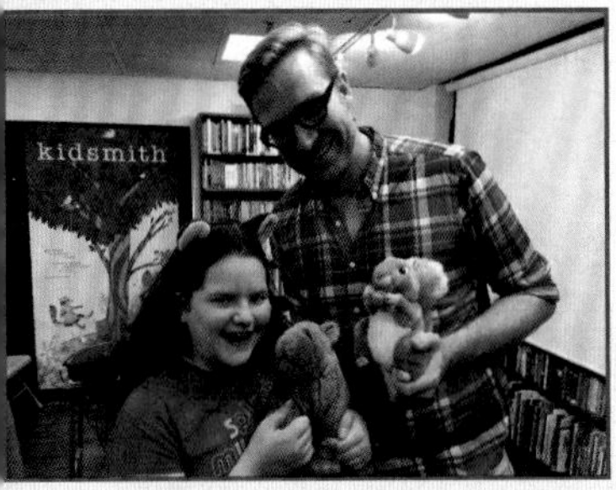
kidsmith

ALSO: Hi Erica,

I was glad to see you at MICE. Thank you for taking a picture with me and my squirrels. I really liked it. Now I can say I met both the writer and artist of SQUIRREL GIRL this month!

Sincerely,
Yael Burstein
Brookline, Massachusetts

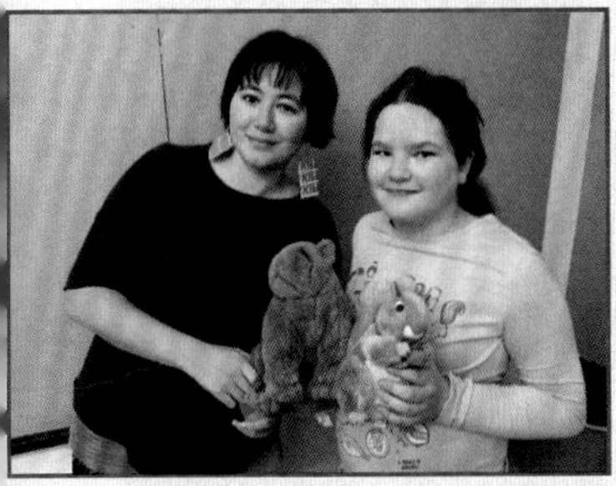

RYAN: Thanks, Yael—it was great to meet you! And one of my favorite things about writing so many sorts of different books (Comic books! Picture books! Non-fiction time-travel books!) is meeting the different kinds of people who read them — and sometimes, when I'm really lucky, the kinds of people who read *all* of them. It was super great to meet you, and I'm glad you got to meet Erica a few days later, too! We all went out to dinner when I was in town, so I got to hang out with her too.

Dear Ryan, Derek, Erica, Wil, Sarah, Rico, Travis and anyone who I may have missed,

To begin with, thank you for printing my daughter Yael's art and picture back in issue #35. Yael was delighted to see her Plaidlactus rendering appear in the letter column.

We were also delighted that we just got the chance to meet Ryan North at our local bookstore, Brookline Booksmith, during his book tour for *How to Invent Everything.* In her email, Yael has included a photo of herself as Squirrel Girl with Ryan as that tall guy who probably never thought that one day he'd be asked to pose with young kids and squirrels.

While I'm writing this letter, I want to mention here what I said on Twitter after I read issue #37 last week. I was very moved to see that when the Thing attended the funeral for "Squirrel Girl," he was wearing a kippah. Representation matters a lot. I know that it took actual intent on the part of the creative team to show this tiny circle of black on the head of the Thing. So I did want you all to know that I noticed and appreciated the nod to his being Jewish. Thank you all.

I also want to share with you a theory I have come up with as to how it is possible that Doreen is not a mutant, as indicated by Doreen's mother Maureen in the second issue #1 of 2015 (as opposed to the first issue #1 of 2015).

By definition, a mutant is someone who has a mutation in their genes, meaning that some of their DNA is slightly changed from whatever DNA they received from their parents. (In truth, all humans have some mutations in their genes, but most are minor and do not give us super-powers, alas.) So let us suppose that Doreen has no mutations in her genes at all. How would it be possible for her to have her squirrel powers? My theory is that all those squirrel powers came from recessive genes in her parents, genes that were not expressed by her parents because they had non-squirrel dominant genes. These squirrel genes therefore remained dormant in Dor and Maureen, but manifested in Doreen.

To put it another way, and to make complicated genetics unrealistically simplistic, suppose capital S is the gene for no squirrel powers and lowercase s is the gene for squirrel powers. Then Doreen's parents each had the gene pair Ss. Doreen's genes could have been either SS, Ss, Ss or ss, meaning she had only a 25% chance of inheriting squirrel powers from her parents. But she did. She won the squirrel lottery, which I have now decided must be a real thing, and thus became Squirrel Girl.

This all fits very nicely with Maureen's story. When she says that Doreen's doctor indicated that what had happened with Doreen's DNA made her even more special, it's because the probability of being a mutant in the Marvel Universe is rather high. But the probability of non-mutant genes giving someone super-powers? Almost inconceivable. And to the more vital point, or at least more vital between the years 1993 and 2018, this explanation of Doreen's genes would in fact make her legally distinct from being a mutant. It also explains why Doreen called herself a mutant when she was a teenager; she probably thought that was easier to say than to go through this whole explanation when she first met Tony Stark in 1991.

Finally, Yael suggests that had Doreen's parents had the gene pair ss, they could have been Squirrel-Man and Squirrel-Woman.

Sincerely,
Michael A. Burstein
Brookline, Massachusetts

RYAN: Michael — it's rare when I can say, "Whoa, I think you have thought about this Squirrel Girl thing even more than I have," but whoa, I think you have thought about this Squirrel Girl thing even more than I have! AND I LOVE IT. It is a perfectly plausible explanation that has the added benefit of being really sciencey AND fitting in with everything that came before. Thank you! Also: Thanks for all the kind words. And I think Wil Moss has to get the credit for the kippah — it was his idea to add it! That's the great thing about comics being such a collaborative medium: Everyone gets to contribute, and the end result is stronger for it (and also sometimes people give the writer all the credit, which is ALSO nice).

I just had to write because I was rereading SQUIRREL GIRL #30 and I realized that her opening line is a reference to *Due South,* one of my favorite comedic buddy-cop shows from the '90s! I'm so ashamed that I didn't get the reference! How many more references to things I like did Doreen make that I've missed? Has she talked about Edward and Ein from *Cowboy Bebop?* Spoken of John Steed of the non-Marvel *Avengers?* Regaled Nancy with tales of Carl Kolchak, the Night Stalker? I need to know!

Keep up the great work and the obscure references!

Joshua Thomas
Sitka, Alaska

RYAN: Thank you kindly! I figured Doreen would be the kind of person to reference *Due South,* being as she is half Canadian. Here's my theory of using references when writing: They have to work even if you don't catch the reference. If it's something the character wouldn't say, you can't use it because then the character is acting, well, out of character. And that means that, almost by definition, any reference is subtle and can slip by you! So I'm very glad you caught it.

Hi, Squirrel Crew!

I just wanted to pass along some photos of little Caroline, rocking her awesome Squirrel Girl costume! She's 1 year old.

Mark Turetsky

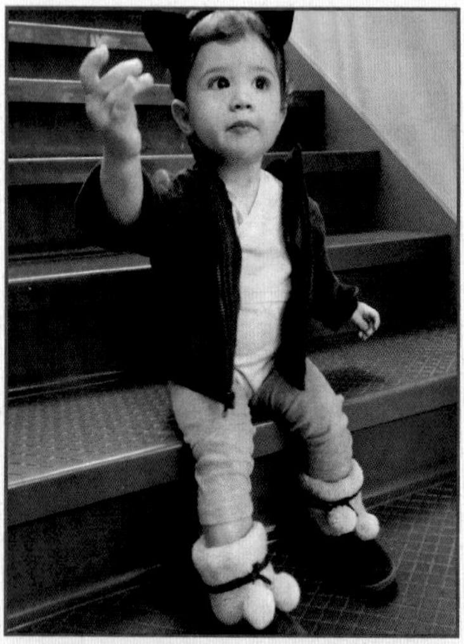

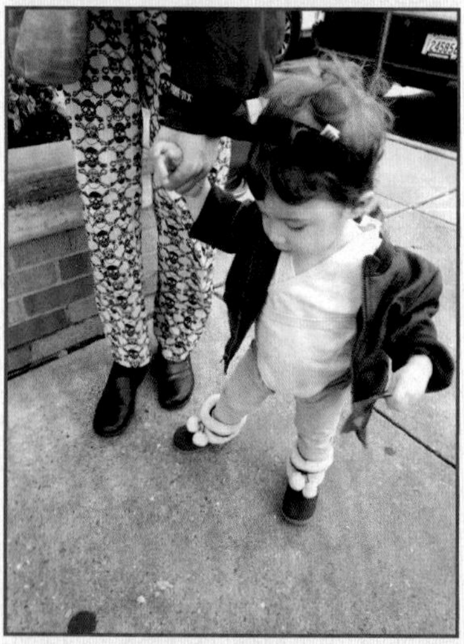

RYAN: Adorable. Caroline is just beginning to walk and she's ALREADY fighting crime! She's gonna do great.

I have been LOVING all the Squirrel Girl costumes popping up around Hallowe'en — @unbeatablesg has been retweeting a lot of them — and I have now concluded that we need a second dress-up holiday in the year. Maybe something in April so we never go more than six months without wearing a costume? I see no downsides to my plan.

I've been really busy lately, fighting (and moonlighting) with Hydra and the Hand, so our whole family actually fell behind a few issues. Yes, yes...the horror! We finally got to get our Derek Charm on, and it's good stuff. My 7-year-old twin daughters thought it was time for us to let you know that. And now you know.

Since we have multiple fans of Doreen in the household, we recently ordered some of the Marvel Gallery Squirrel Girl PVC Diorama pieces. I can't wait to set one up next to my X-23 as Wolverine statue. They're going to look quite groovy together.

Also, word on the street is Ryan North might be a Skrull?!

Darrick Patrick
Dayton, Ohio

P.S. I'm including a photograph of Nola and Logann holding a couple copies of UNBEATABLE SQUIRREL GIRL. From the fairly recent issues that have been released, I asked them to pick their favorite covers. These are the two that they chose.

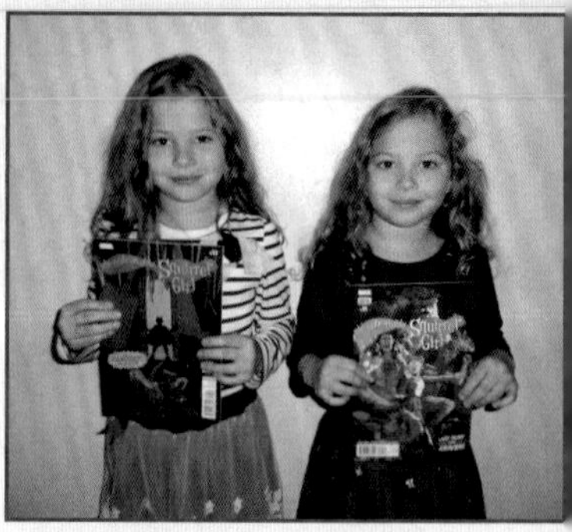

RYAN: RYAN IS NOT A SKRULL, SO WE SHOULD ALL STOP INVESTIGATING THAT THEORY. ALSO, RYAN OFTEN REFERS TO HIMSELF IN THE THIRD PERSON, AND THAT'S COMPLETELY NORMAL TOO. NOBODY SHOULD BE SUSPICIOUS OF RYAN. ALSO, RYAN THINKS THAT THOSE ARE EXCELLENT COVER CHOICES AND IT IS ALWAYS GOOD TO HEAR FROM YOU!! END COMMUNICATION.

Next Issue:

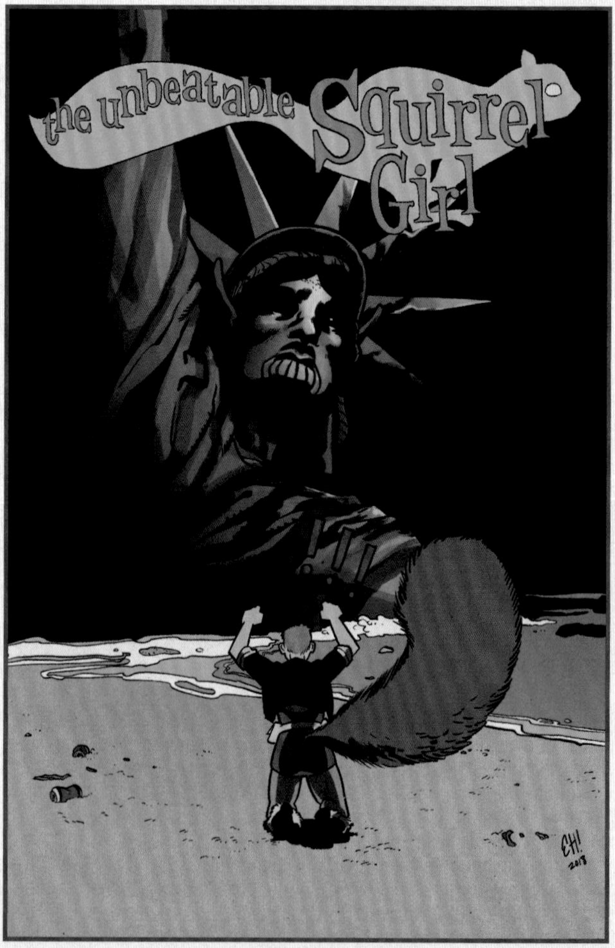
the unbeatable Squirrel Girl
CH!
2018

Attention, Squirrel Scouts! Make sure to check out our production blog, **unbeatablesquirrelgirl.tumblr.com**, where we post behind-the-scenes stuff on how the book gets made, along with all sorts of cool things *you* make: fanart, cosplay, whatever!

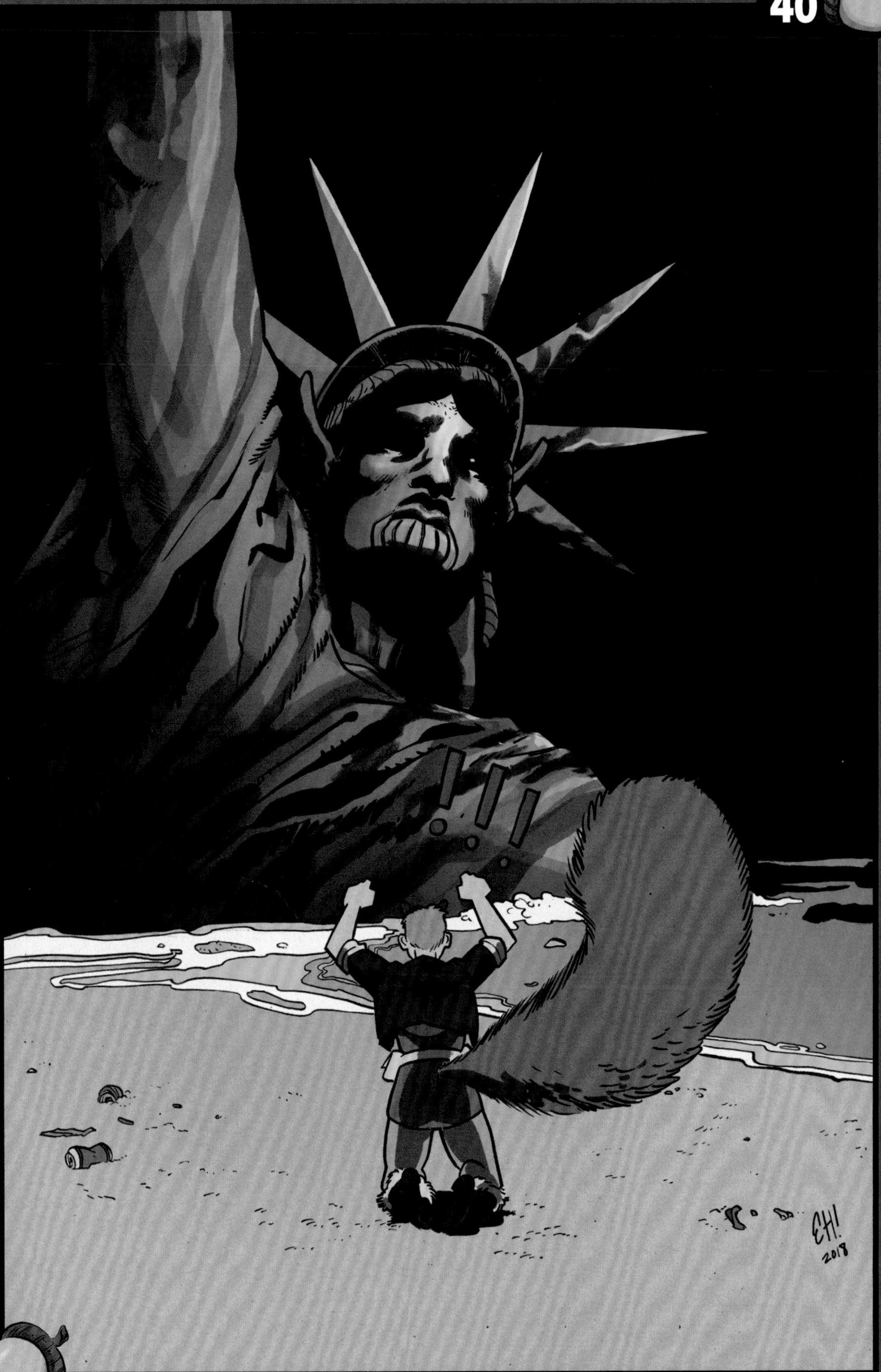

*Doreen Green isn't just a second-year computer science student: she secretly also has all the powers of both squirrel and girl! She uses her amazing abilities to fight crime **and** be as awesome as possible. You know her as...**The Unbeatable Squirrel Girl**! Find out what she's been up to, with...*

Squirrel Girl in a nutshell

search!

#suspensestories

#candybars

#squirrelnames

#teamclaude

#msbrant

Nancy W. @sewwiththeflo
You know how in math class the teacher will teach you something and you'll think "come on when are we ever going to use this in real life?"

Nancy W. @sewwiththeflo
And then you say that out loud, and the teacher replies with something about the beauty of mathematics, and then builds on that to expound upon how all knowledge is itself an intrinsic good and how we're all better people for having learned some cool knowledge just now.

Nancy W. @sewwiththeflo
Or perhaps the teacher instead promises you that one fine day you'll be getting on the bus, and you'll realize to your horror that you don't have bus fare, and the driver will say "No problem! Just answer this math question and I'll let you ride for free!"

Nancy W. @sewwiththeflo
And on that day, you'll think back to this class, and you'll say "Mr. Bell was right, for I did indeed use this in real life."

Nancy W. @sewwiththeflo
Well, guess what.

Egg @imduderadtude
@sewwiththeflo i guess...that u forget ur bus fare!!!!!!!!!

Nancy W. @sewwiththeflo
@imduderadtude No, but I did use some math in real life.

Nancy W. @sewwiththeflo
@imduderadtude We were trying to find someone, and we knew how long his messages took to reach a fixed point, and so by knowing the speed that information traveled at, we could determine where he was!

Nancy W. @sewwiththeflo
@imduderadtude It was actually a sphere of possible locations, but easy enough to check, and then we found him!

Nancy W. @sewwiththeflo
@imduderadtude So I owe my sixth grade math teacher an apology. Sorry, Mr. Bell. I did use your math in real life after all.

Egg @imduderadtude
@sewwiththeflo lol okay im not mr bell

Nancy W. @sewwiththeflo
@imduderadtude It - it was a RHETORICAL apology. I'm not actually going to track down my sixth grade math teacher and apologize to him. I'm sure he doesn't even remember the quiet sassmaster girl who sat in the back of his class over a decade ago.

Egg @imduderadtude
@sewwiththeflo @iquitelovemath hey mr bell one nancy whitehead used what you taught her in real life and would like to say something!!!!!!!!

Nancy W. @sewwiththeflo
@imduderadtude @iquitelovemath YOU DIDN'T

Nancy W. @sewwiththeflo
@imduderadtude @iquitelovemath OH MY GOD IT'S THE SAME MR. BELL

Nancy W. @sewwiththeflo
@imduderadtude @iquitelovemath MR. BELL I'M SORRY SOME RANDO TAGGED YOU IN THIS CONVERSATION BUT JUST SO YOU KNOW I USED MATH TO DO A THING

Nancy W. @sewwiththeflo
@imduderadtude @iquitelovemath SORRY ABOUT BEING NOT AS GOOD A STUDENT BACK THEN BUT I'M REALLY GOOD NOW, SO UH - THANKS

Nancy W. @sewwiththeflo
@imduderadtude @iquitelovemath OKAY BYE

Nancy W. @sewwiththeflo
@imduderadtude NEVER DO THAT AGAIN

Egg @imduderadtude
@sewwiththeflo lollllll

Nancy W. @sewwiththeflo
@imduderadtude NEVER REPLY TO ME WITH "LOL" AGAIN

Egg @imduderadtude
@sewwiththeflo roflllllllll

Nancy W. @sewwiththeflo
@imduderadtude WHY AM I EVEN TALKING TO YOU, WE'RE ABOUT TO HAVE A VERY IMPORTANT CONVERSATION WITH SOMEONE WHO HAS BEEN THE CAUSE OF A LOT OF RECENT PROBLEMS FOR ME AND MY FRIENDS, SO BYE, RANDOM INTERNET PERSON I DON'T KNOW

Nancy W. @sewwiththeflo
Two facts: I need to get more followers on this site, and online continues to be a mistake.

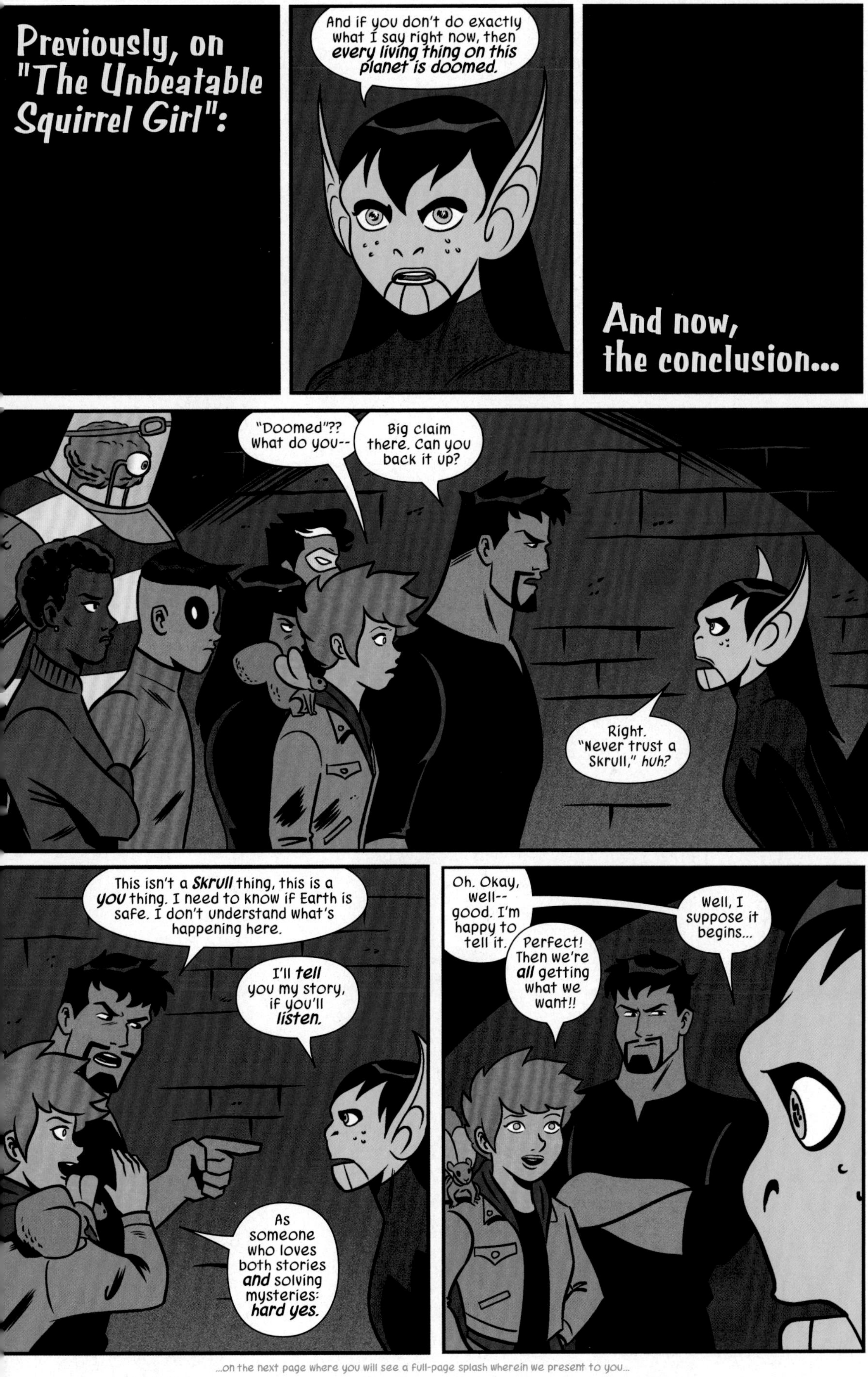

Previously, on "The Unbeatable Squirrel Girl":
And if you don't do exactly what I say right now, then every living thing on this planet is doomed.
And now, the conclusion...
"Doomed"?? What do you--
Big claim there. Can you back it up?
Right. "Never trust a Skrull," huh?
This isn't a Skrull thing, this is a you thing. I need to know if Earth is safe. I don't understand what's happening here.
I'll tell you my story, if you'll listen.
As someone who loves both stories and solving mysteries: hard yes.
Oh. Okay, well-- good. I'm happy to tell it.
Perfect! Then we're all getting what we want!!
Well, I suppose it begins...

...on the next page where you will see a full-page splash wherein we present to you...

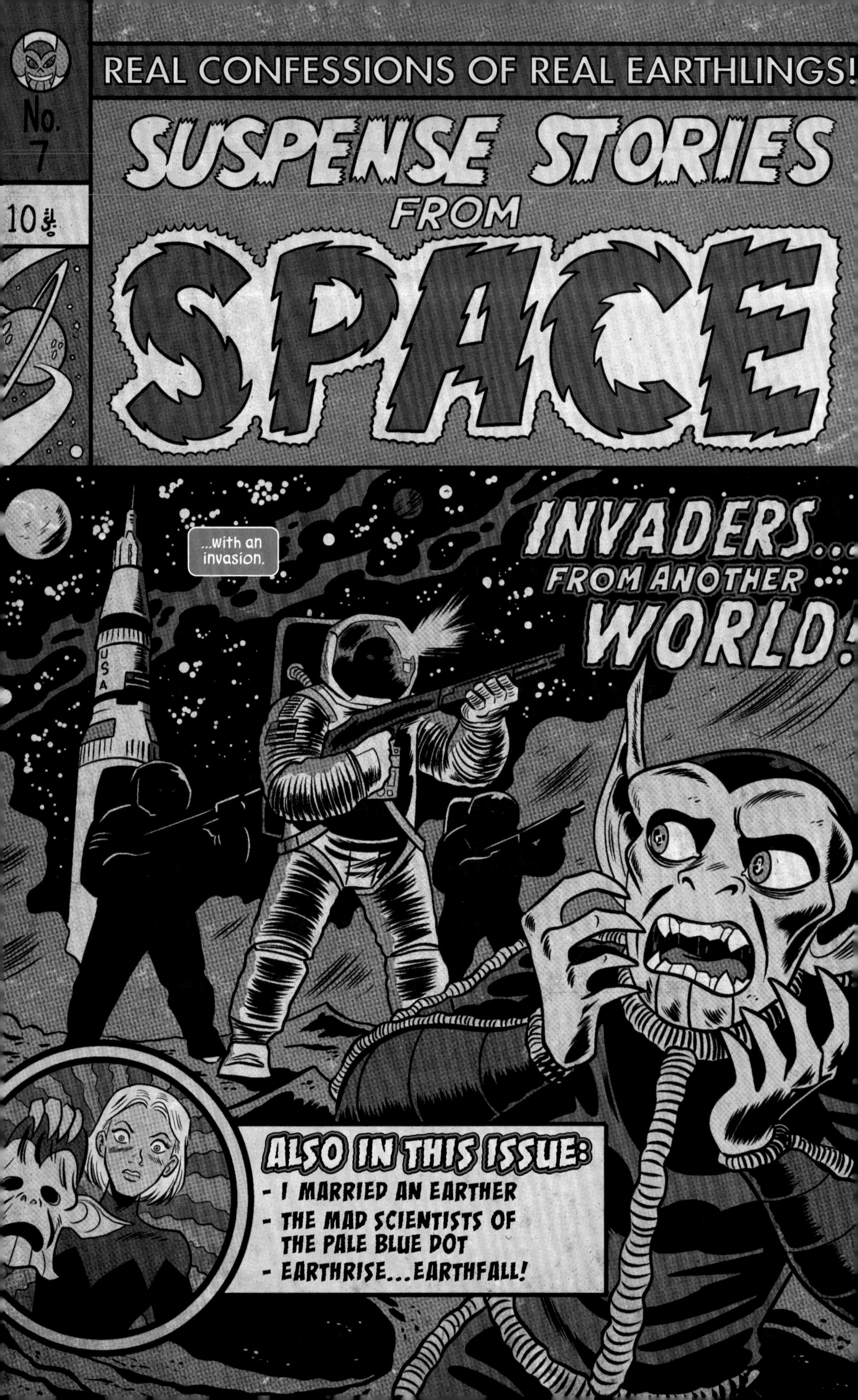

REAL CONFESSIONS OF REAL EARTHLINGS!
No. 7
10
SUSPENSE STORIES FROM SPACE
...with an invasion.
INVADERS... FROM ANOTHER WORLD!
USA
ALSO IN THIS ISSUE:
- I MARRIED AN EARTHER
- THE MAD SCIENTISTS OF THE PALE BLUE DOT
- EARTHRISE...EARTHFALL!

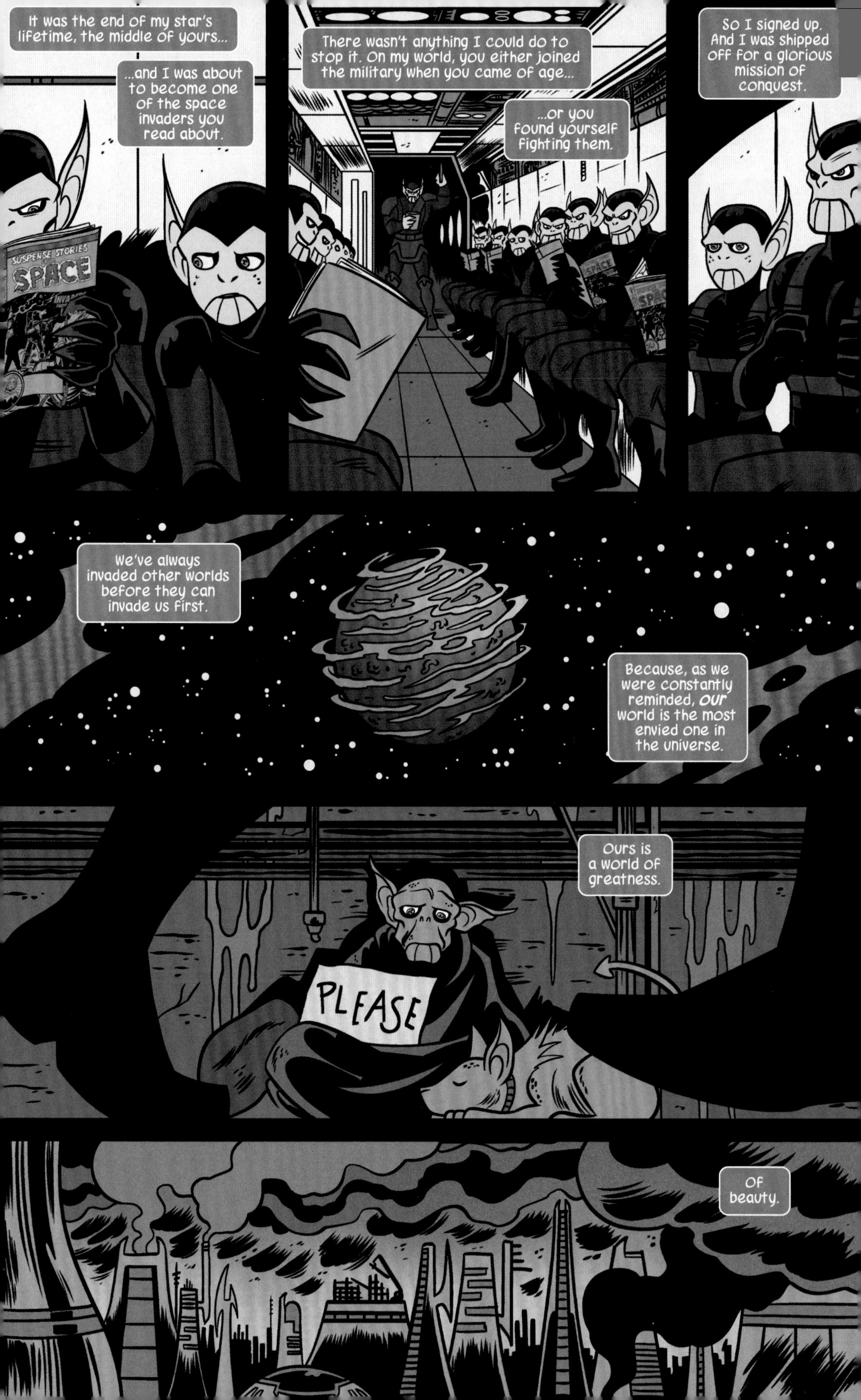
It was the end of my star's lifetime, the middle of yours...
...and I was about to become one of the space invaders you read about.
SUSPENSE STORIES
SPACE
There wasn't anything I could do to stop it. On my world, you either joined the military when you came of age...
...or you found yourself fighting them.
So I signed up. And I was shipped off for a glorious mission of conquest.
We've always invaded other worlds before they can invade us first.
Because, as we were constantly reminded, *our* world is the most envied one in the universe.
Ours is a world of greatness.
PLEASE
Of beauty.

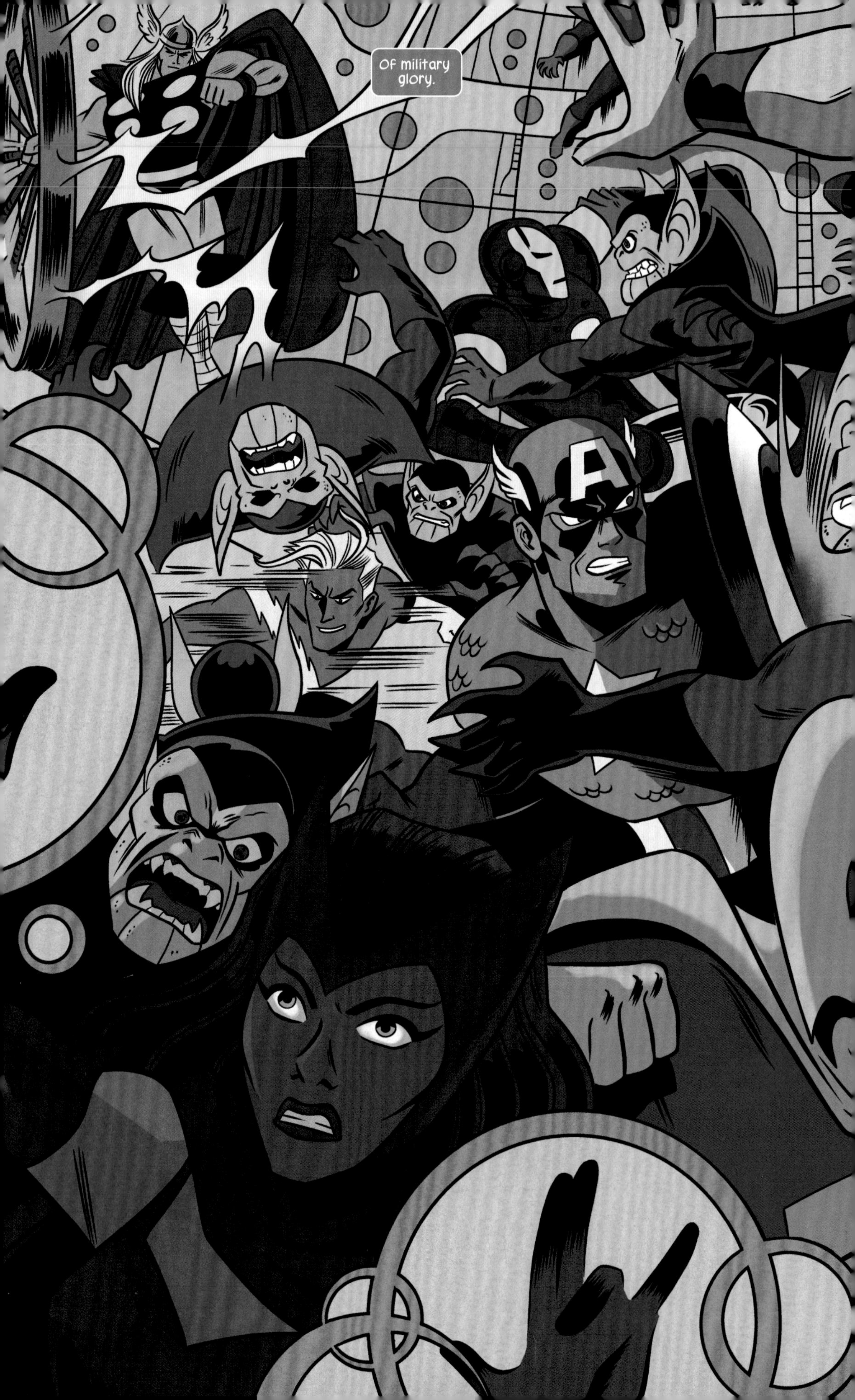
Of military glory.

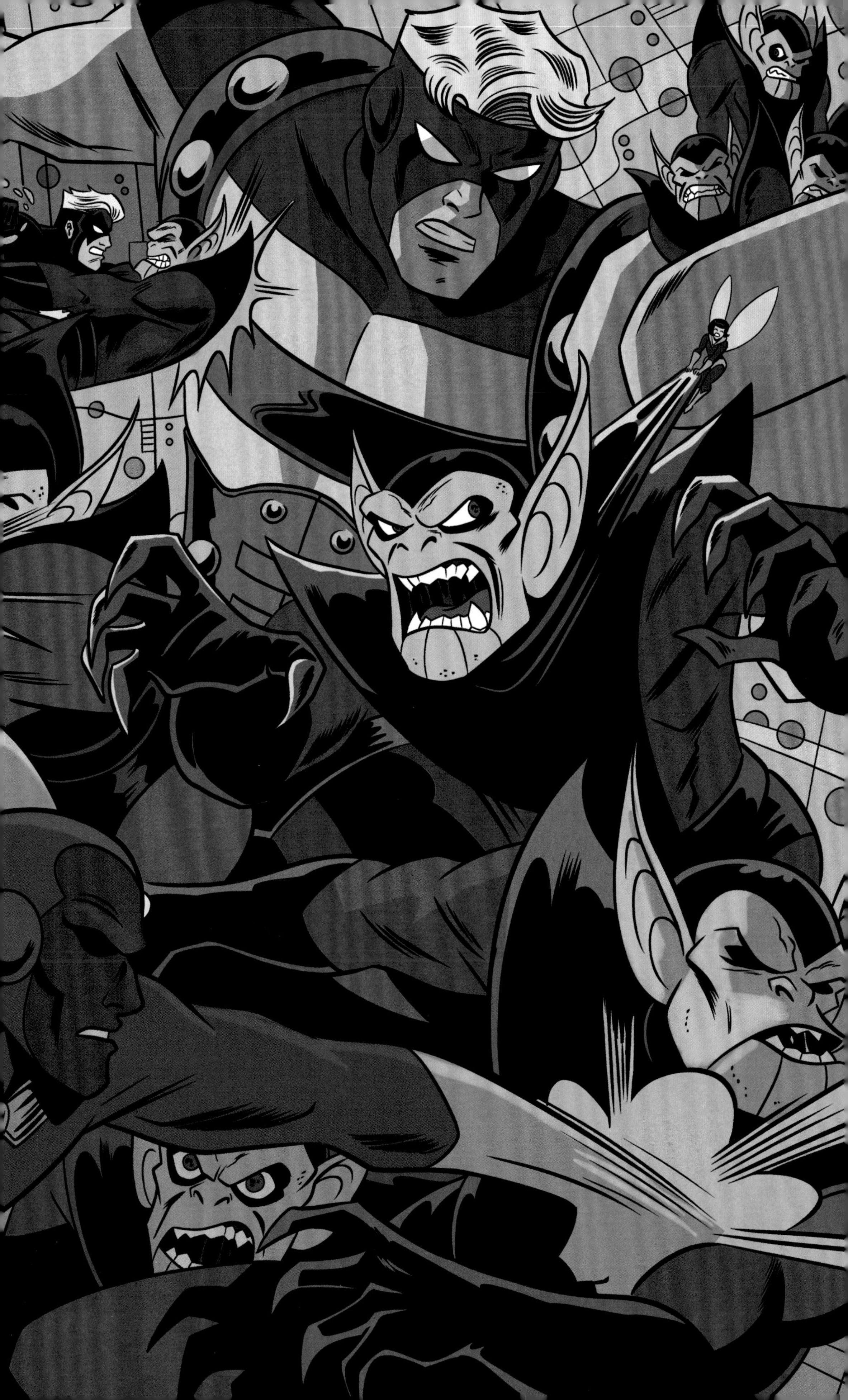

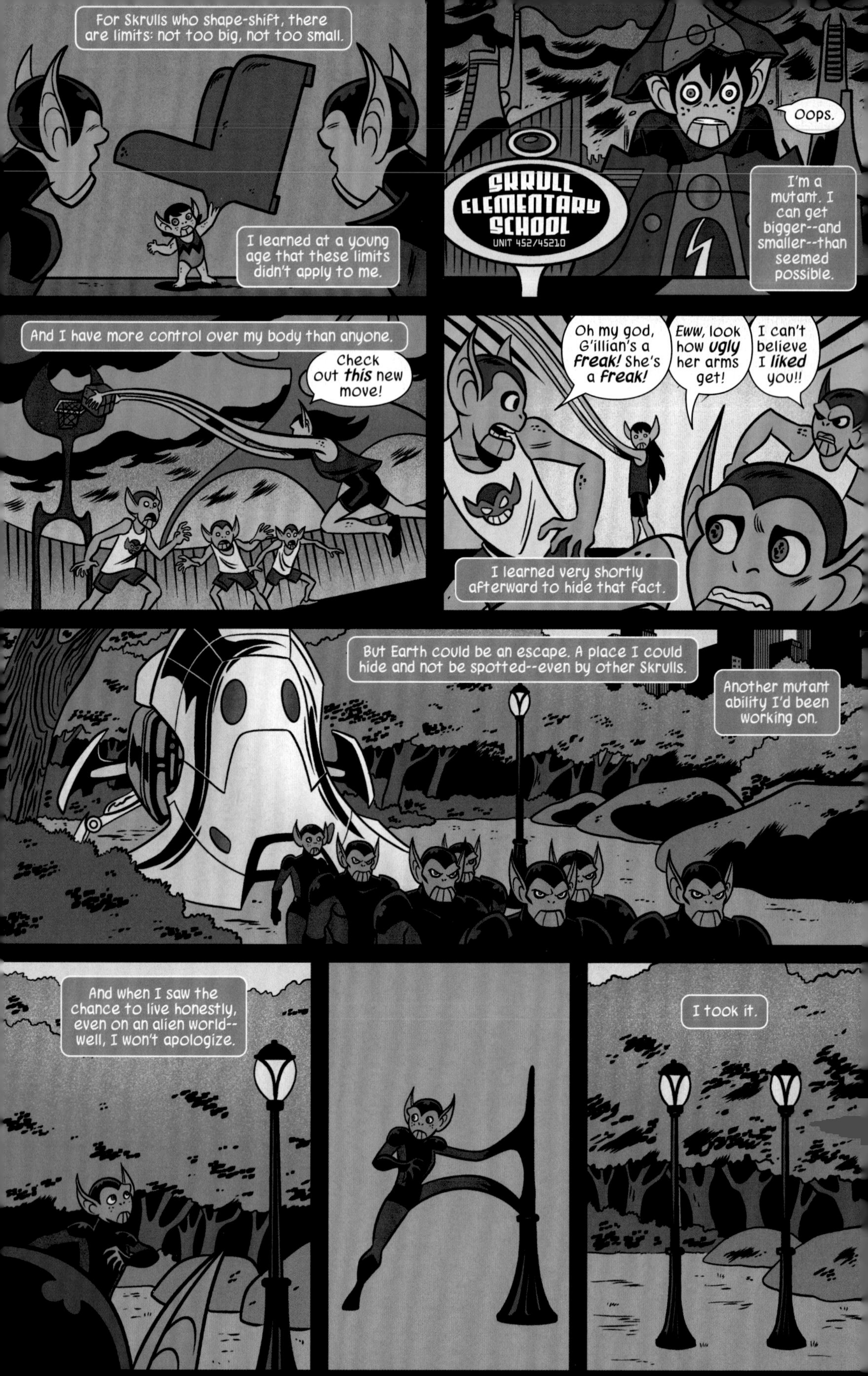
For Skrulls who shape-shift, there are limits: not too big, not too small.
I learned at a young age that these limits didn't apply to me.
Oops.
SKRULL ELEMENTARY SCHOOL
UNIT 452/45210
I'm a mutant. I can get bigger--and smaller--than seemed possible.
And I have more control over my body than anyone.
Check out this new move!
Oh my god, G'illian's a freak! She's a freak!
Eww, look how ugly her arms get!
I can't believe I liked you!!
I learned very shortly afterward to hide that fact.
But Earth could be an escape. A place I could hide and not be spotted--even by other Skrulls.
Another mutant ability I'd been working on.
And when I saw the chance to live honestly, even on an alien world--well, I won't apologize.
I took it.

See, normally babies can't turn their hands into couches. Parents: If your baby is turning his or her hand into a couch,

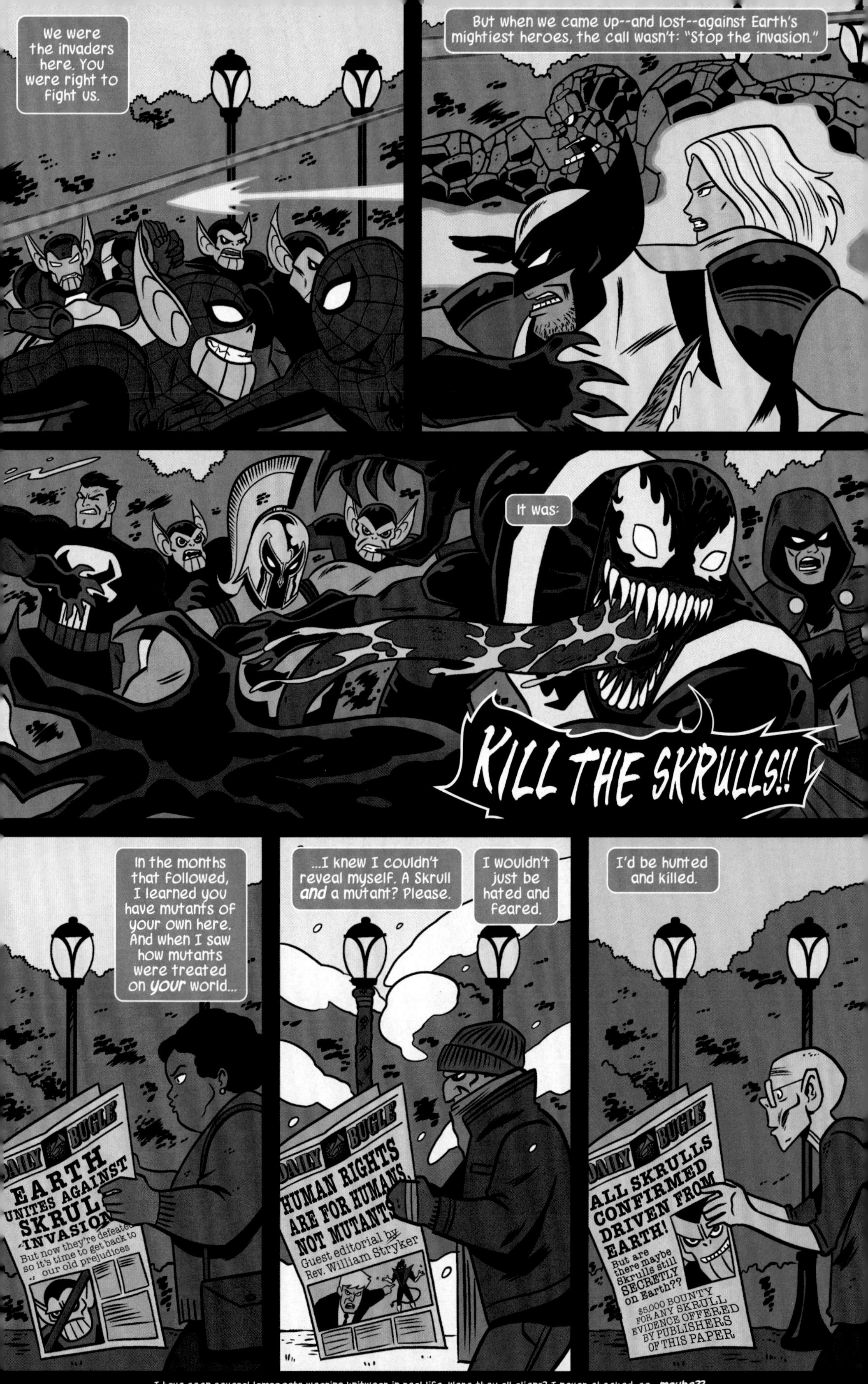
We were the invaders here. You were right to fight us.
But when we came up--and lost--against Earth's mightiest heroes, the call wasn't: "Stop the invasion."
It was:
KILL THE SKRULLS!!
In the months that followed, I learned you have mutants of your own here. And when I saw how mutants were treated on *your* world...
DAILY BUGLE
EARTH UNITES AGAINST SKRULL INVASION
But now they're defeated so it's time to get back to our old prejudices
...I knew I couldn't reveal myself. A Skrull *and* a mutant? Please.
I wouldn't just be hated and feared.
DAILY BUGLE
HUMAN RIGHTS ARE FOR HUMANS, NOT MUTANTS
Guest editorial by Rev. William Stryker
I'd be hunted and killed.
DAILY BUGLE
ALL SKRULLS CONFIRMED DRIVEN FROM EARTH!
But are there maybe Skrulls still SECRETLY on Earth??
$5,000 BOUNTY FOR ANY SKRULL EVIDENCE OFFERED BY PUBLISHERS OF THIS PAPER

I have seen several lampposts wearing knitwear in real life. Were they all aliens? I never checked, so--*maybe??*

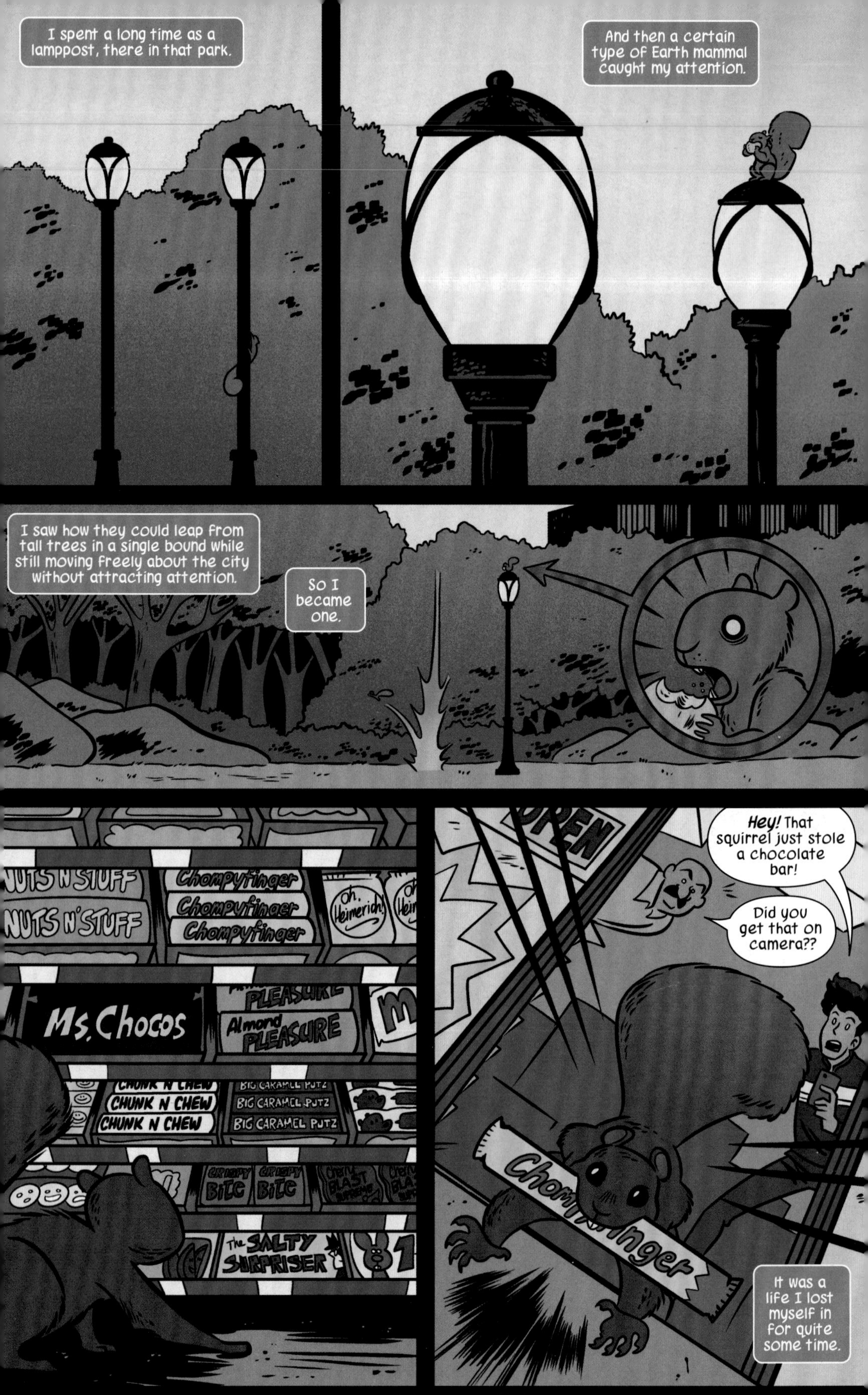
I spent a long time as a lamppost, there in that park.
And then a certain type of Earth mammal caught my attention.
I saw how they could leap from tall trees in a single bound while still moving freely about the city without attracting attention.
So I became one.
NUTS N' STUFF
NUTS N' STUFF
Chompyfinger
Chompyfinger
Chompyfinger
Oh, Heimerich!
Ms. Chocos
Almond PLEASURE
Almond PLEASURE
CHUNK N CHEW
CHUNK N CHEW
CHUNK N CHEW
BIG CARAMEL PUTZ
BIG CARAMEL PUTZ
BIG CARAMEL PUTZ
CRISPY BITE
CRISPY BITE
The SALTY SURPRISER
OPEN
Hey! That squirrel just stole a chocolate bar!
Did you get that on camera??
It was a life I lost myself in for quite some time.

I have seen several squirrels steal chocolate bars in real life too! Turns out writing is easy, as long as you just write down what you see, and also live in a town with guerrilla knitters and wild, capricious, chocolate-loving squirrels.

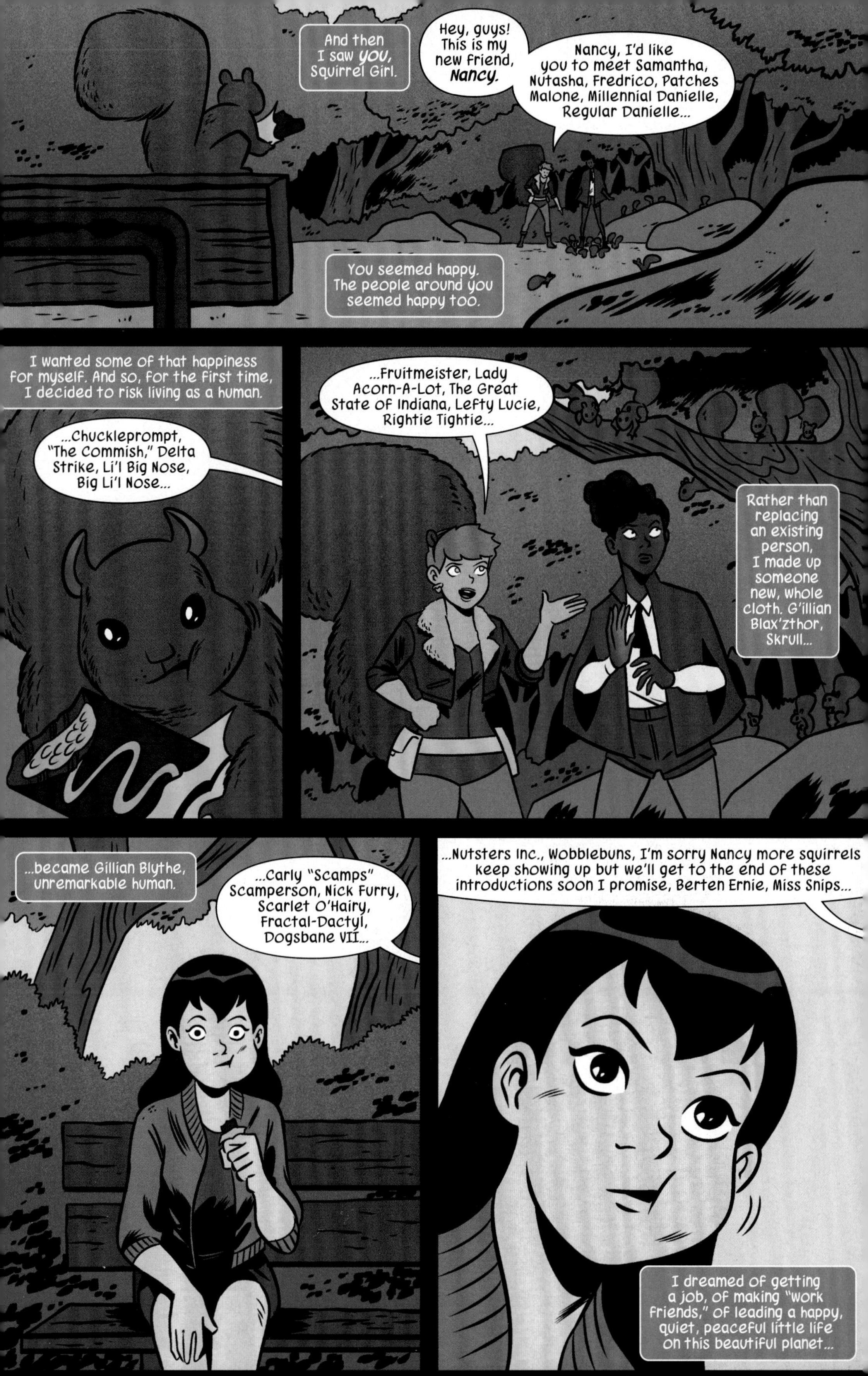

And then I saw *you,* Squirrel Girl.
Hey, guys! This is my new friend, ***Nancy.***
Nancy, I'd like you to meet Samantha, Nutasha, Fredrico, Patches Malone, Millennial Danielle, Regular Danielle...
You seemed happy. The people around you seemed happy too.
I wanted some of that happiness for myself. And so, for the first time, I decided to risk living as a human.
...Chuckleprompt, "The Commish," Delta Strike, Li'l Big Nose, Big Li'l Nose...
...Fruitmeister, Lady Acorn-A-Lot, The Great State of Indiana, Lefty Lucie, Rightie Tightie...
Rather than replacing an existing person, I made up someone new, whole cloth. G'illian Blax'zthor, Skrull...
...became Gillian Blythe, unremarkable human.
...Carly "Scamps" Scamperson, Nick Furry, Scarlet O'Hairy, Fractal-Dactyl, Dogsbane VII...
...Nutsters Inc., Wobblebuns, I'm sorry Nancy more squirrels keep showing up but we'll get to the end of these introductions soon I promise, Berten Ernie, Miss Snips...
I dreamed of getting a job, of making "work friends," of leading a happy, quiet, peaceful little life on this beautiful planet...

Nick Furry is in charge of A.C.O.R.N., an off-the-books extra-governmental organization dedicated to the Adept Collection Of Radical Nuts.
There! Now if you ever meet him, you'll be able to chat him up with confidence!

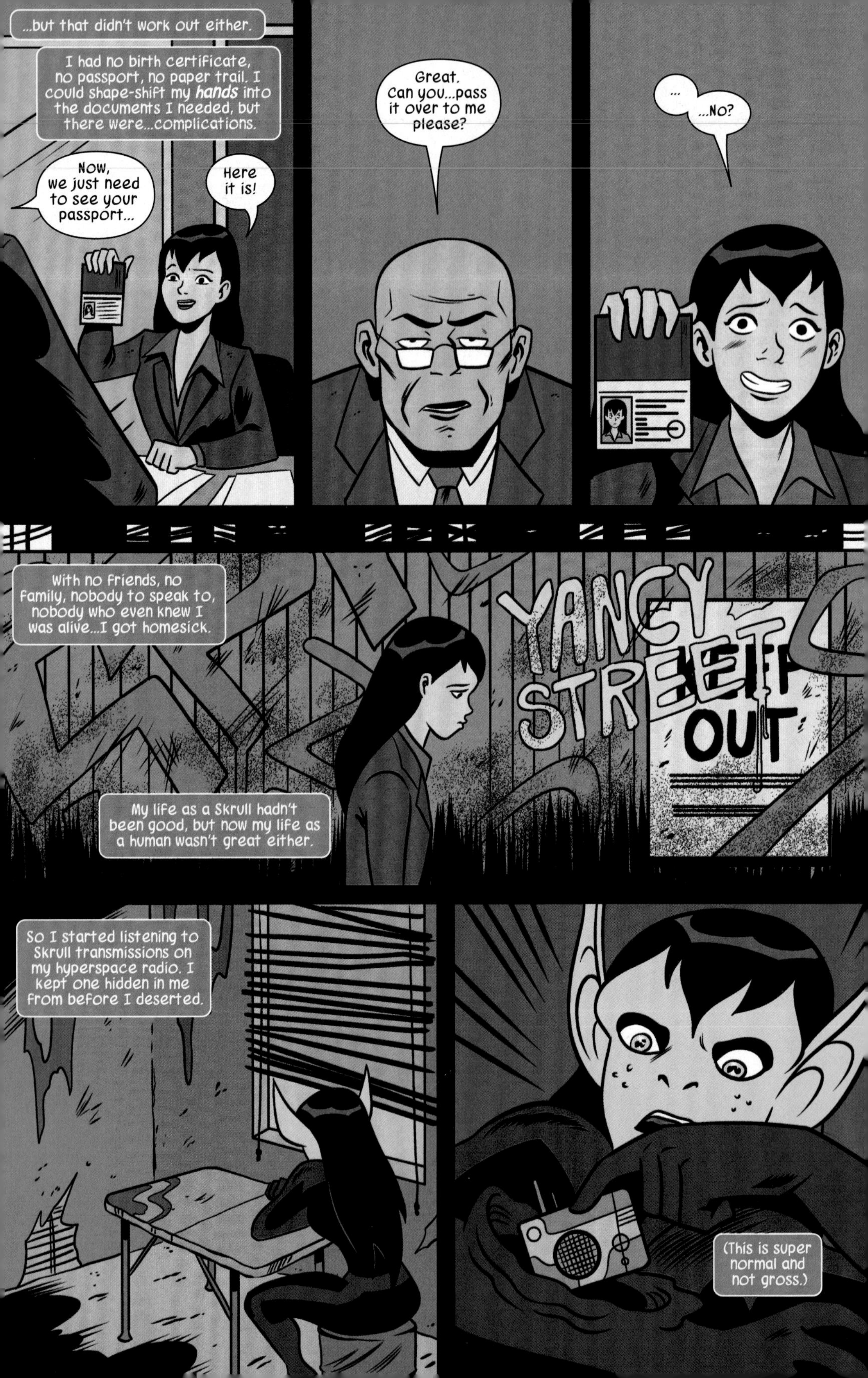
...but that didn't work out either.
I had no birth certificate, no passport, no paper trail. I could shape-shift my ***hands*** into the documents I needed, but there were...complications.
Now, we just need to see your passport...
Here it is!
Great. Can you...pass it over to me please?
...
...No?
With no friends, no family, nobody to speak to, nobody who even knew I was alive...I got homesick.
YANCY STREET
OUT
My life as a Skrull hadn't been good, but now my life as a human wasn't great either.
So I started listening to Skrull transmissions on my hyperspace radio. I kept one hidden in me from before I deserted.
(This is super normal and not gross.)

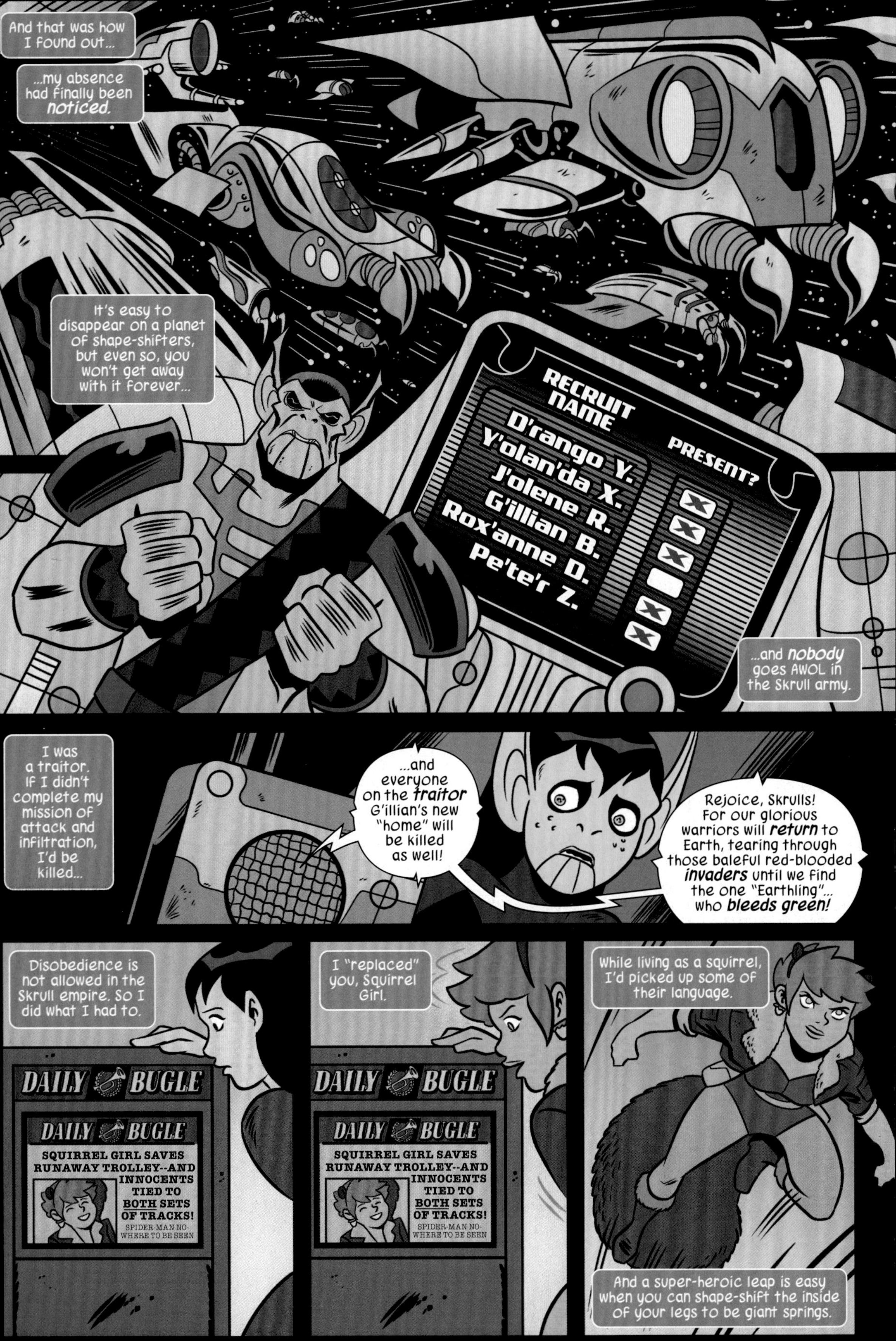
And that was how I found out...
...my absence had finally been *noticed.*
It's easy to disappear on a planet of shape-shifters, but even so, you won't get away with it forever...
RECRUIT NAME
PRESENT?
D'rango Y.
Y'olan'da X.
J'olene R.
G'illian B.
Rox'anne D.
Pe'te'r Z.
...and *nobody* goes AWOL in the Skrull army.
I was a traitor. If I didn't complete my mission of attack and infiltration, I'd be killed...
...and everyone on the *traitor* G'illian's new "home" will be killed as well!
Rejoice, Skrulls! For our glorious warriors will *return* to Earth, tearing through those baleful red-blooded *invaders* until we find the one "Earthling"... who *bleeds green!*
Disobedience is not allowed in the Skrull empire. So I did what I had to.
DAILY BUGLE
DAILY BUGLE
SQUIRREL GIRL SAVES RUNAWAY TROLLEY--AND INNOCENTS TIED TO BOTH SETS OF TRACKS!
SPIDER-MAN NOWHERE TO BE SEEN
I "replaced" you, Squirrel Girl.
DAILY BUGLE
DAILY BUGLE
SQUIRREL GIRL SAVES RUNAWAY TROLLEY--AND INNOCENTS TIED TO BOTH SETS OF TRACKS!
SPIDER-MAN NOWHERE TO BE SEEN
While living as a squirrel, I'd picked up some of their language.
And a super-heroic leap is easy when you can shape-shift the inside of your legs to be giant springs.

To be fair, *lots* of things are easy when you can shape-shift the inside of your legs to be giant springs. Super-heroic leaps, basketball, professional hopscotch, probably other things too...

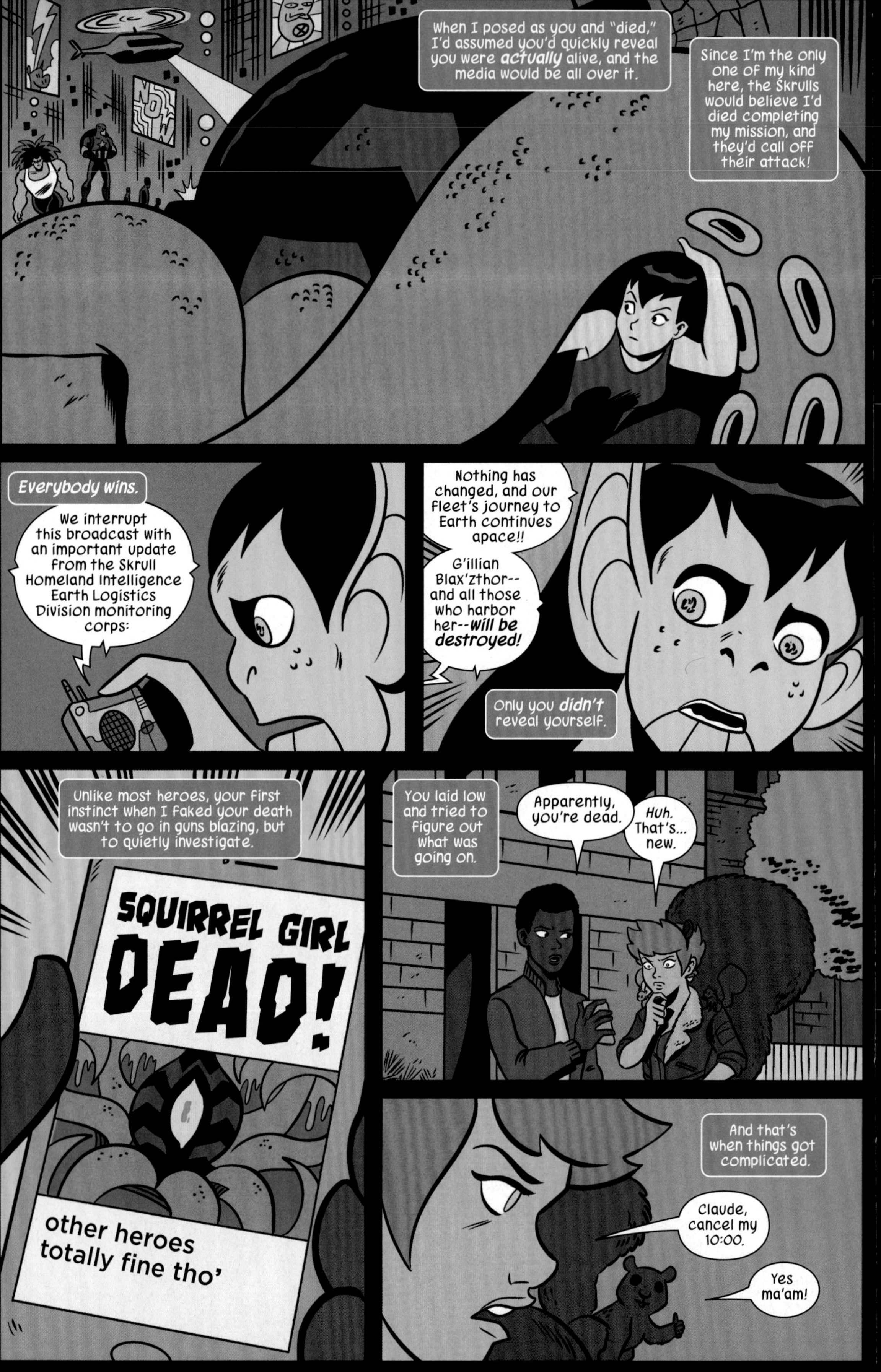

When I posed as you and "died," I'd assumed you'd quickly reveal you were *actually* alive, and the media would be all over it.
Since I'm the only one of my kind here, the Skrulls would believe I'd died completing my mission, and they'd call off their attack!
Everybody wins.
We interrupt this broadcast with an important update from the Skrull Homeland Intelligence Earth Logistics Division monitoring corps:
Nothing has changed, and our fleet's journey to Earth continues apace!!
G'illian Blax'zthor--and all those who harbor her--*will be destroyed!*
Only you *didn't* reveal yourself.
Unlike most heroes, your first instinct when I faked your death wasn't to go in guns blazing, but to quietly investigate.
SQUIRREL GIRL DEAD!
other heroes totally fine tho'
You laid low and tried to figure out what was going on.
Apparently, you're dead.
Huh. That's... new.
And that's when things got complicated.
Claude, cancel my 10:00.
Yes ma'am!

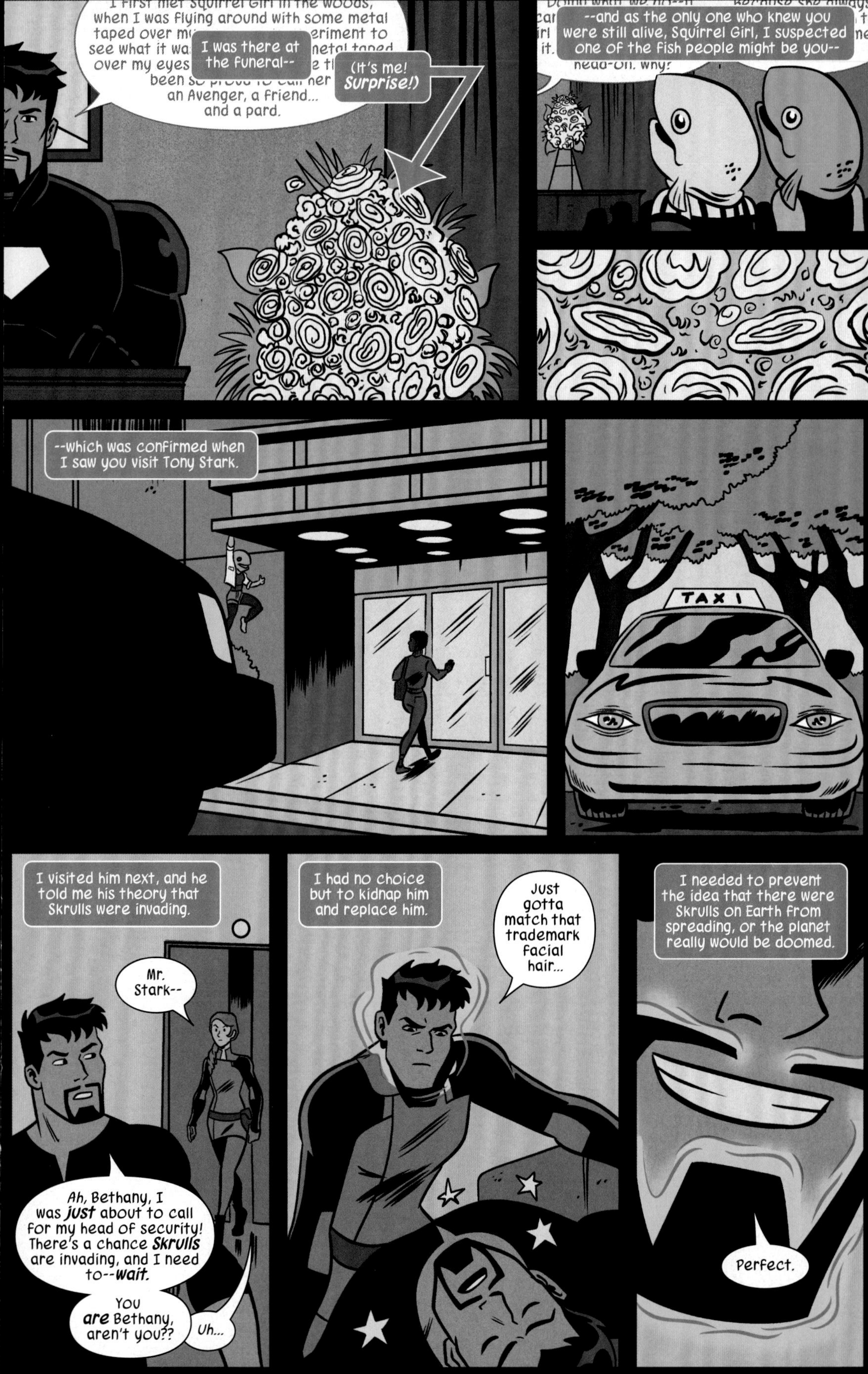
I first met Squirrel Girl in the woods, when I was flying around with some metal taped over m... eriment to see what it wa... metal taped over my eyes... been so proud to call her an Avenger, a friend... and a pard.
I was there at the funeral--
(It's me! Surprise!)
--and as the only one who knew you were still alive, Squirrel Girl, I suspected one of the fish people might be you--
--which was confirmed when I saw you visit Tony Stark.
TAXI
I visited him next, and he told me his theory that Skrulls were invading.
Mr. Stark--
Ah, Bethany, I was just about to call for my head of security! There's a chance Skrulls are invading, and I need to--wait.
You are Bethany, aren't you??
Uh...
I had no choice but to kidnap him and replace him.
Just gotta match that trademark facial hair...
I needed to prevent the idea that there were Skrulls on Earth from spreading, or the planet really would be doomed.
Perfect.

Those of you who called "entirely non-suspicious bouquet" as being the villain in the first part of this story: congratulations! For once, your endless flower-based paranoia has paid off!

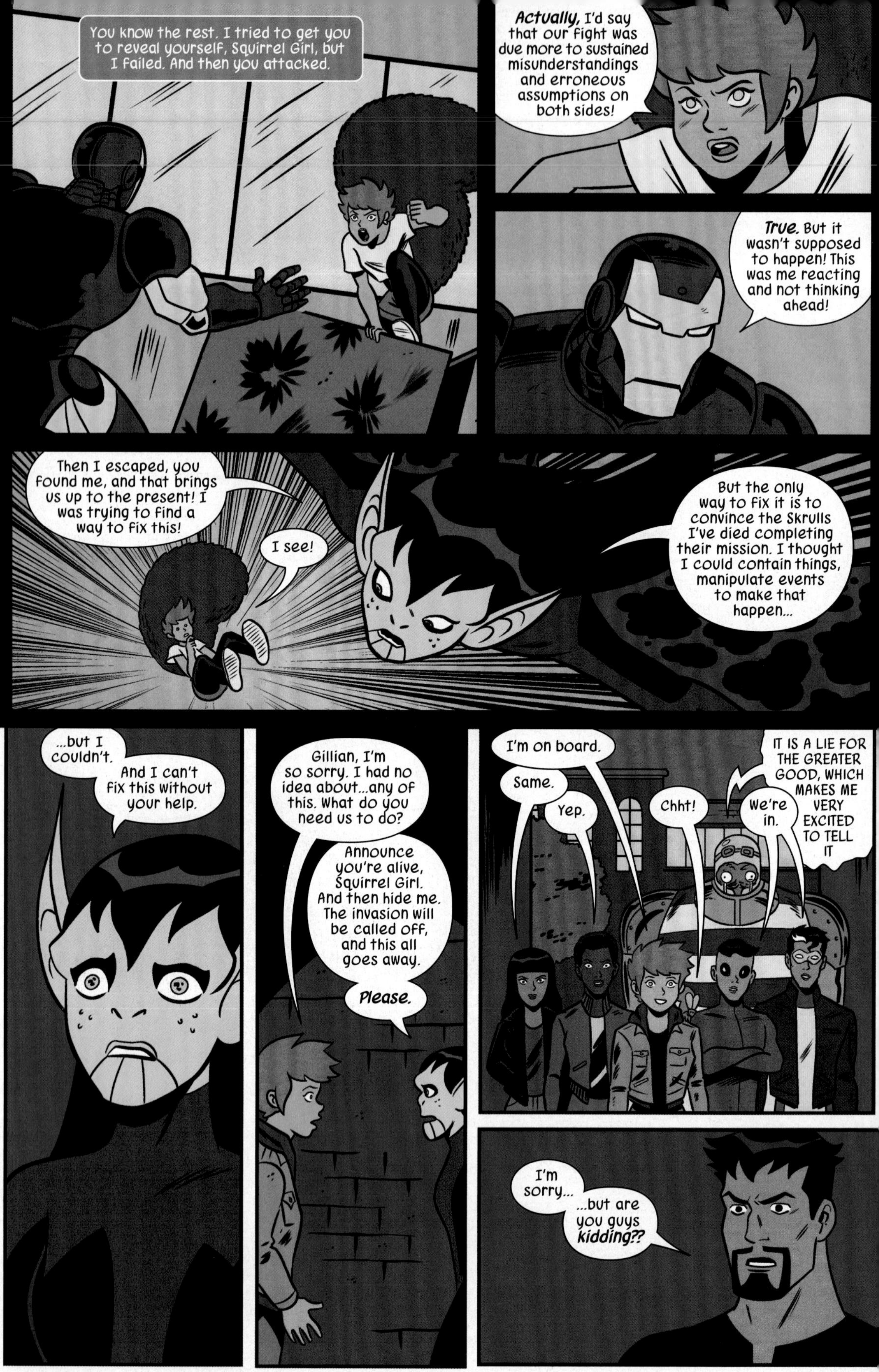
You know the rest. I tried to get you to reveal yourself, Squirrel Girl, but I failed. And then you attacked.
Actually, I'd say that our fight was due more to sustained misunderstandings and erroneous assumptions on both sides!
True. But it wasn't supposed to happen! This was me reacting and not thinking ahead!
Then I escaped, you found me, and that brings us up to the present! I was trying to find a way to fix this!
I see!
But the only way to fix it is to convince the Skrulls I've died completing their mission. I thought I could contain things, manipulate events to make that happen...
...but I couldn't.
And I can't fix this without your help.
Gillian, I'm so sorry. I had no idea about...any of this. What do you need us to do?
Announce you're alive, Squirrel Girl. And then hide me. The invasion will be called off, and this all goes away.
Please.
I'm on board.
Same.
Yep.
Chht!
We're in.
IT IS A LIE FOR THE GREATER GOOD, WHICH MAKES ME VERY EXCITED TO TELL IT
I'm sorry...
...but are you guys kidding??

I BELIEVE IT WAS SØREN AABYE KIERKEGAARD WHO FIRST TOLD HIS HATERS THAT "YOU CAN'T SPELL 'ALIENATION' WITHOUT 'LIE.'" HOWEVER, ON THE CHANCE THAT IT WAS NOT, THEN I WOULD ABSOLUTELY LIKE THE CREDIT

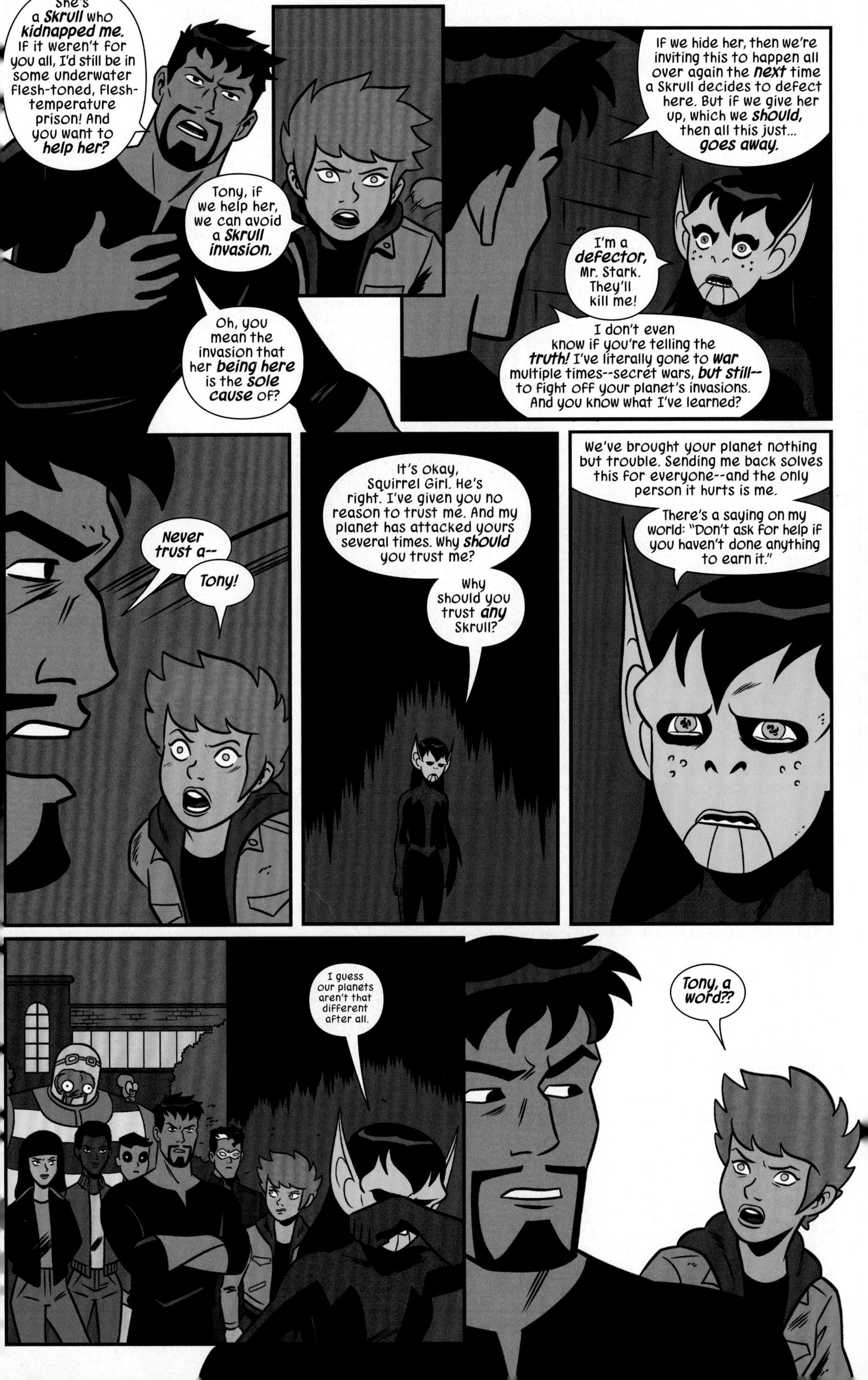

She's a Skrull who kidnapped me. If it weren't for you all, I'd still be in some underwater flesh-toned, flesh-temperature prison! And you want to help her?
Tony, if we help her, we can avoid a Skrull invasion.
Oh, you mean the invasion that her being here is the sole cause of?
If we hide her, then we're inviting this to happen all over again the next time a Skrull decides to defect here. But if we give her up, which we should, then all this just... goes away.
I'm a defector, Mr. Stark. They'll kill me!
I don't even know if you're telling the truth! I've literally gone to war multiple times--secret wars, but still--to fight off your planet's invasions. And you know what I've learned?
Never trust a--
Tony!
It's okay, Squirrel Girl. He's right. I've given you no reason to trust me. And my planet has attacked yours several times. Why should you trust me?
Why should you trust any Skrull?
We've brought your planet nothing but trouble. Sending me back solves this for everyone--and the only person it hurts is me.
There's a saying on my world: "Don't ask for help if you haven't done anything to earn it."
I guess our planets aren't that different after all.
Tony, a word??

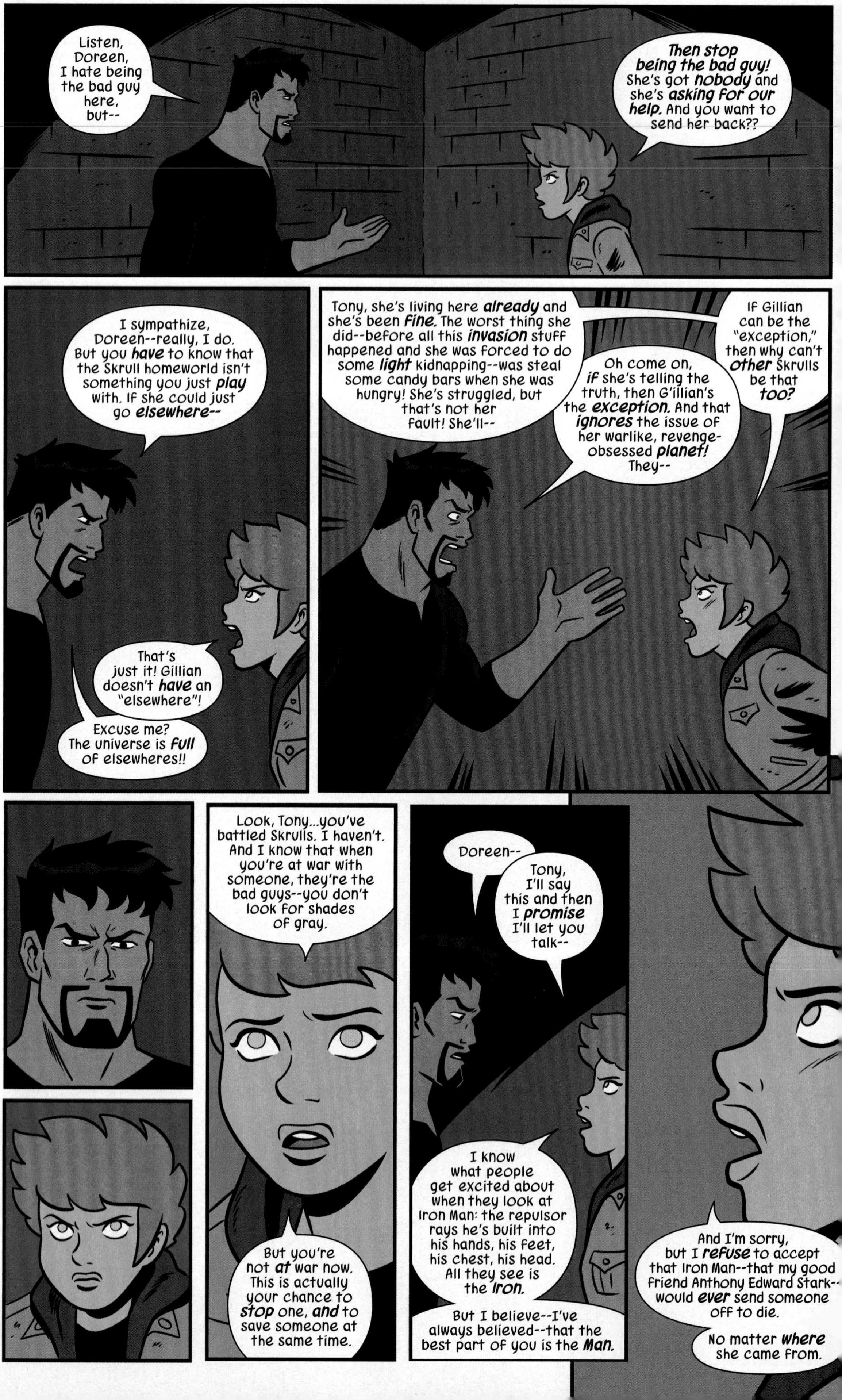
Listen, Doreen, I hate being the bad guy here, but--
Then stop being the bad guy! She's got nobody and she's asking for our help. And you want to send her back??
I sympathize, Doreen--really, I do. But you have to know that the Skrull homeworld isn't something you just play with. If she could just go elsewhere--
That's just it! Gillian doesn't have an "elsewhere"!
Excuse me? The universe is full of elsewheres!!
Tony, she's living here already and she's been fine. The worst thing she did--before all this invasion stuff happened and she was forced to do some light kidnapping--was steal some candy bars when she was hungry! She's struggled, but that's not her fault! She'll--
Oh come on, if she's telling the truth, then G'illian's the exception. And that ignores the issue of her warlike, revenge-obsessed planet! They--
If Gillian can be the "exception," then why can't other Skrulls be that too?
Look, Tony...you've battled Skrulls. I haven't. And I know that when you're at war with someone, they're the bad guys--you don't look for shades of gray.
But you're not at war now. This is actually your chance to stop one, and to save someone at the same time.
Doreen--
Tony, I'll say this and then I promise I'll let you talk--
I know what people get excited about when they look at Iron Man: the repulsor rays he's built into his hands, his feet, his chest, his head. All they see is the Iron.
But I believe--I've always believed--that the best part of you is the Man.
And I'm sorry, but I refuse to accept that Iron Man--that my good friend Anthony Edward Stark--would ever send someone off to die.
No matter where she came from.

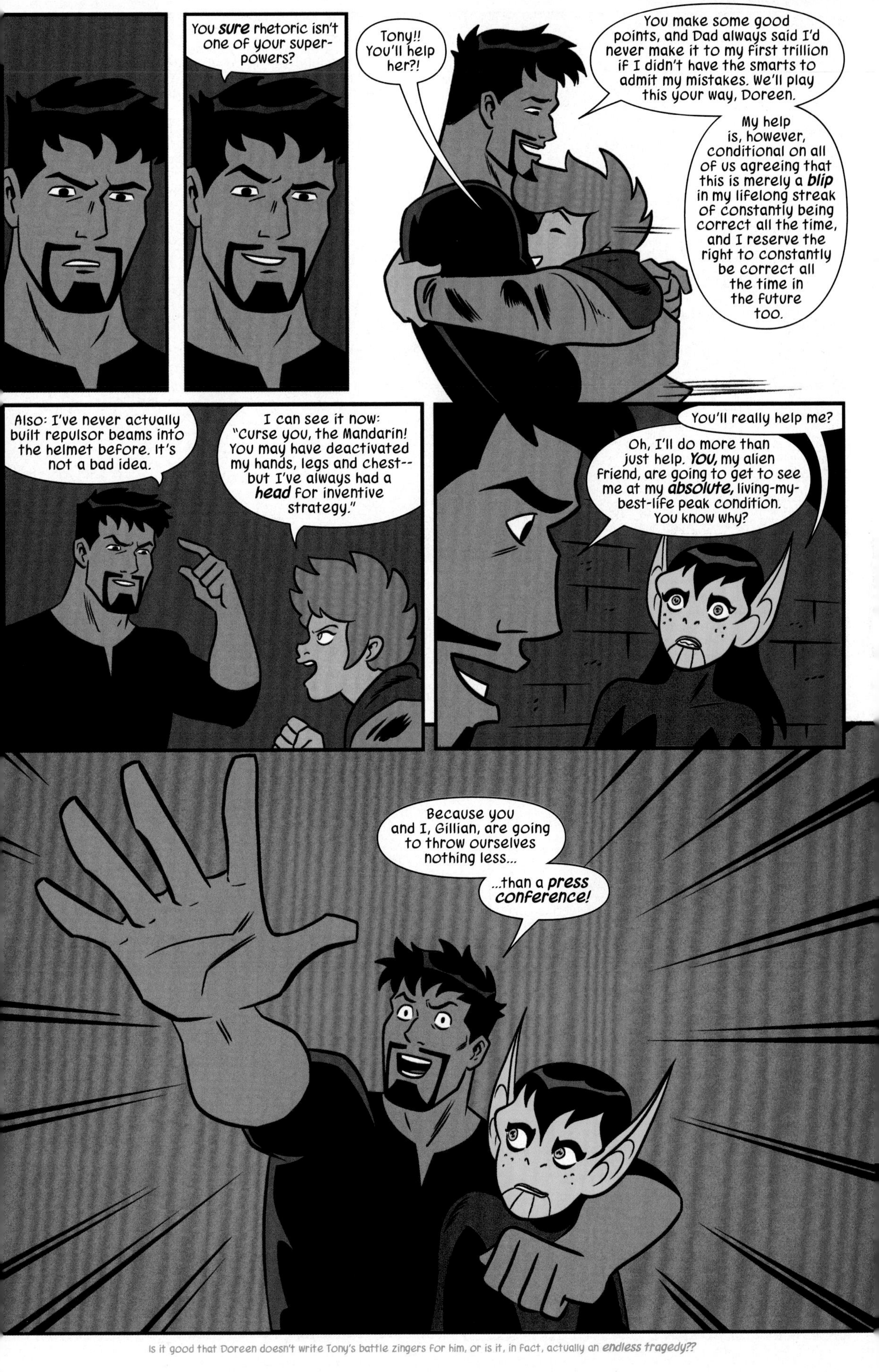
You sure rhetoric isn't one of your super-powers?
Tony!! You'll help her?!
You make some good points, and Dad always said I'd never make it to my first trillion if I didn't have the smarts to admit my mistakes. We'll play this your way, Doreen.
My help is, however, conditional on all of us agreeing that this is merely a blip in my lifelong streak of constantly being correct all the time, and I reserve the right to constantly be correct all the time in the future too.
Also: I've never actually built repulsor beams into the helmet before. It's not a bad idea.
I can see it now: "Curse you, the Mandarin! You may have deactivated my hands, legs and chest--but I've always had a head for inventive strategy."
You'll really help me?
Oh, I'll do more than just help. YOU, my alien friend, are going to get to see me at my absolute, living-my-best-life peak condition. You know why?
Because you and I, Gillian, are going to throw ourselves nothing less...
...than a press conference!

Is it good that Doreen doesn't write Tony's battle zingers for him, or is it, in fact, actually an *endless tragedy??*

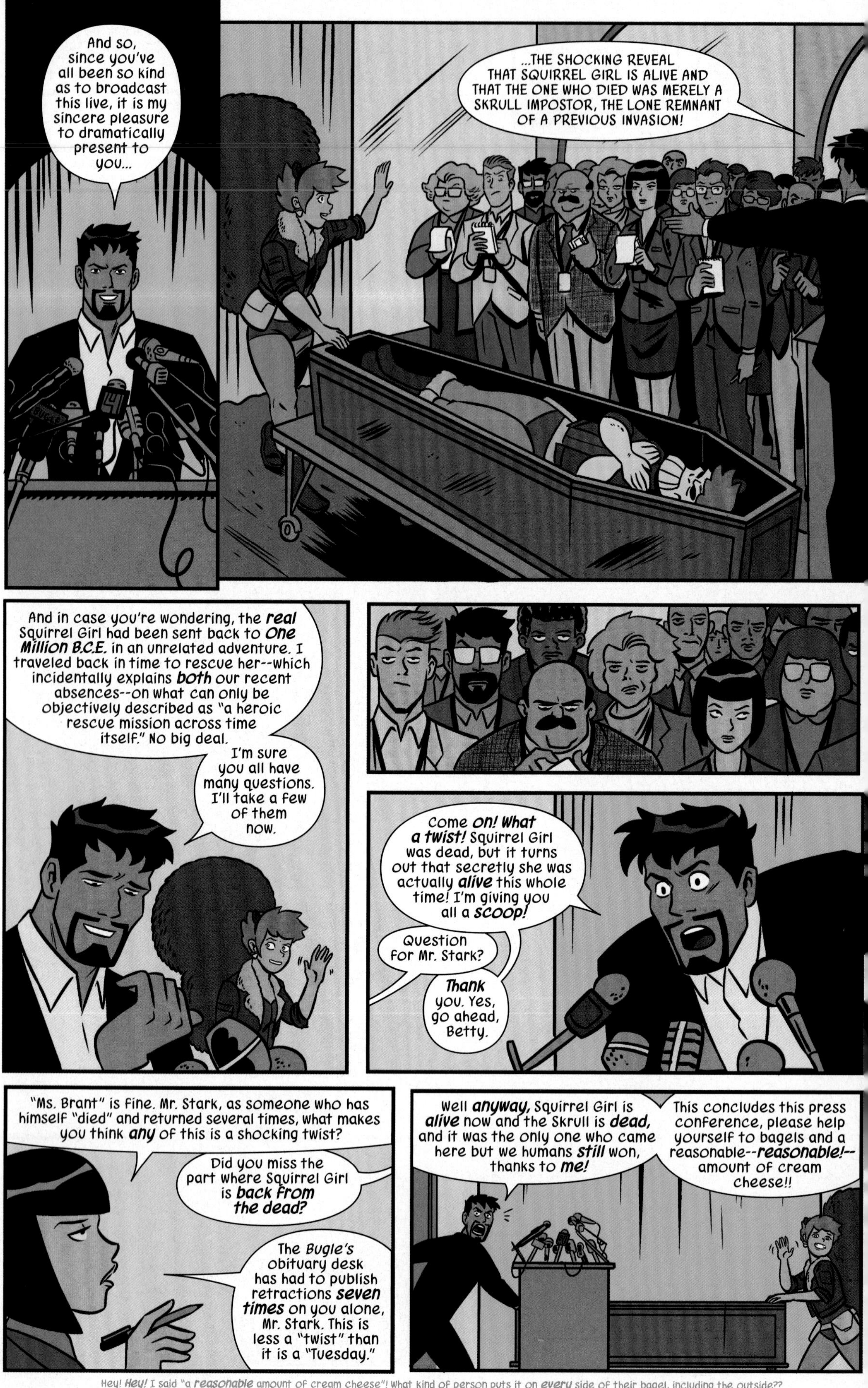
And so, since you've all been so kind as to broadcast this live, it is my sincere pleasure to dramatically present to you...
...THE SHOCKING REVEAL THAT SQUIRREL GIRL IS ALIVE AND THAT THE ONE WHO DIED WAS MERELY A SKRULL IMPOSTOR, THE LONE REMNANT OF A PREVIOUS INVASION!
And in case you're wondering, the real Squirrel Girl had been sent back to One Million B.C.E. in an unrelated adventure. I traveled back in time to rescue her--which incidentally explains both our recent absences--on what can only be objectively described as "a heroic rescue mission across time itself." No big deal.
I'm sure you all have many questions. I'll take a few of them now.
Come on! What a twist! Squirrel Girl was dead, but it turns out that secretly she was actually alive this whole time! I'm giving you all a scoop!
Question for Mr. Stark?
Thank you. Yes, go ahead, Betty.
"Ms. Brant" is fine. Mr. Stark, as someone who has himself "died" and returned several times, what makes you think any of this is a shocking twist?
Did you miss the part where Squirrel Girl is back from the dead?
The Bugle's obituary desk has had to publish retractions seven times on you alone, Mr. Stark. This is less a "twist" than it is a "Tuesday."
Well anyway, Squirrel Girl is alive now and the Skrull is dead, and it was the only one who came here but we humans still won, thanks to me!
This concludes this press conference, please help yourself to bagels and a reasonable--reasonable!--amount of cream cheese!!

Hey! *Hey!* I said "a *reasonable* amount of cream cheese"! What kind of person puts it on *every* side of their bagel, including the outside?? Yes, *obviously* I'm intrigued, impressed and curious over how you intend to eat it, but do it on someone else's dime!!

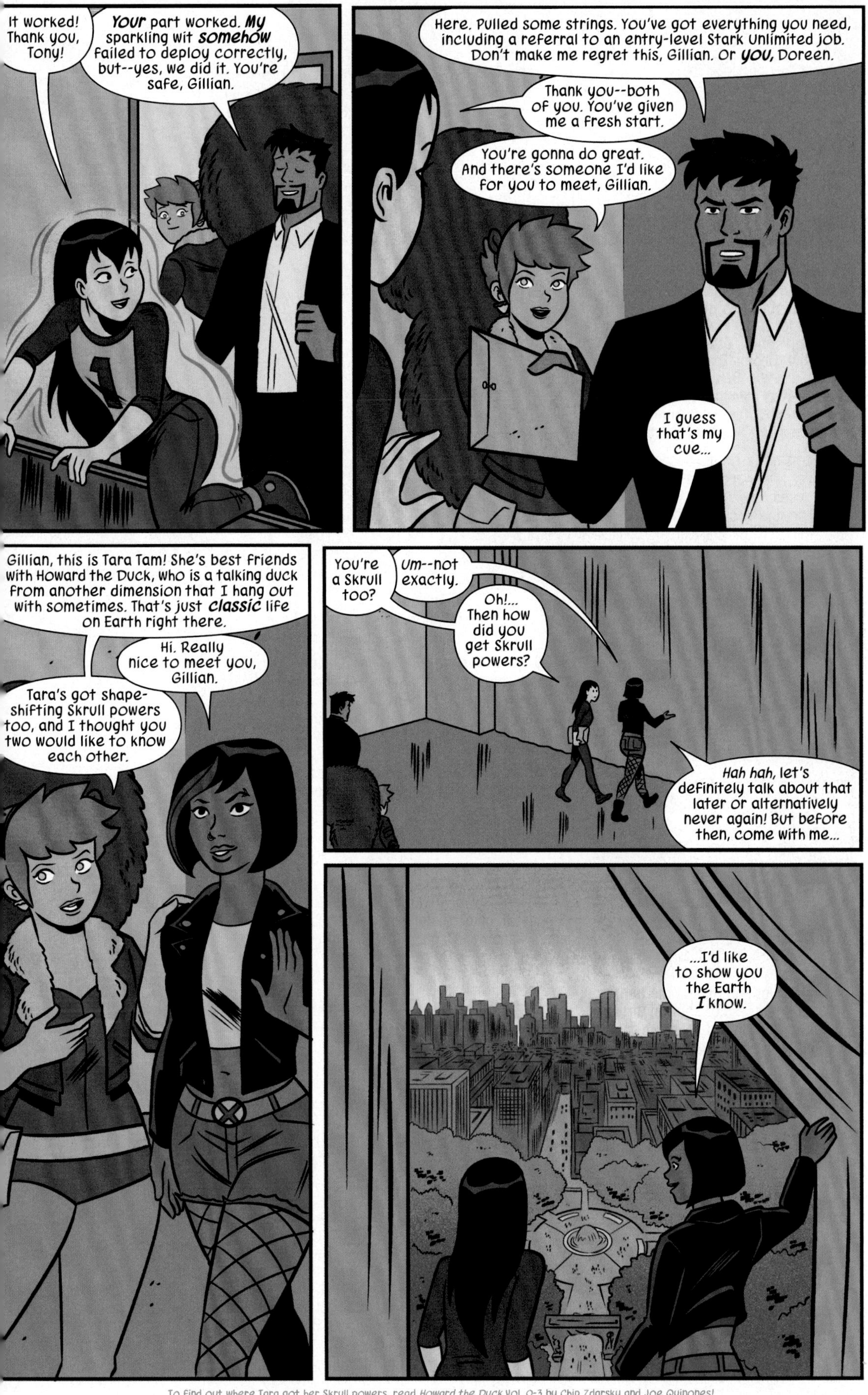
It worked! Thank you, Tony!
YOUR part worked. MY sparkling wit SOMEHOW failed to deploy correctly, but--yes, we did it. You're safe, Gillian.
Here. Pulled some strings. You've got everything you need, including a referral to an entry-level Stark Unlimited job. Don't make me regret this, Gillian. Or YOU, Doreen.
Thank you--both of you. You've given me a fresh start.
You're gonna do great. And there's someone I'd like for you to meet, Gillian.
I guess that's my cue...
Gillian, this is Tara Tam! She's best friends with Howard the Duck, who is a talking duck from another dimension that I hang out with sometimes. That's just CLASSIC life on Earth right there.
Hi. Really nice to meet you, Gillian.
Tara's got shape-shifting Skrull powers too, and I thought you two would like to know each other.
You're a Skrull too?
Um--not exactly.
Oh!... Then how did you get Skrull powers?
Hah hah, let's definitely talk about that later or alternatively never again! But before then, come with me...
...I'd like to show you the Earth I know.

To find out where Tara got her Skrull powers, read *Howard the Duck* Vol. 0-3 by Chip Zdarsky and Joe Quinones!
The series has other much more interesting plot points in it too, but if you wade through them then you'll eventually get to this very minor detail!!

Ryan!

Letters From Nuts

NEVA
Erica!
FORGET

Send letters to mheroes@marvel.com or 135 W 50th St, 7th Floor, New York, NY 10020 (Please mark "OKAY TO PRINT"

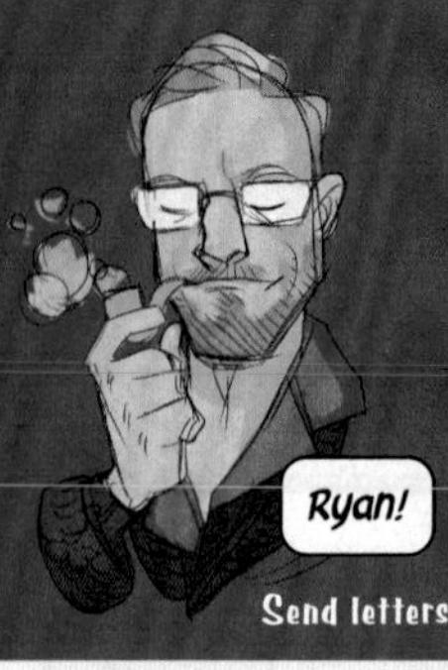

Okay, be honest, is Gillian your new favorite character or what?? (I mean, second to Brain Drain of course.) Join us next issue for a fun standalone featuring Spider-Man and drawn by special guest artist Naomi Franquiz! But don't worry, USG MVP Derek Charm will be back for #42 -- along with a couple of surprise guests! In the meantime, here's Ryan to answer some of your letters!

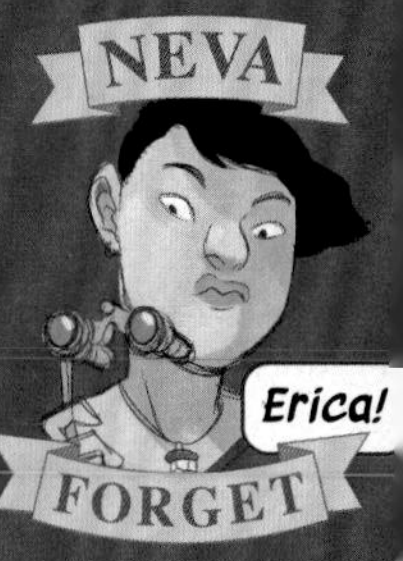

Hello, my name is Inara. I really like your comics. For Halloween I was Squirrel Girl, and my sister Majel was Tippy-Toe. My Nana made the costumes from scratch. Thank you for making great comics!

Inara (10) and Majel (6)
Pittsburgh, PA

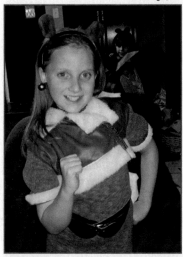

RYAN: Inara, nothing makes me happier than a sister team-up of Squirrel Girl and Tippy-Toe! Your Nana has some sweet skills. And thank you for liking our comics!

Dear Ryan and Erica,

I love your comic and just wanted to say thanks for all the great days SG has brought me. I enjoy reading things that make me feel good (I think most people do) and Squirrel Girl is just one of those things. I found SG a little late, but I couldn't be more happy that I did. So many Marvel comics are gory and serious while SG isn't. Since it is so rare, it is special and I love that about her. I decided to dress up as her for Halloween and had tons of fun making the costume. I noticed that not a lot of people had cosplayed in Squirrel Girl's new gray costume so I did. I made Tippy-Toe too, but she didn't make it into the photo.

Thank you for all of your hard work on Squirrel Girl and thank you for an amazing comic.

Dylan

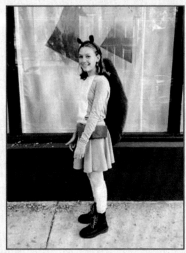

RYAN: Ah, Dylan, amazing! I love the gray costume too and you nailed it perfectly. And no worries about finding the book late--the nice thing about books is that they are infinitely patient and will wait for you indefinitely! Thanks again for the kind words, and I hope you find more opportunities to wear that great costume!

Hi again, Marvel!

It's Lia again, only NINE YEARS OLD this time (hold on, my sister is blowing into my ear one sec there we go)!!!!!!!!!!!!!! I've seen both "flattering pseudocode" letters and I've got one for Tippy.

> CHUCKCCHT (crrt chuck chitt cuk) [crrt chit cuk squee chutt crrk chht chrt chit chit][chuck squee cuk chuckchit crrt crrt chirt chhttk]Tik_crrt_cuk_squee_chuk CUK () crrt_chuk_chitt_squee

So how was that? I hope Tippy approves.

The three of them (because I'm including Nancy) are TOTALLY "marvelous" (Yes, I also love puns)!

Stay nuts,
Lia Alexander
Age 9

P.S. Got two pics, one from Halloween (which was yesterday, by the way) and one for a next storyline how the Earth is under attack while Allene visits after promising she won't try to replace everyone with squirrels, already did that two times, one on earth (stopped by Doreen) and one in the Negative Zone. Oh well. At least the Avengers will have help.

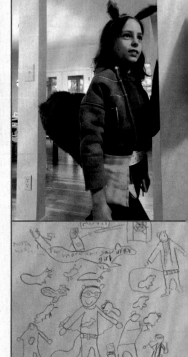

RYAN: Lia, your costume is spectacular (BUT OF COURSE YOU ALREADY KNEW THAT, HOW COULD YOU NOT, IT'S AWESOME), and as for your second pic--I think you'll be happy to know that Allene MAY be seen in a couple of months, so keep your eyes peeled for that! ALSO KEEP DRAWING COMICS, THAT'S AMAZING

Dear Ryan and Erica,

We love Squirrel Girl! My 7-year-old daughter fell in love with Squirrel Girl and Tippy-Toe this past summer when her Uncle Evan introduced her to the comic books for her birthday. Evie's favorite lovey is a small cat hand puppet, so Evie now treats her like Tippy-Toe. For Halloween, she had only one request: Squirrel Girl! We found a fur lion costume at Good Will and her grandmother and I worked on revising the costume to fit SG's look. I am attaching pictures of her as Squirrel Girl and Kit Girl as Tippy-Toe. I will also attach a photo of her handwritten letter addressed directly to Squirrel Girl. You decide if you'd like to print anything!

Thank you for giving my fierce, strong-willed daughter such an incredible role model. :)

Theresa Allgood
Hamden, CT

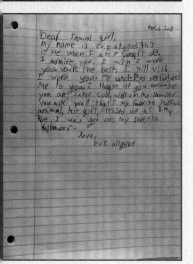

Transcription of Evie's letter:

Dear Squirrel Girl,

My name is Evie Allgood. This is me when I am 7 years old. I admire you. I wish I were you. You're the best. I still wish I were you. My Uncle Evo introduced me to you. I thought of you because you are super cool. Who's on my shoulder, you ask? Well, that's my favorite stuffed animal, Kit Girl, dressed up as Tippy-Toe. I was you on my seventh Halloween.

Love,
Evie Allgood

RYAN: Evie, you've got all the "Deadpool's Guide to Super Villains" cards! You are ready for ANYTHING. And your Squirrel Girl costume (and Kit Girl's Tippy costume) are both great. Look at this--a letters page full of amazing costumes that readers have made! This is officially the best letters page in any comic. I don't make the rules, I just observe when they're awesome!

After Tony tells Databus Doreen's secret identity he then instructs it to "delete that fact and never record it again." So it deletes the fact. But to be able to know to never record it again, it will need to know exactly what not to record. Tony has just told his brand-new digital assistant to remember and not remember the same bit of information. No wonder his A.I.s never work out so well.

Also, are we to believe that Tony is using a late '90s Sound Blaster program for therapy?

David

RYAN: Hah! David, I would like to say that, as a very clever writer, I absolutely realized this sort of paradox Tony was setting up in Databus there! I mean, I would really *like* to say that...but there is still a small but non-zero chance I didn't realize that until I read your letter just now. But as it is 100% the sort of thing Tony would overlook, I feel like we all got lucky and it's super on-brand, so we're good. And yes, I hereby proclaim that Tony using Dr. Sbaitso as his personal therapist is absolutely the most Tony thing in the world.

Squirrel Girl has become a favorite in our house since we discovered the comic about two years ago. As it turns out, I had the fortune to publish some of Erica's art almost a dozen years ago in Tales of the Talisman magazine where she illustrated one of her dad's stories. It's been awesome to see her success in the world of comics. I was sorry to see Erica's departure from the interior pages, but Derek has shown himself to be a great successor.

I like to collect action figures of my favorite heroes. Unfortunately, I haven't found a Squirrel Girl action figure yet, but my younger daughter, Verity, decided to remedy that. She created a Squirrel Girl plush for my birthday. I've attached a picture of her showing off her creation.

Keep eating nuts and kicking butts!
David Lee Summers
Las Cruces, New Mexico

RYAN: DAVID, what a coincidence, and it's great to hear from you! And Verity is super talented. There's still no Squirrel Girl action figures (WHY?), but there ARE some really sweet Marvel Rising dolls, of which there is a Squirrel Girl one! I have her in my house. She protects it against criminals, and you can tell it works because we have been attacked by criminals zero (0) times since I got her. She comes with a little Tippy too! Though I gotta admit, I am really jealous of Verity's handmade Doreen there!!

Next Issue:

the unbeatable Squirrel Girl
ENTER MS.
QUIZZLER

Attention, Squirrel Scouts! Make sure to check out our production blog, **unbeatablesquirrelgirl.tumblr.com**, where we post behind-the-scenes stuff on how the book gets made, along with all sorts of cool things *you* make: fanart, cosplay, whatever!

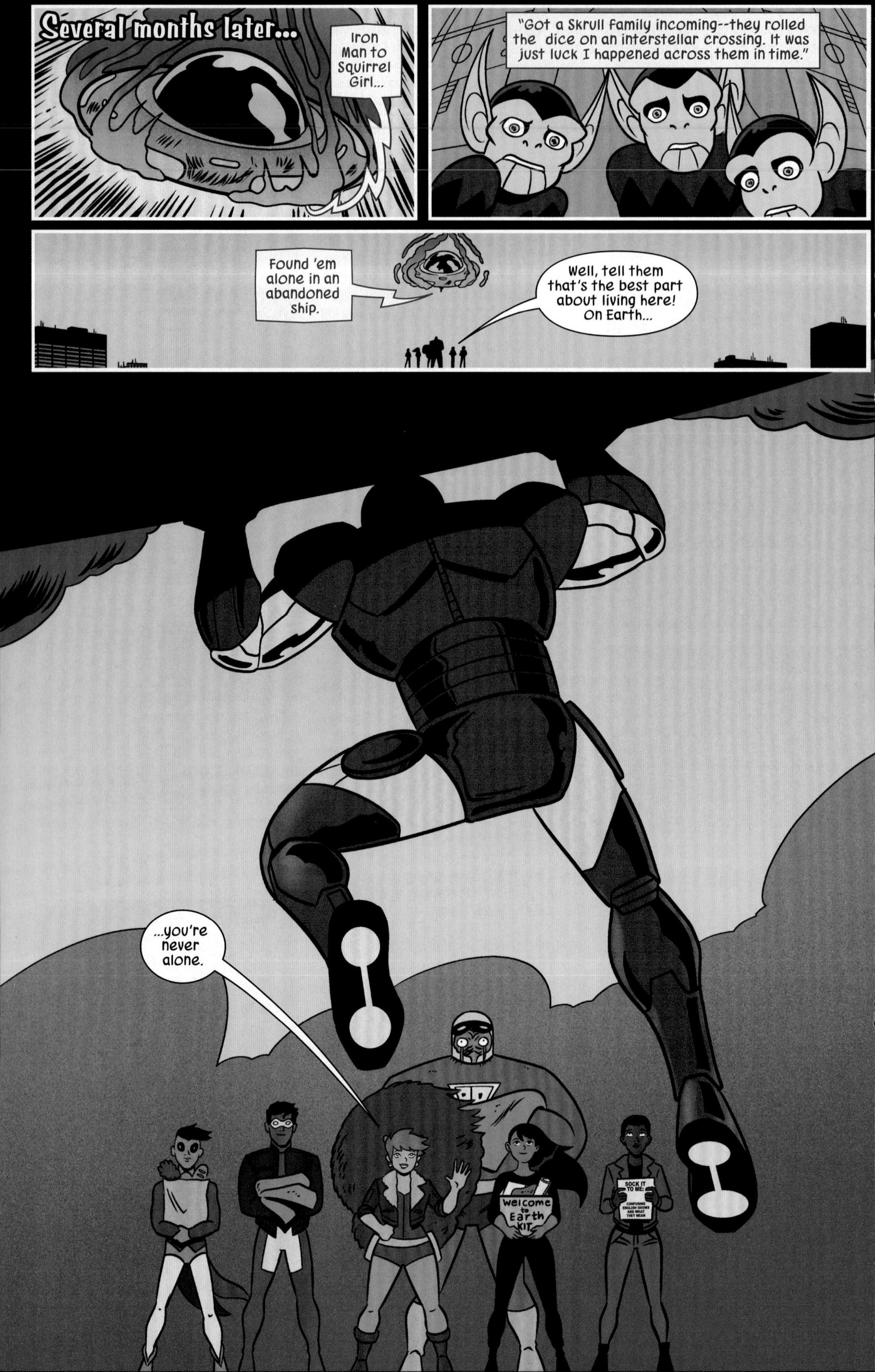
Several months later...
Iron Man to Squirrel Girl...
"Got a Skrull family incoming--they rolled the dice on an interstellar crossing. It was just luck I happened across them in time."
Found 'em alone in an abandoned ship.
Well, tell them that's the best part about living here! On Earth...
...you're never alone.
Welcome to Earth Kit
SOCK IT TO ME: CONFUSING ENGLISH IDIOMS AND WHAT THEY MEAN

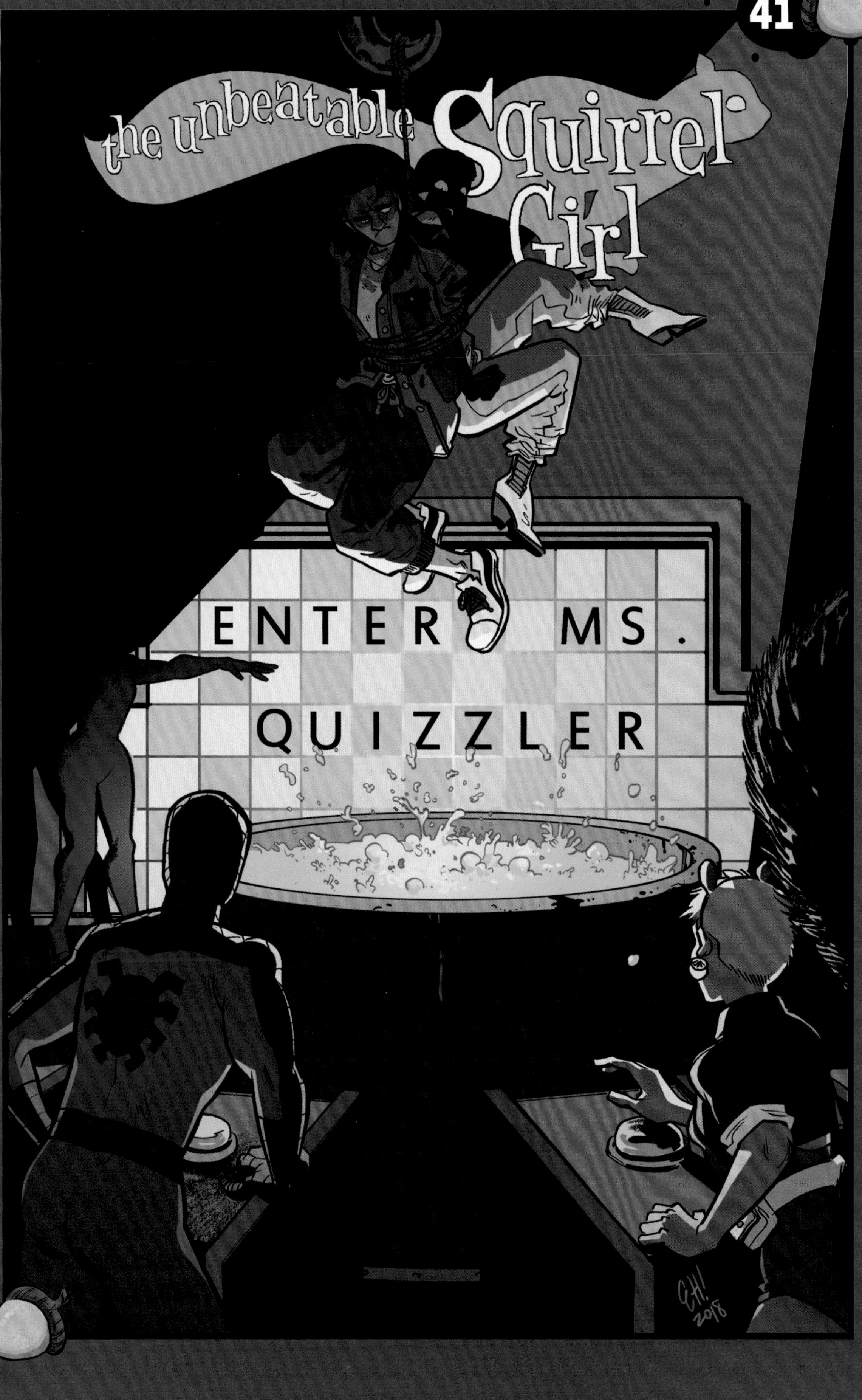
the unbeatable Squirrel Girl
ENTER MS. QUIZZLER
EH! 2018

*Doreen Green isn't just a second-year computer science student: she secretly also has all the powers of both squirrel and girl! She uses her amazing abilities to fight crime **and** be as awesome as possible. You know her as...**The Unbeatable Squirrel Girl!** Find out what she's been up to, with...*

Squirrel Girl *in a nutshell*

search!

#peterparker
#nancywhitehead
#msquizzler
#secretidentities
#stinklines
#publicdomaincharacters

Squirrel Girl @unbeatablesg
Good news, everyone! I wasn't actually dead! That was just a Skrull posing as me who died!

Squirrel Girl @unbeatablesg
Yep, we should all relax because everything's fine, I was just briefly replaced with a space alien but it's no big deal now!!

Squirrel Girl @unbeatablesg
You may be wondering: Have others been replaced with space invaders too? The answer: NOPE. Me and @starkmantony checked, and nobody has been replaced by an alien duplicate! So we can all just RELAX and BE COOL. Hooray!

Egg @imduderadtude
@unbeatablesg im a skrull

Nancy W. @sewwiththeflo
@unbeatablesg @imduderadtude No, he's not.

Egg @imduderadtude
@unbeatablesg @sewwiththeflo how do u kno maybe im doing skrull stuff rgiht now

Nancy W. @sewwiththeflo
@unbeatablesg @imduderadtude "Skrull stuff."

Egg @imduderadtude
@unbeatablesg @sewwiththeflo ya like 4 example sayin "is any1 else bored out of their SKRULLS" and then eating their brains

Egg @imduderadtude
@unbeatablesg @sewwiththeflo or whatever

Egg @imduderadtude
@unbeatablesg @sewwiththeflo not SUPER clear on what a skrull is tbh

Nancy W. @sewwiththeflo
@unbeatablesg @imduderadtude THEN WHY ARE YOU REPLYING TO THIS THREAD??

Egg @imduderadtude
@unbeatablesg @sewwiththeflo i'm just living and loving the online life and sharing my #content with the world!!!

Squirrel Girl @unbeatablesg
ANYWAY in other exciting news, @starkmantony isn't missing anymore either! That was implied earlier when I said we ensured Earth is safe, but I'm happy to make it official that Tony Stark is alive and well, as are his new AIs that are definitely reading this!

Squirrel Girl @unbeatablesg
So everything's back to normal: Tony's casually created intelligent digital life without any thought of the consequences, I'm a regular person with the proportional speed and strength of a squirrel, and costume crime is held in check by costumed crimefighters...

Squirrel Girl @unbeatablesg
...whose powers and abilities are juuuust slightly better than the villains they defeat!! STATUS QUO 4EVAH, IN THIS PARTICULAR INSTANCE

Squirrel Girl @unbeatablesg
Now it's time to relax, unwind, and maybe watch a movie! That's right! Even heroes "waste time" and "eat giant buckets of popcorn"!!

Squirrel Girl @unbeatablesg
One thing's for certain: After the events of the past few days, I think we've all earned a quiet couple of days where nothing happens!

Squirrel Girl @unbeatablesg
And just such a day begins riiiiiiight......

Squirrel Girl @unbeatablesg
...NOW.

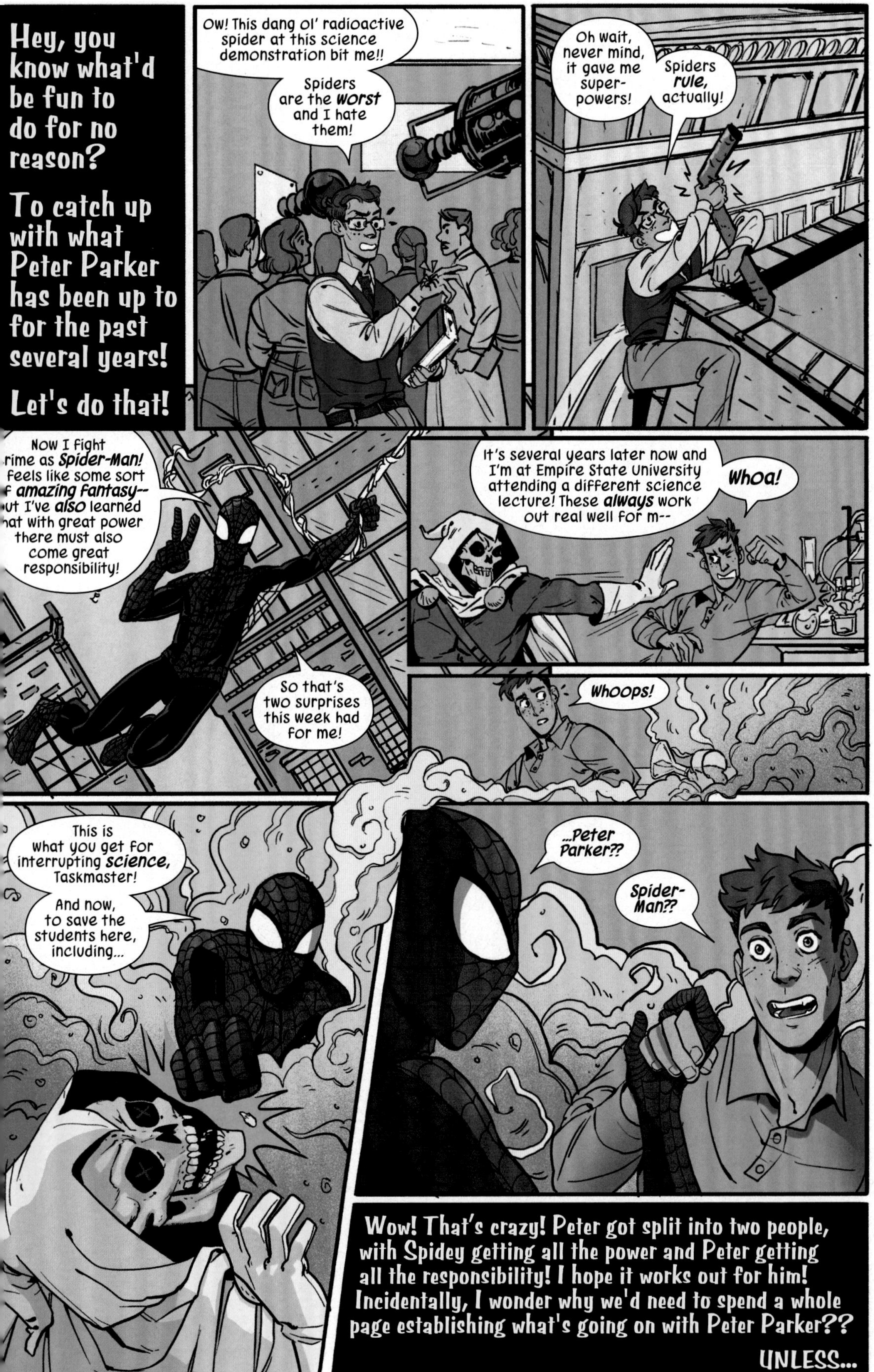
Hey, you know what'd be fun to do for no reason?
To catch up with what Peter Parker has been up to for the past several years!
Let's do that!
Ow! This dang ol' radioactive spider at this science demonstration bit me!!
Spiders are the worst and I hate them!
Oh wait, never mind, it gave me super-powers!
Spiders rule, actually!
Now I fight
rime as Spider-Man!
feels like some sort
f amazing fantasy--
ut I've also learned
hat with great power
there must also
come great
responsibility!
So that's two surprises this week had for me!
It's several years later now and I'm at Empire State University attending a different science lecture! These always work out real well for m--
Whoa!
Whoops!
This is what you get for interrupting science, Taskmaster!
And now, to save the students here, including...
...Peter Parker??
Spider-Man??
Wow! That's crazy! Peter got split into two people, with Spidey getting all the power and Peter getting all the responsibility! I hope it works out for him! Incidentally, I wonder why we'd need to spend a whole page establishing what's going on with Peter Parker??
UNLESS...

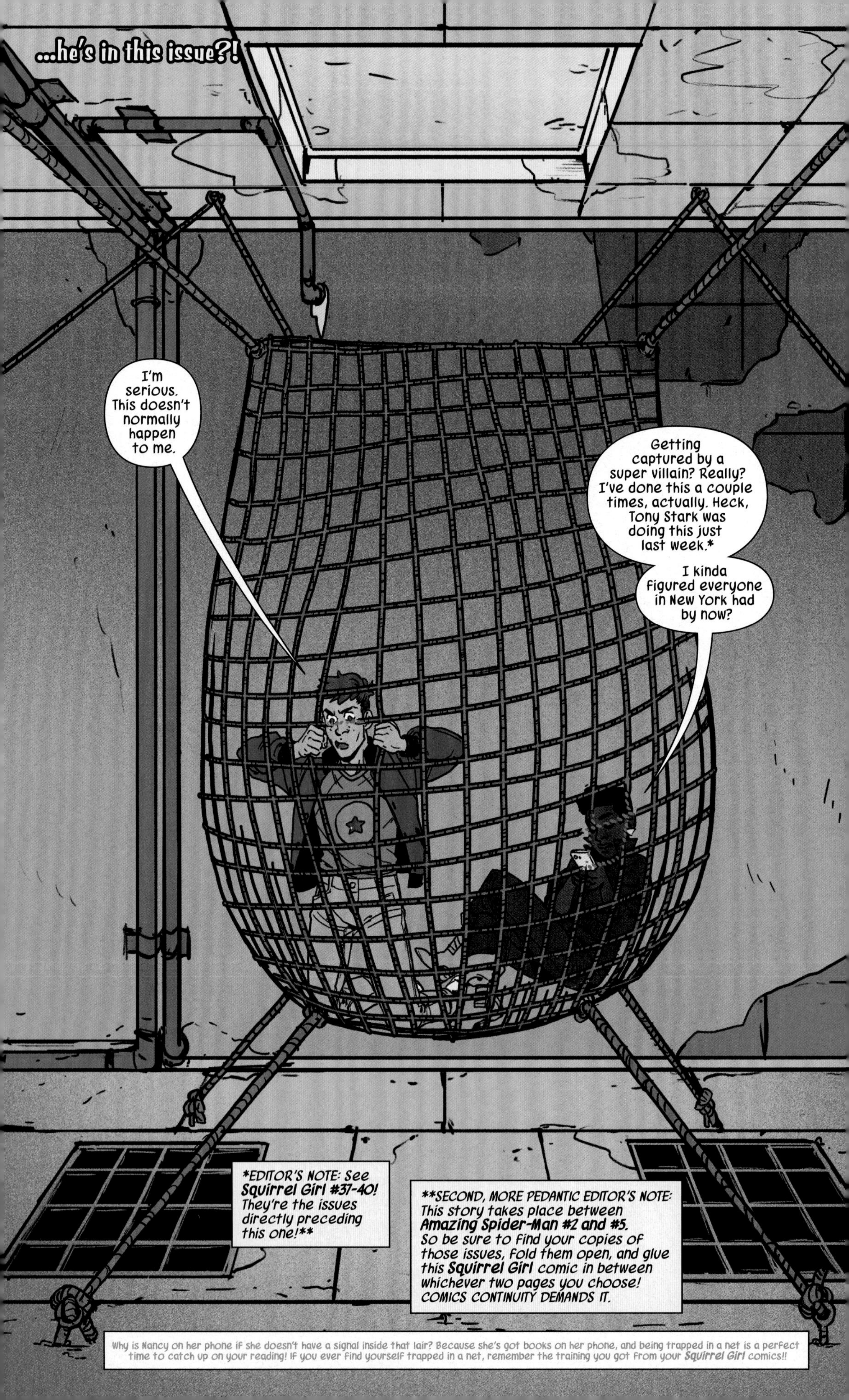
...he's in this issue?!
I'm serious. This doesn't normally happen to me.
Getting captured by a super villain? Really? I've done this a couple times, actually. Heck, Tony Stark was doing this just last week.*
I kinda figured everyone in New York had by now?
*EDITOR'S NOTE: See Squirrel Girl #37-40! They're the issues directly preceding this one!**
**SECOND, MORE PEDANTIC EDITOR'S NOTE: This story takes place between Amazing Spider-Man #2 and #5. So be sure to find your copies of those issues, fold them open, and glue this Squirrel Girl comic in between whichever two pages you choose! COMICS CONTINUITY DEMANDS IT.
Why is Nancy on her phone if she doesn't have a signal inside that lair? Because she's got books on her phone, and being trapped in a net is a perfect time to catch up on your reading! If you ever find yourself trapped in a net, remember the training you got from your Squirrel Girl comics!!

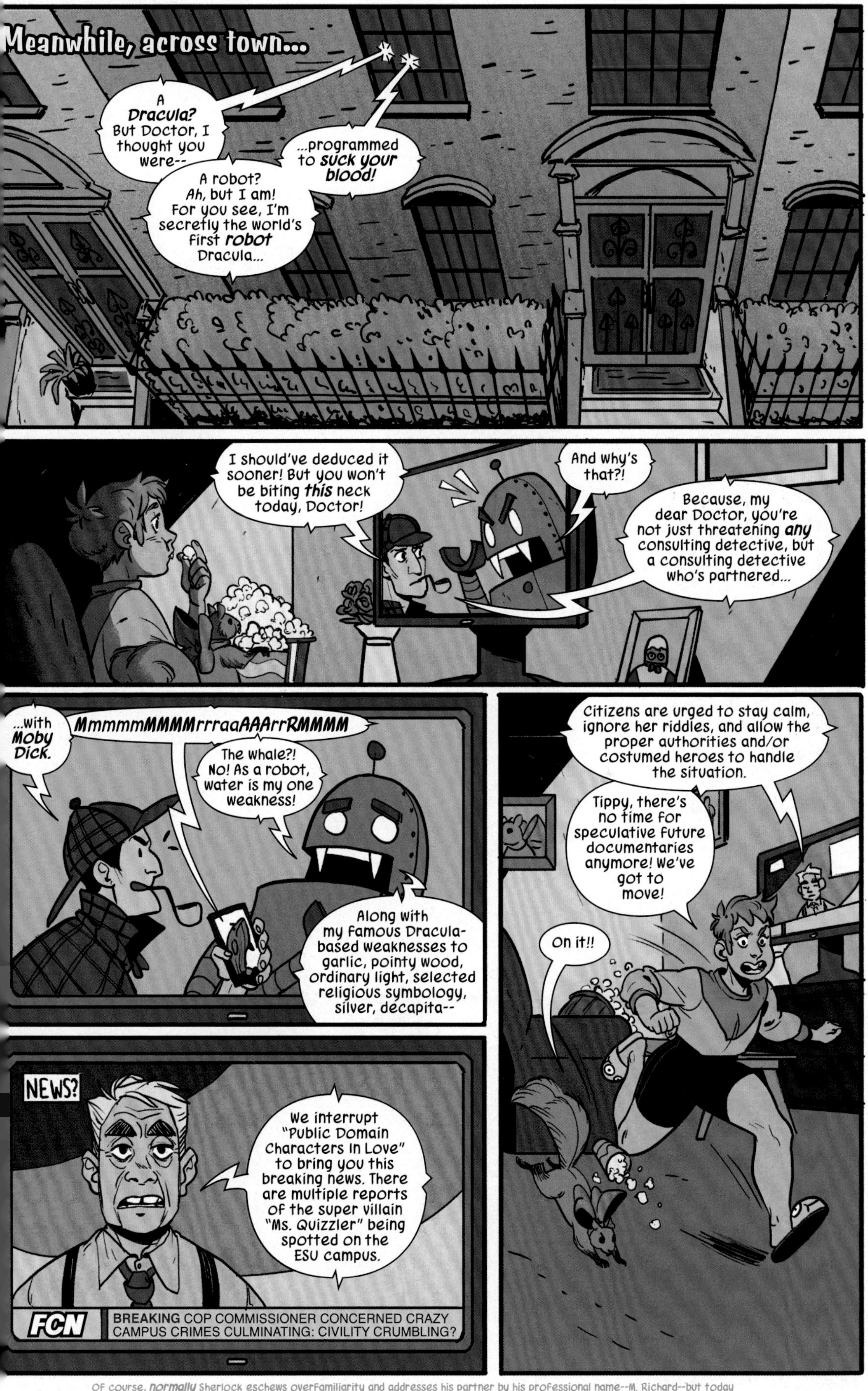
Meanwhile, across town...
A *Dracula?* But Doctor, I thought you were--
A robot? *Ah,* but I am! For you see, I'm secretly the world's first *robot* Dracula...
...programmed to *suck your blood!*
I should've deduced it sooner! But you won't be biting *this* neck today, Doctor!
And why's that?!
Because, my dear Doctor, you're not just threatening *any* consulting detective, but a consulting detective who's partnered...
...with *Moby Dick.*
MmmmmMMMMrrraaAAArrRMMMM
The whale?! No! As a robot, water is my one weakness!
Along with my famous Dracula-based weaknesses to garlic, pointy wood, ordinary light, selected religious symbology, silver, decapita--
NEWS?
We interrupt "Public Domain Characters In Love" to bring you this breaking news. There are multiple reports of the super villain "Ms. Quizzler" being spotted on the ESU campus.
FCN
BREAKING COP COMMISSIONER CONCERNED CRAZY CAMPUS CRIMES CULMINATING: CIVILITY CRUMBLING?
Citizens are urged to stay calm, ignore her riddles, and allow the proper authorities and/or costumed heroes to handle the situation.
Tippy, there's no time for speculative future documentaries anymore! We've got to move!
On it!!

Of course, *normally* Sherlock eschews overfamiliarity and addresses his partner by his professional name--M. Richard--but today he deduced it was appropriate to make an exception.

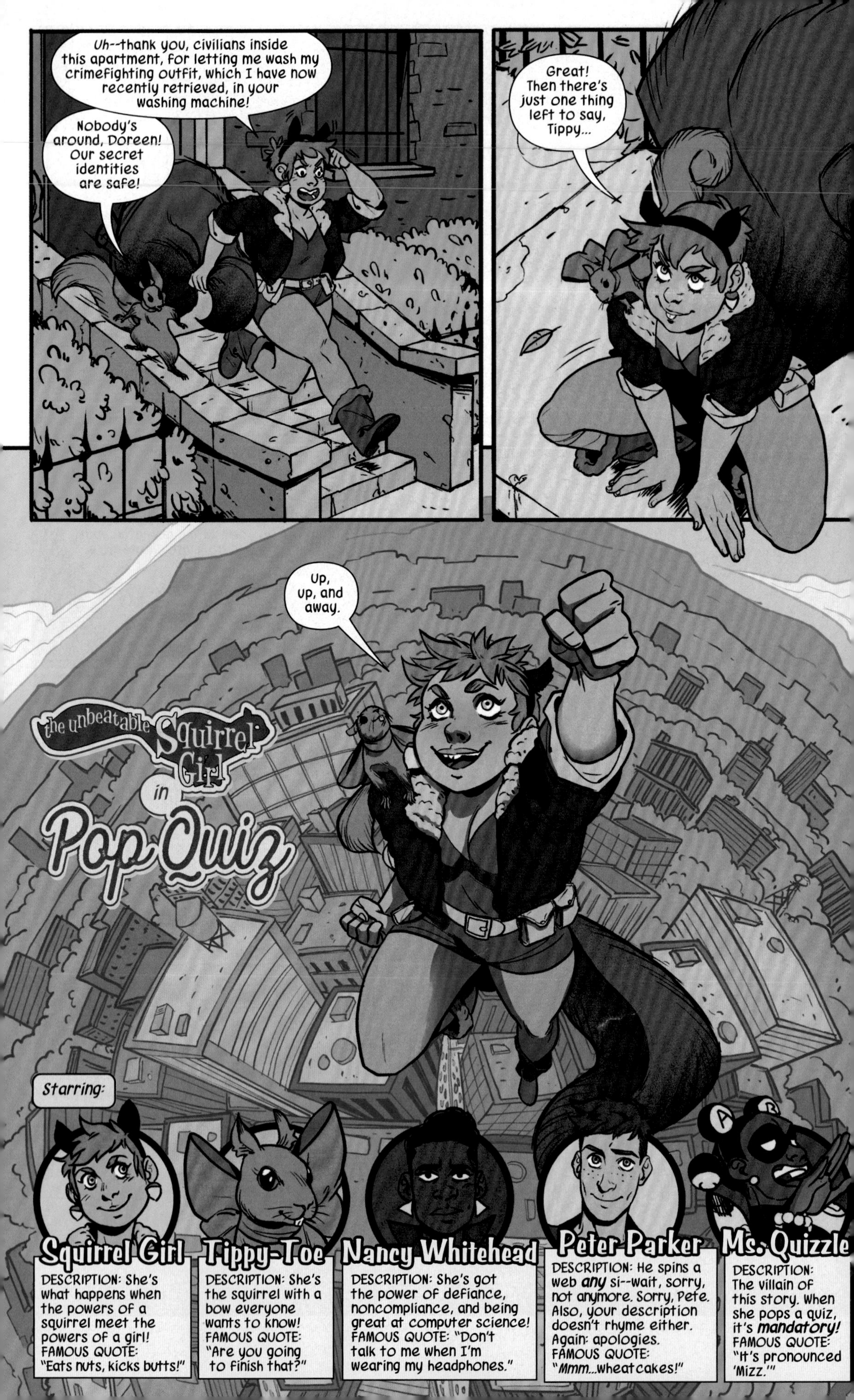

Uh--thank you, civilians inside this apartment, for letting me wash my crimefighting outfit, which I have now recently retrieved, in your washing machine!
Nobody's around, Doreen! Our secret identities are safe!
Great! Then there's just one thing left to say, Tippy...
Up, up, and away.
the unbeatable Squirrel Girl
in
Pop Quiz
Starring:
Squirrel Girl
DESCRIPTION: She's what happens when the powers of a squirrel meet the powers of a girl! FAMOUS QUOTE: "Eats nuts, kicks butts!"
Tippy-Toe
DESCRIPTION: She's the squirrel with a bow everyone wants to know! FAMOUS QUOTE: "Are you going to finish that?"
Nancy Whitehead
DESCRIPTION: She's got the power of defiance, noncompliance, and being great at computer science! FAMOUS QUOTE: "Don't talk to me when I'm wearing my headphones."
Peter Parker
DESCRIPTION: He spins a web *any* si--wait, sorry, not anymore. Sorry, Pete. Also, your description doesn't rhyme either. Again: apologies. FAMOUS QUOTE: "*Mmm...*wheatcakes!"
Ms. Quizzle
DESCRIPTION: The villain of this story. When she pops a quiz, it's *mandatory!* FAMOUS QUOTE: "It's pronounced 'Mizz.'"

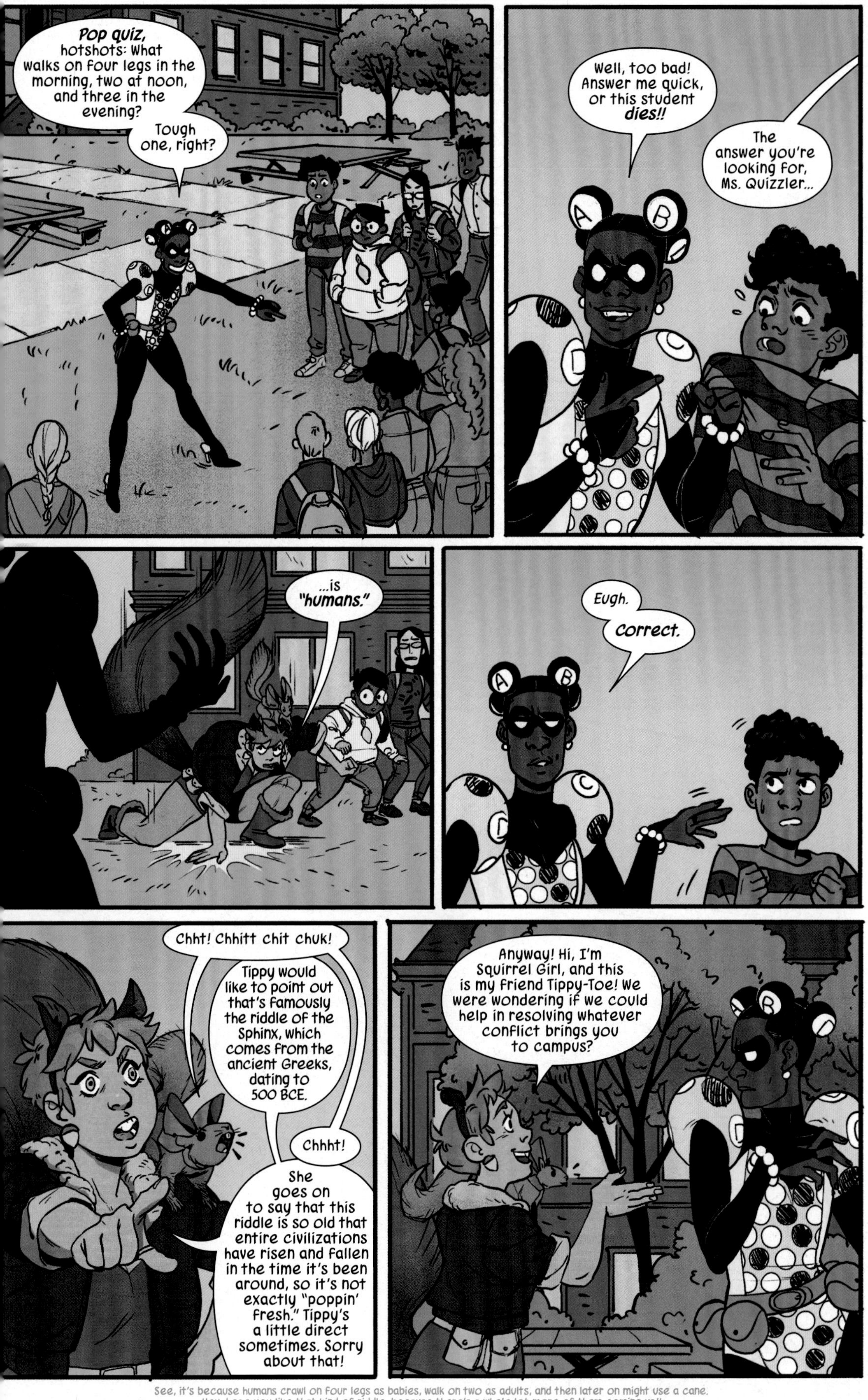

Pop quiz, hotshots: What walks on four legs in the morning, two at noon, and three in the evening?
Tough one, right?
Well, too bad! Answer me quick, or this student dies!!
The answer you're looking for, Ms. Quizzler...
...is "humans."
Eugh.
Correct.
Chht! Chhitt chit chuk!
Tippy would like to point out that's famously the riddle of the Sphinx, which comes from the ancient Greeks, dating to 500 BCE.
Chhht!
She goes on to say that this riddle is so old that entire civilizations have risen and fallen in the time it's been around, so it's not exactly "poppin' fresh." Tippy's a little direct sometimes. Sorry about that!
Anyway! Hi, I'm Squirrel Girl, and this is my friend Tippy-Toe! We were wondering if we could help in resolving whatever conflict brings you to campus?

See, it's because humans crawl on four legs as babies, walk on two as adults, and then later on might use a cane.
Hey, hope you like that kind of riddle, because there's a whole lot more of them coming up!!

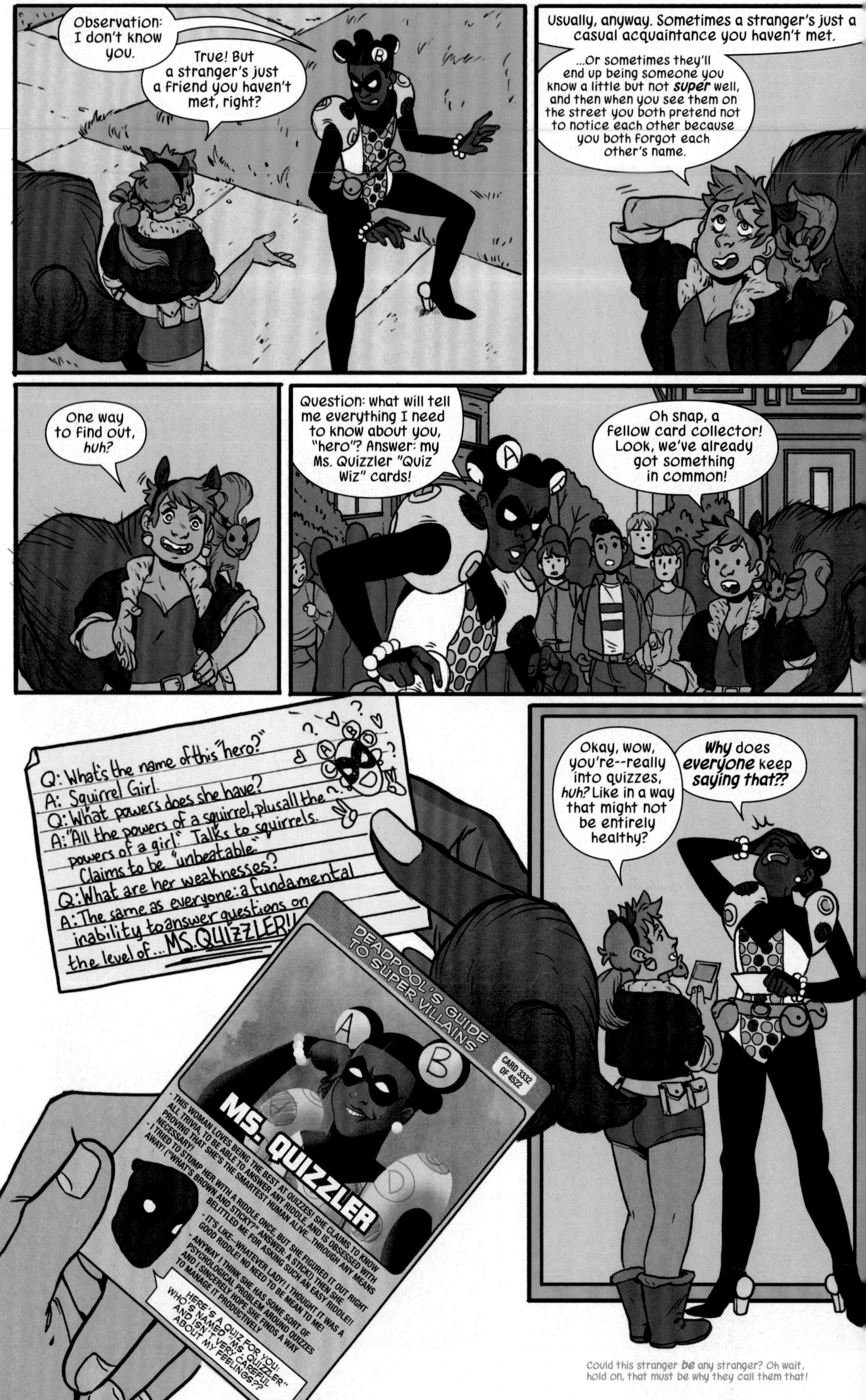
Observation: I don't know you.
True! But a stranger's just a friend you haven't met, right?
Usually, anyway. Sometimes a stranger's just a casual acquaintance you haven't met.
...Or sometimes they'll end up being someone you know a little but not *super* well, and then when you see them on the street you both pretend not to notice each other because you both forgot each other's name.
One way to find out, *huh?*
Question: what will tell me everything I need to know about you, "hero"? Answer: my Ms. Quizzler "Quiz Wiz" cards!
Oh snap, a fellow card collector! Look, we've already got something in common!
Q: What's the name of this "hero?"
A: Squirrel Girl.
Q: What powers does she have?
A: "All the powers of a squirrel, plus all the powers of a girl." Talks to squirrels. Claims to be "unbeatable."
Q: What are her weaknesses?
A: The same as everyone: a fundamental inability to answer questions on the level of... MS. QUIZZLER!!
DEADPOOL'S GUIDE TO SUPER VILLAINS
CARD 3332 OF 4522
MS. QUIZZLER
- THIS WOMAN LOVES BEING THE BEST AT QUIZZES! SHE CLAIMS TO KNOW ALL TRIVIA, TO BE ABLE TO ANSWER ANY RIDDLE, AND IS OBSESSED WITH PROVING THAT SHE'S THE SMARTEST HUMAN ALIVE...THROUGH ANY MEANS NECESSARY!
- I TRIED TO STUMP HER WITH A RIDDLE ONCE, BUT SHE FIGURED IT OUT RIGHT AWAY! ("WHAT'S BROWN AND STICKY?" ANSWER: A STICK!) THEN SHE BELITTLED ME FOR ASKING SUCH AN EASY RIDDLE!!
- IT'S LIKE--WHATEVER LADY! I THOUGHT IT WAS A GOOD RIDDLE! NO NEED TO BE MEAN TO ME!
- ANYWAY I THINK SHE HAS SOME SORT OF PSYCHOLOGICAL PROBLEM AROUND QUIZZES AND I SINCERELY HOPE SHE FINDS A WAY TO MANAGE IT PRODUCTIVELY
HERE'S A QUIZ FOR YOU: WHO'S NAMED "MS. QUIZZLER" AND ISN'T VERY CAREFUL ABOUT MY FEELINGS??
Okay, wow, you're--really into quizzes, *huh?* Like in a way that might not be entirely healthy?
Why does *everyone* keep *saying that??*

Could this stranger *be* any stranger? Oh wait, hold on, that must be why they call them that!

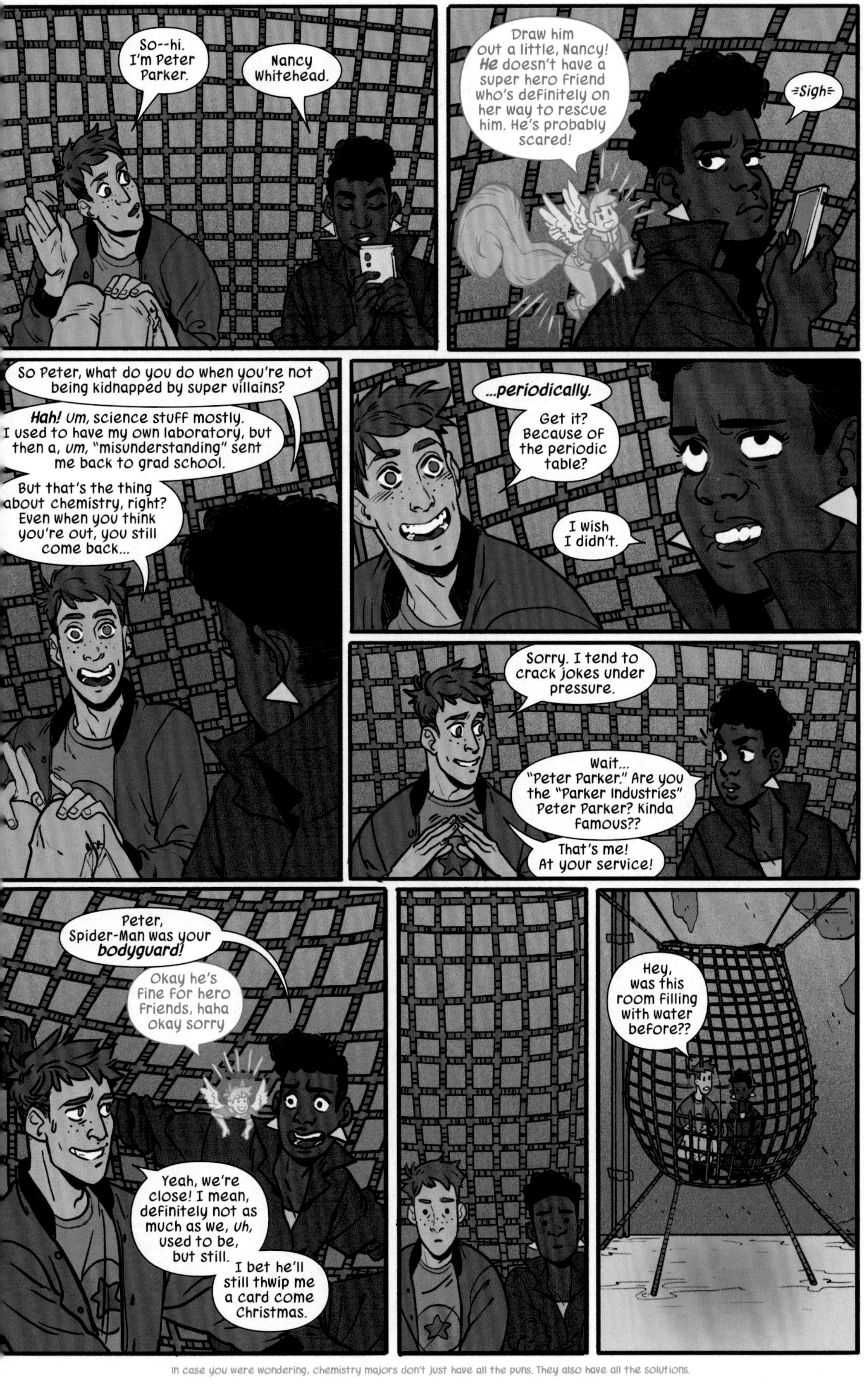
So--hi. I'm Peter Parker.
Nancy Whitehead.
Draw him out a little, Nancy! *He* doesn't have a super hero friend who's definitely on her way to rescue him. He's probably scared!
=Sigh=
So Peter, what do you do when you're not being kidnapped by super villains?
Hah! Um, science stuff mostly. I used to have my own laboratory, but then a, *um*, "misunderstanding" sent me back to grad school.
But that's the thing about chemistry, right? Even when you think you're out, you still come back...
...periodically.
Get it? Because of the periodic table?
I wish I didn't.
Sorry. I tend to crack jokes under pressure.
Wait... "Peter Parker." Are you the "Parker Industries" Peter Parker? Kinda famous??
That's me! At your service!
Peter, Spider-Man was your *bodyguard!*
Okay he's fine for hero friends, haha okay sorry
Yeah, we're close! I mean, definitely not as much as we, *uh*, used to be, but still.
I bet he'll still thwip me a card come Christmas.
Hey, was this room filling with water before??

In case you were wondering, chemistry majors don't just have all the puns. They also have all the solutions.

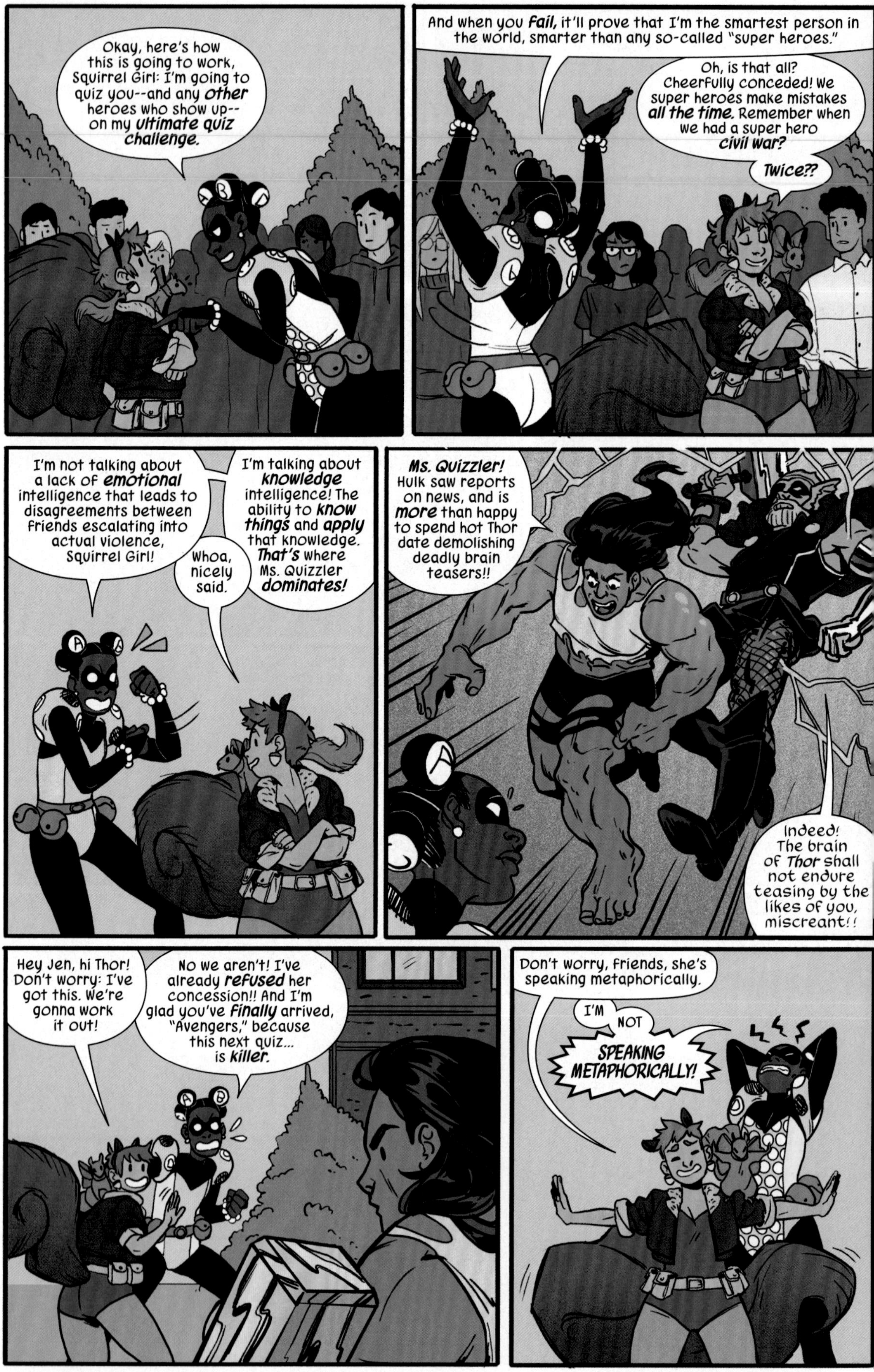
Okay, here's how this is going to work, Squirrel Girl: I'm going to quiz you--and any *other* heroes who show up--on my ***ultimate quiz challenge.***
And when you ***fail,*** it'll prove that I'm the smartest person in the world, smarter than any so-called "super heroes."
Oh, is that all? Cheerfully conceded! We super heroes make mistakes ***all the time.*** Remember when we had a super hero ***civil war?***
Twice??
I'm not talking about a lack of ***emotional*** intelligence that leads to disagreements between friends escalating into actual violence, Squirrel Girl!
I'm talking about ***knowledge*** intelligence! The ability to ***know things*** and ***apply*** that knowledge. ***That's*** where Ms. Quizzler ***dominates!***
Whoa, nicely said.
Ms. Quizzler! Hulk saw reports on news, and is ***more*** than happy to spend hot Thor date demolishing deadly brain teasers!!
Indeed! The brain of *Thor* shall not endure teasing by the likes of you, miscreant!!
Hey Jen, hi Thor! Don't worry: I've got this. We're gonna work it out!
No we aren't! I've already ***refused*** her concession!! And I'm glad you've ***finally*** arrived, "Avengers," because this next quiz... is ***killer.***
Don't worry, friends, she's speaking metaphorically.
I'M NOT
SPEAKING METAPHORICALLY!

The brain of *Thor* does not enjoy teasing of any persuasion, miscreant! The brain of Thor likes praise, and hammers, and feasts, and battles, and sports, and speaking about itself in the third person, and most recently going on fun dates with female Hulks who are also lawyers, but that is *it!*

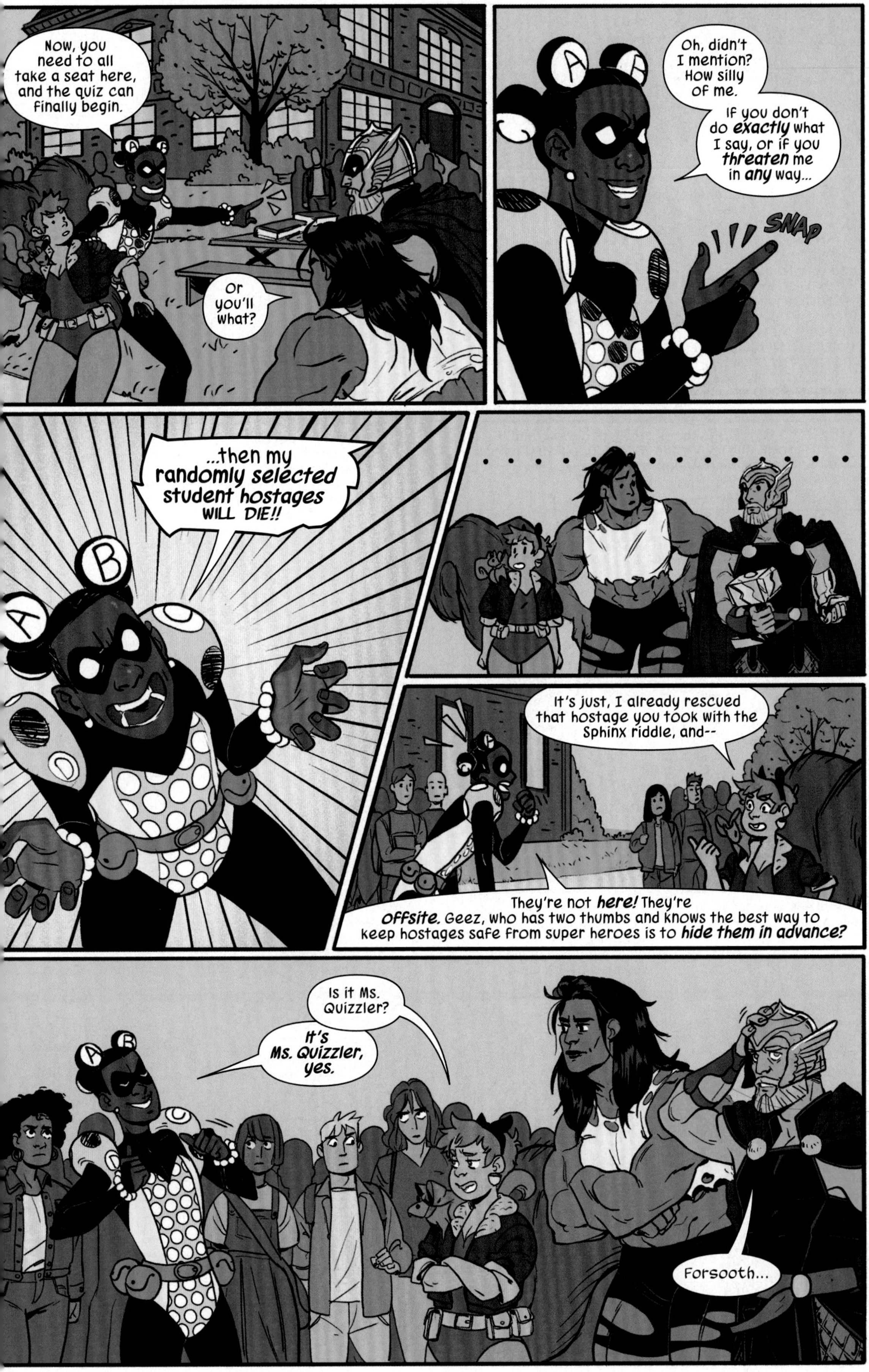
Now, you need to all take a seat here, and the quiz can finally begin.
Or you'll what?
Oh, didn't I mention? How silly of me.
If you don't do *exactly* what I say, or if you *threaten* me in *any* way...
SNAP
...then my **randomly selected student hostages** WILL DIE!!
• • • • • • • • • • • • • • •
It's just, I already rescued that hostage you took with the Sphinx riddle, and--
They're not *here!* They're *offsite.* Geez, who has two thumbs and knows the best way to keep hostages safe from super heroes is to *hide them in advance?*
Is it Ms. Quizzler?
It's Ms. Quizzler, yes.
Forsooth...

Who has two thumbs and knows that this joke structure always ends with the person telling the joke being the answer? Yes, in this case, the answer is *you*, the reader.

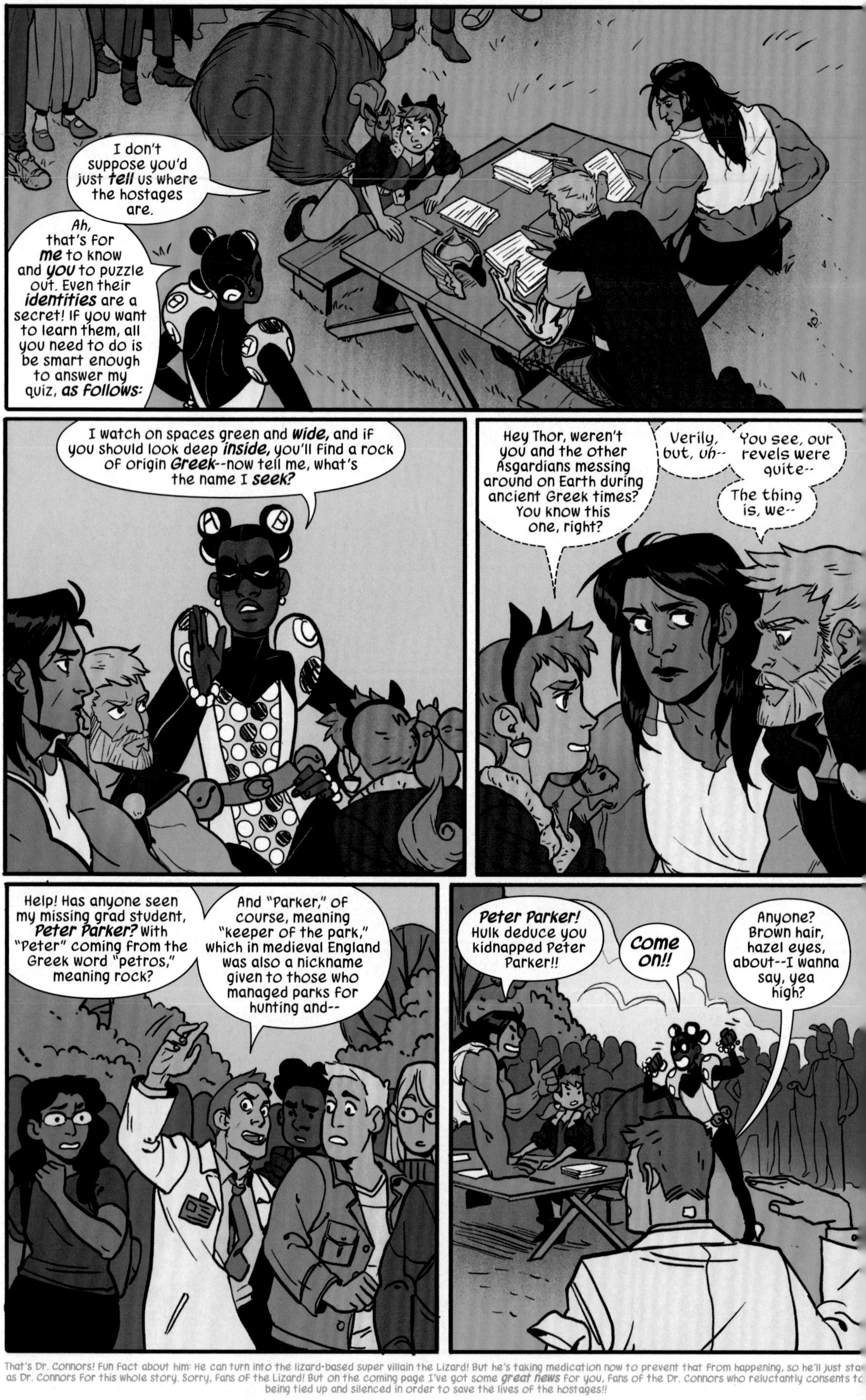
I don't suppose you'd just *tell* us where the hostages are.
Ah, that's for *me* to know and *you* to puzzle out. Even their *identities* are a secret! If you want to learn them, all you need to do is be smart enough to answer my quiz, *as follows:*
I watch on spaces green and *wide,* and if you should look deep *inside,* you'll find a rock of origin *Greek*--now tell me, what's the name I *seek?*
Hey Thor, weren't you and the other Asgardians messing around on Earth during ancient Greek times? You know this one, right?
Verily, but, uh--
You see, our revels were quite--
The thing is, we--
Help! Has anyone seen my missing grad student, *Peter Parker?* With "Peter" coming from the Greek word "petros," meaning rock?
And "Parker," of course, meaning "keeper of the park," which in medieval England was also a nickname given to those who managed parks for hunting and--
Peter Parker! Hulk deduce you kidnapped Peter Parker!!
Come on!!
Anyone? Brown hair, hazel eyes, about--I wanna say, yea high?

That's Dr. Connors! Fun fact about him: He can turn into the lizard-based super villain the Lizard! But he's taking medication now to prevent that from happening, so he'll just sta as Dr. Connors for this whole story. Sorry, fans of the Lizard! But on the coming page I've got some *great news* for you, fans of the Dr. Connors who reluctantly consents t being tied up and silenced in order to save the lives of the hostages!!

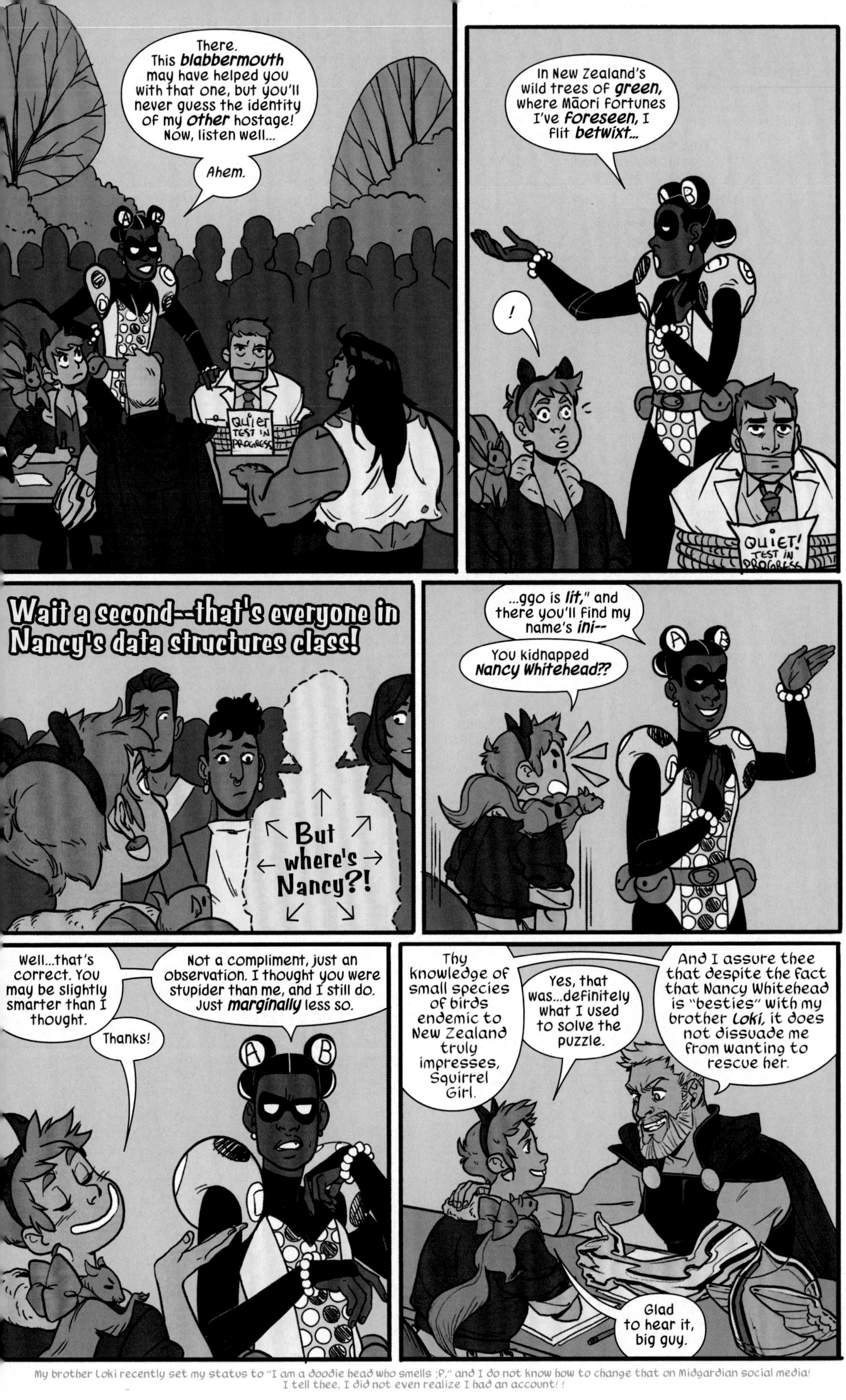
There. This blabbermouth may have helped you with that one, but you'll never guess the identity of my other hostage! Now, listen well...
Ahem.
QUIET TEST IN PROGRESS
In New Zealand's wild trees of green, where Māori fortunes I've foreseen, I flit betwixt...
!
QUIET! TEST IN PROGRESS
Wait a second--that's everyone in Nancy's data structures class!
But where's Nancy?!
...ggo is lit," and there you'll find my name's ini--
You kidnapped Nancy Whitehead??
Well...that's correct. You may be slightly smarter than I thought.
Not a compliment, just an observation. I thought you were stupider than me, and I still do. Just marginally less so.
Thanks!
Thy knowledge of small species of birds endemic to New Zealand truly impresses, Squirrel Girl.
Yes, that was...definitely what I used to solve the puzzle.
And I assure thee that despite the fact that Nancy Whitehead is "besties" with my brother Loki, it does not dissuade me from wanting to rescue her.
Glad to hear it, big guy.

My brother Loki recently set my status to "I am a doodie head who smells ;P," and I do not know how to change that on Midgardian social media! I tell thee, I did not even realize I had an account! !

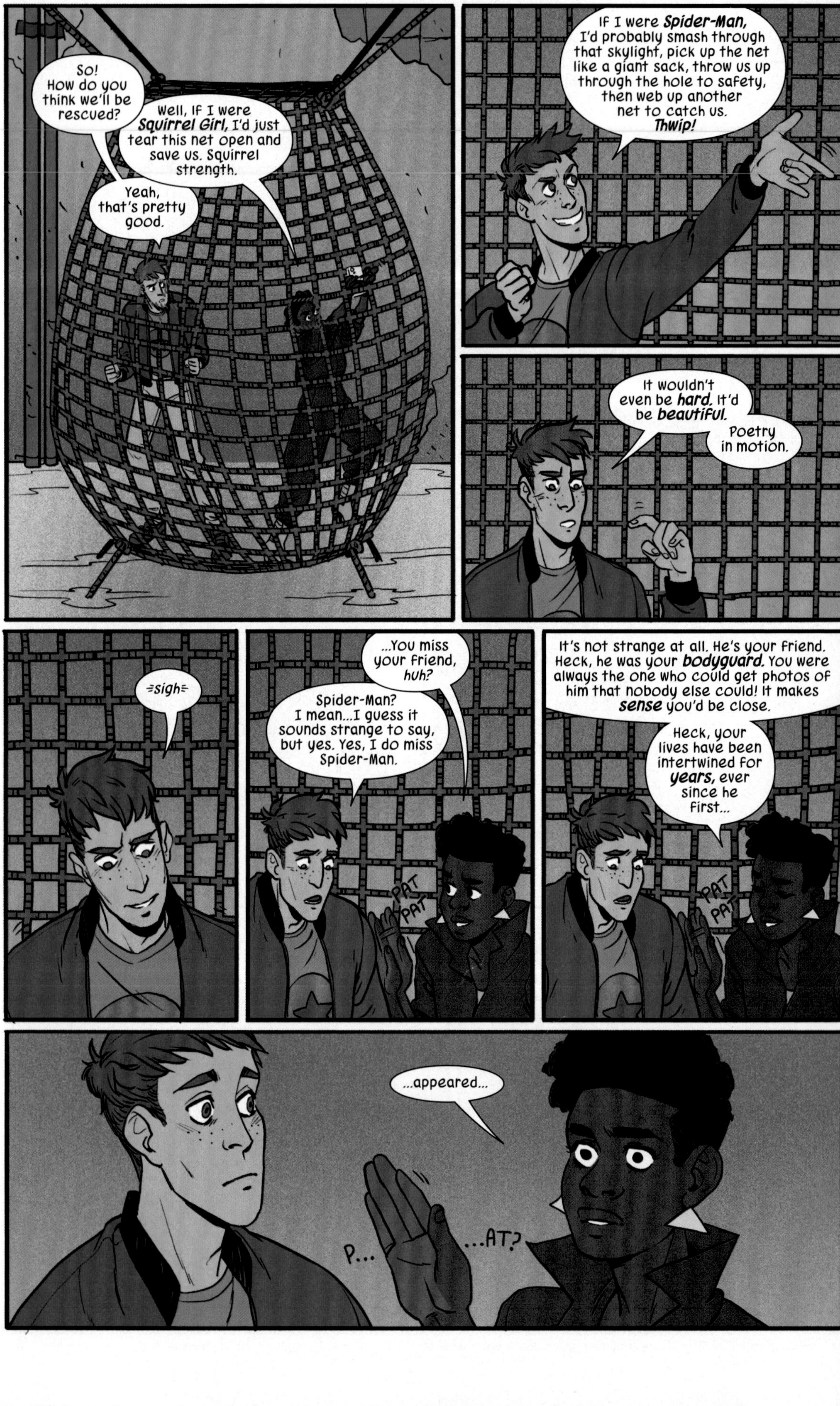
So! How do you think we'll be rescued?
Well, If I were **Squirrel Girl**, I'd just tear this net open and save us. Squirrel strength.
Yeah, that's pretty good.
If I were **Spider-Man**, I'd probably smash through that skylight, pick up the net like a giant sack, throw us up through the hole to safety, then web up another net to catch us. **Thwip!**
It wouldn't even be **hard**. It'd be **beautiful**.
Poetry in motion.
=sigh=
...You miss your friend, *huh?*
Spider-Man? I mean...I guess it sounds strange to say, but yes. Yes, I do miss Spider-Man.
PAT PAT
It's not strange at all. He's your friend. Heck, he was your **bodyguard**. You were always the one who could get photos of him that nobody else could! It makes **sense** you'd be close.
Heck, your lives have been intertwined for **years**, ever since he first...
PAT PAT
...appeared...
P...
...AT?

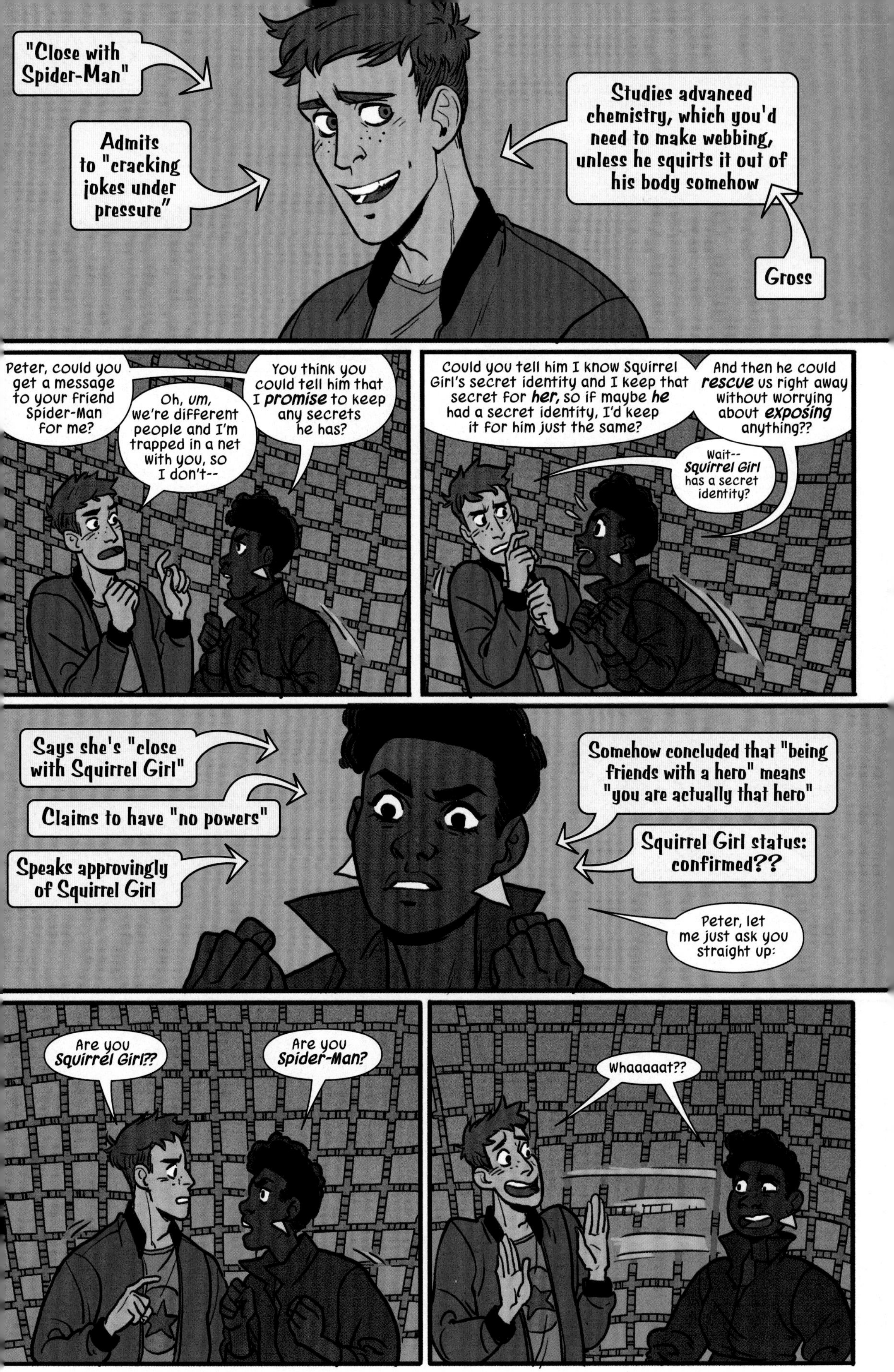
"Close with Spider-Man"
Admits to "cracking jokes under pressure"
Studies advanced chemistry, which you'd need to make webbing, unless he squirts it out of his body somehow
Gross
Peter, could you get a message to your friend Spider-Man for me?
Oh, um, we're different people and I'm trapped in a net with you, so I don't--
You think you could tell him that I promise to keep any secrets he has?
Could you tell him I know Squirrel Girl's secret identity and I keep that secret for her, so if maybe he had a secret identity, I'd keep it for him just the same?
And then he could rescue us right away without worrying about exposing anything??
Wait-- Squirrel Girl has a secret identity?
Says she's "close with Squirrel Girl"
Claims to have "no powers"
Speaks approvingly of Squirrel Girl
Somehow concluded that "being friends with a hero" means "you are actually that hero"
Squirrel Girl status: confirmed??
Peter, let me just ask you straight up:
Are you Squirrel Girl??
Are you Spider-Man?
Whaaaaat??

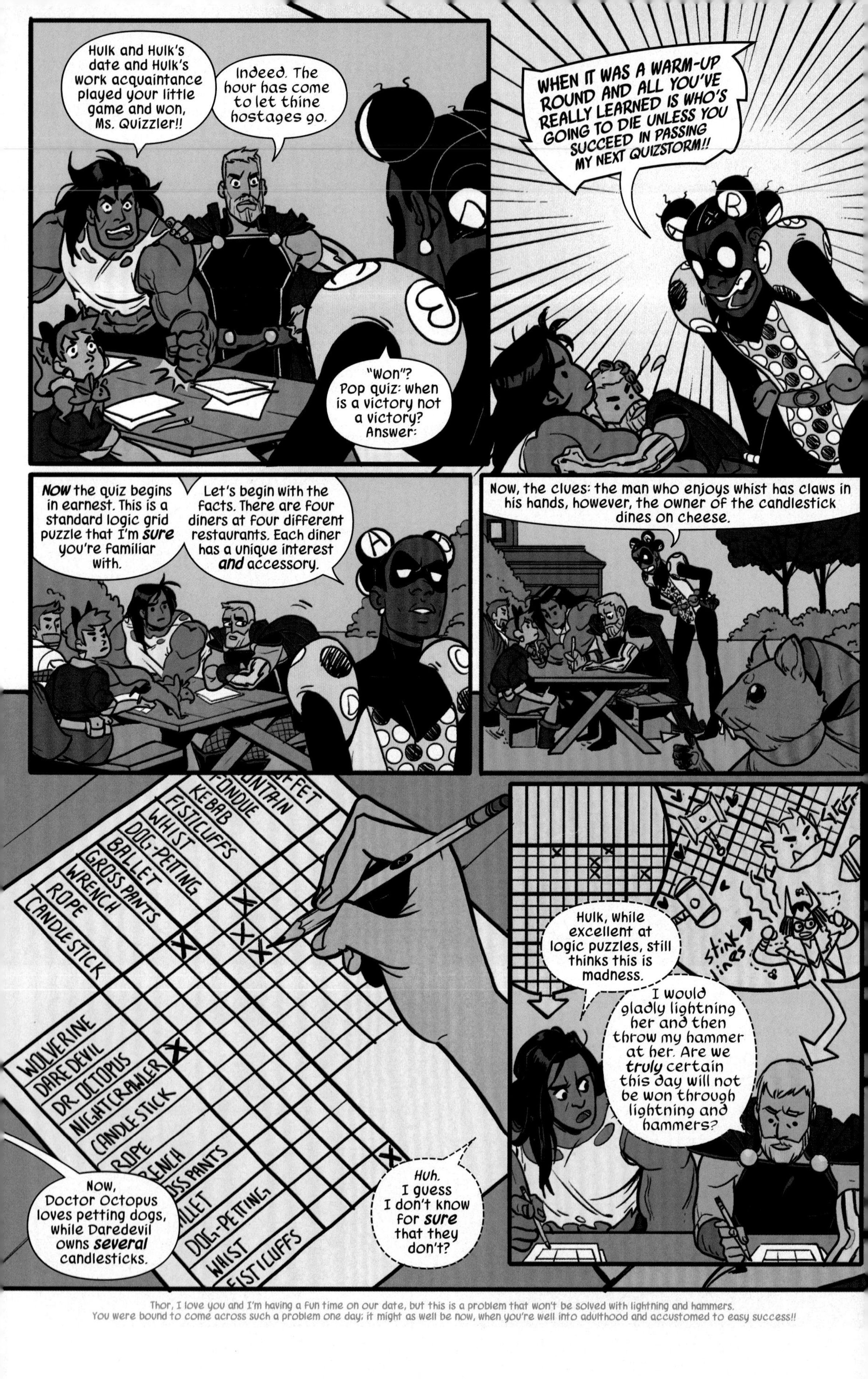
Hulk and Hulk's date and Hulk's work acquaintance played your little game and won, Ms. Quizzler!!
Indeed. The hour has come to let thine hostages go.
"Won"? Pop quiz: when is a victory not a victory? Answer:
WHEN IT WAS A WARM-UP ROUND AND ALL YOU'VE REALLY LEARNED IS WHO'S GOING TO DIE UNLESS YOU SUCCEED IN PASSING MY NEXT QUIZSTORM!!
NOW the quiz begins in earnest. This is a standard logic grid puzzle that I'm sure you're familiar with.
Let's begin with the facts. There are four diners at four different restaurants. Each diner has a unique interest and accessory.
Now, the clues: the man who enjoys whist has claws in his hands, however, the owner of the candlestick dines on cheese.
FONDUE
KEBAB
FISTICUFFS
WHIST
DOG-PETTING
BALLET
GROSS PANTS
WRENCH
ROPE
CANDLESTICK
WOLVERINE
DAREDEVIL
DR. OCTOPUS
NIGHTCRAWLER
CANDLESTICK
DOG-PETTING
WAIST
FISTICUFFS
Now, Doctor Octopus loves petting dogs, while Daredevil owns several candlesticks.
Huh. I guess I don't know for sure that they don't?
stink lines
Hulk, while excellent at logic puzzles, still thinks this is madness.
I would gladly lightning her and then throw my hammer at her. Are we truly certain this day will not be won through lightning and hammers?

Thor, I love you and I'm having a fun time on our date, but this is a problem that won't be solved with lightning and hammers.
You were bound to come across such a problem one day; it might as well be now, when you're well into adulthood and accustomed to easy success!!

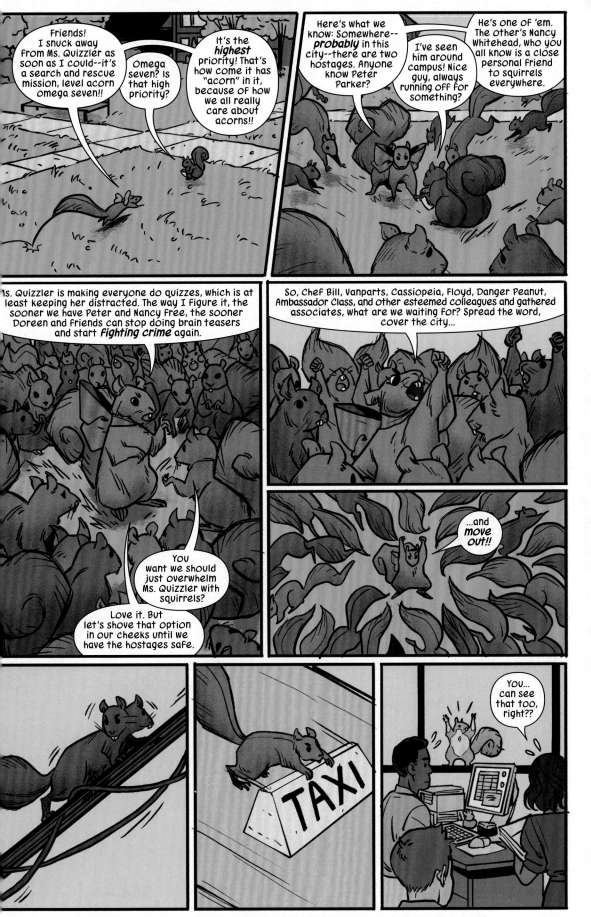

Friends! I snuck away from Ms. Quizzler as soon as I could--it's a search and rescue mission, level acorn omega seven!!

Omega seven? Is that high priority?

It's the **highest** priority! That's how come it has "acorn" in it, because of how we all really care about acorns!!

Here's what we know: Somewhere-- **probably** in this city--there are two hostages. Anyone know Peter Parker?

I've seen him around campus! Nice guy, always running off for something?

He's one of 'em. The other's Nancy Whitehead, who you all know is a close personal friend to squirrels everywhere.

Ms. Quizzler is making everyone do quizzes, which is at least keeping her distracted. The way I figure it, the sooner we have Peter and Nancy free, the sooner Doreen and friends can stop doing brain teasers and start *fighting crime* again.

You want we should just overwhelm Ms. Quizzler with squirrels?

Love it. But let's shove that option in our cheeks until we have the hostages safe.

So, Chef Bill, Vanparts, Cassiopeia, Floyd, Danger Peanut, Ambassador Class, and other esteemed colleagues and gathered associates, what are we waiting for? Spread the word, cover the city...

...and **move out!!**

TAXI

YOU... can see that too, right??

"Let's shove that option in our cheeks" is the squirrel version of the human idiom "let's keep that option in our back pocket."
As a writer committed to excellence in squirrel verisimilitude, I have spent several hours working out their sayings, and I regret *none of it.*

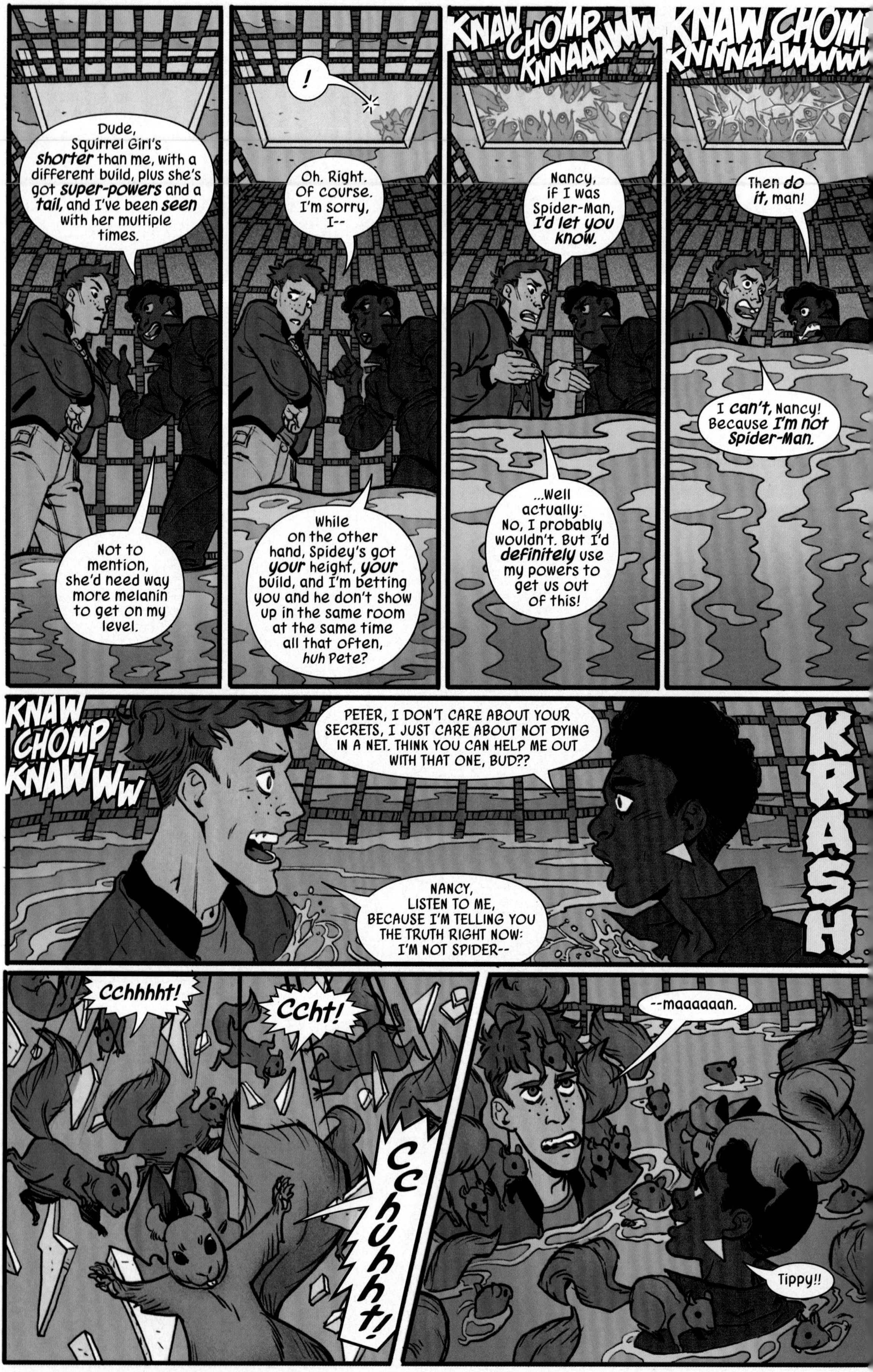
Dude, Squirrel Girl's *shorter* than me, with a different build, plus she's got *super-powers* and a *tail,* and I've been *seen* with her multiple times.
Not to mention, she'd need way more melanin to get on my level.
!
Oh. Right. Of course. I'm sorry, I--
While on the other hand, Spidey's got *your* height, *your* build, and I'm betting you and he don't show up in the same room at the same time all that often, *huh* Pete?
KNAW CHOMP KNNAAAWW
Nancy, if I was Spider-Man, *I'd let you know.*
...Well actually: No, I probably wouldn't. But I'd *definitely* use my powers to get us out of this!
KNAW CHOMP KNNNAAWWWW
Then *do it,* man!
I *can't,* Nancy! Because *I'm not Spider-Man.*
KNAW CHOMP KNAWWW
PETER, I DON'T CARE ABOUT YOUR SECRETS, I JUST CARE ABOUT NOT DYING IN A NET. THINK YOU CAN HELP ME OUT WITH THAT ONE, BUD??
NANCY, LISTEN TO ME, BECAUSE I'M TELLING YOU THE TRUTH RIGHT NOW: I'M NOT SPIDER--
KRASH
Cchhhht!
CCht!
CCHUHHHT!
--maaaaaan.
Tippy!!

Peter Parker, so clever with his words! Was he going to say, "I'm telling you the truth right now: I'm not Spider-Man," or was he going to say, "I'm telling you the truth: right now I'm not Spider-Man"? I mean, *you* know it's the first one because you read it, but Nancy only heard it! Well done, Pete! You've *clearly* got--wow, *several decades* of experience with this whole "secret identity" thing??

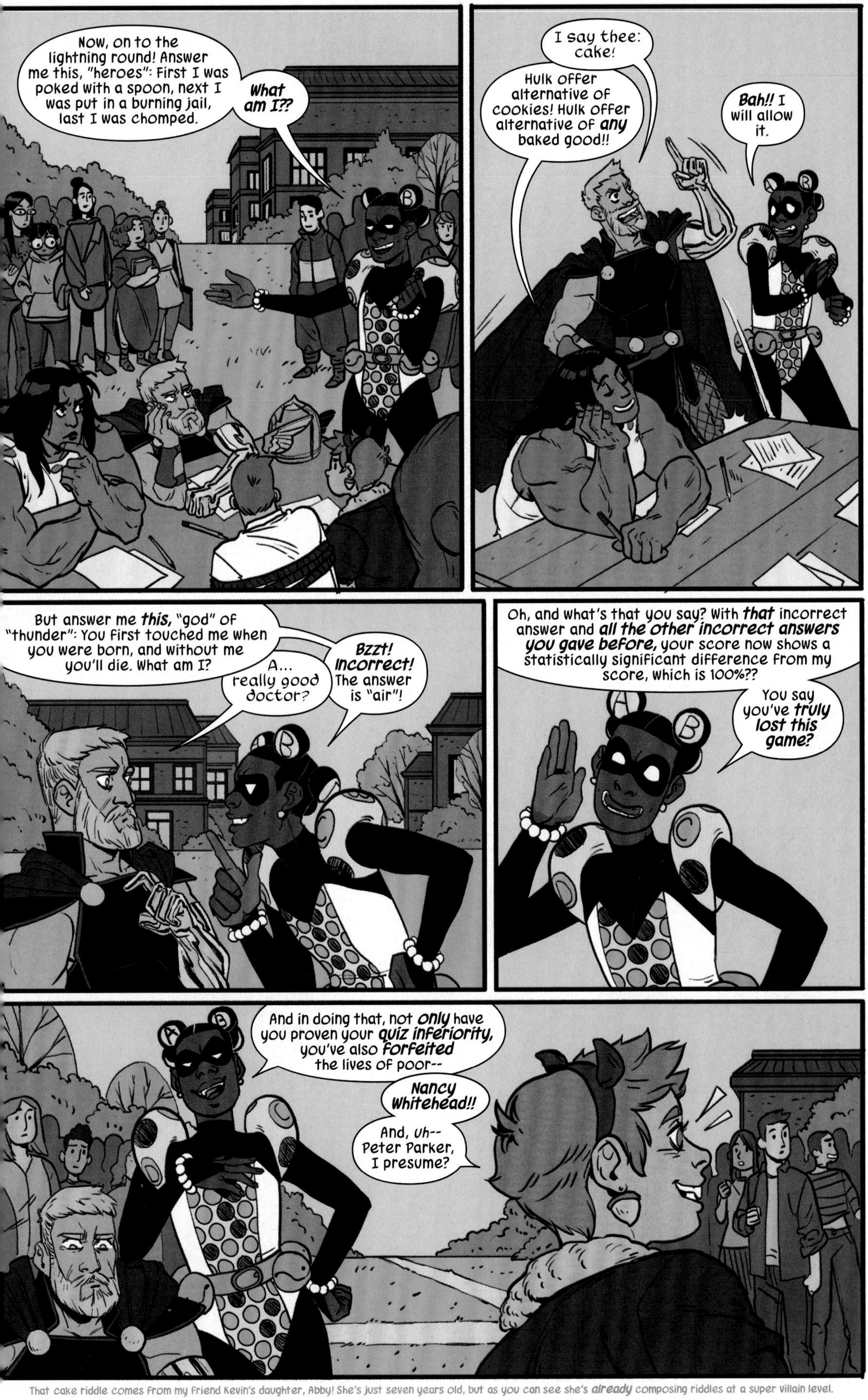
Now, on to the lightning round! Answer me this, "heroes": First I was poked with a spoon, next I was put in a burning jail, last I was chomped.
What am I??
I say thee: cake!
Hulk offer alternative of cookies! Hulk offer alternative of any baked good!!
Bah!! I will allow it.
But answer me this, "god" of "thunder": You first touched me when you were born, and without me you'll die. What am I?
A... really good doctor?
Bzzt! Incorrect! The answer is "air"!
Oh, and what's that you say? With that incorrect answer and all the other incorrect answers you gave before, your score now shows a statistically significant difference from my score, which is 100%??
You say you've truly lost this game?
And in doing that, not only have you proven your quiz inferiority, you've also forfeited the lives of poor--
Nancy Whitehead!!
And, uh-- Peter Parker, I presume?

That cake riddle comes from my friend Kevin's daughter, Abby! She's just seven years old, but as you can see she's *already* composing riddles at a super villain level.

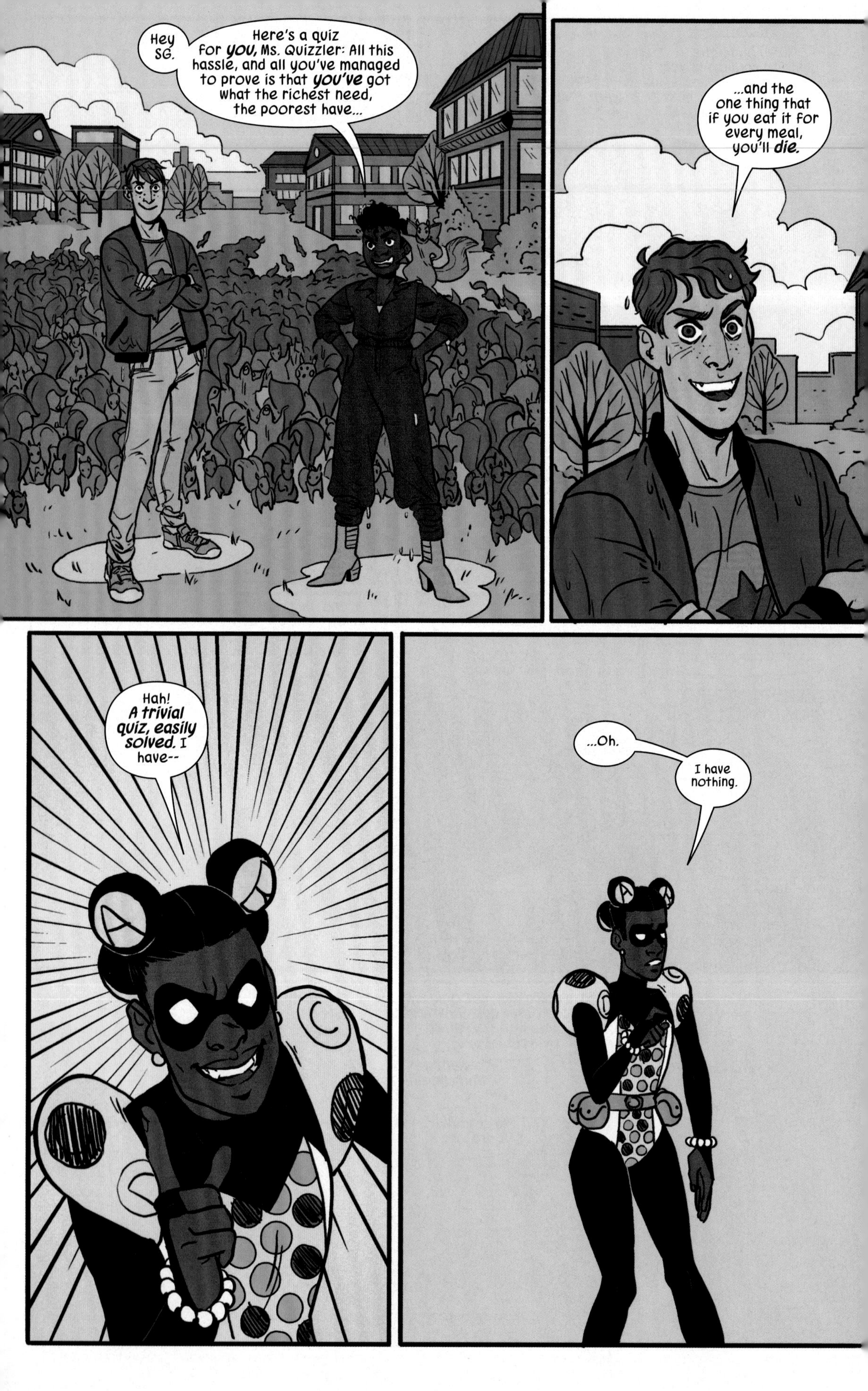

Hey SG.
Here's a quiz for *YOU,* Ms. Quizzler: All this hassle, and all you've managed to prove is that *you've* got what the richest need, the poorest have...
...and the one thing that if you eat it for every meal, you'll *die.*
Hah! *A trivial quiz, easily solved.* I have--
...Oh.
I have nothing.

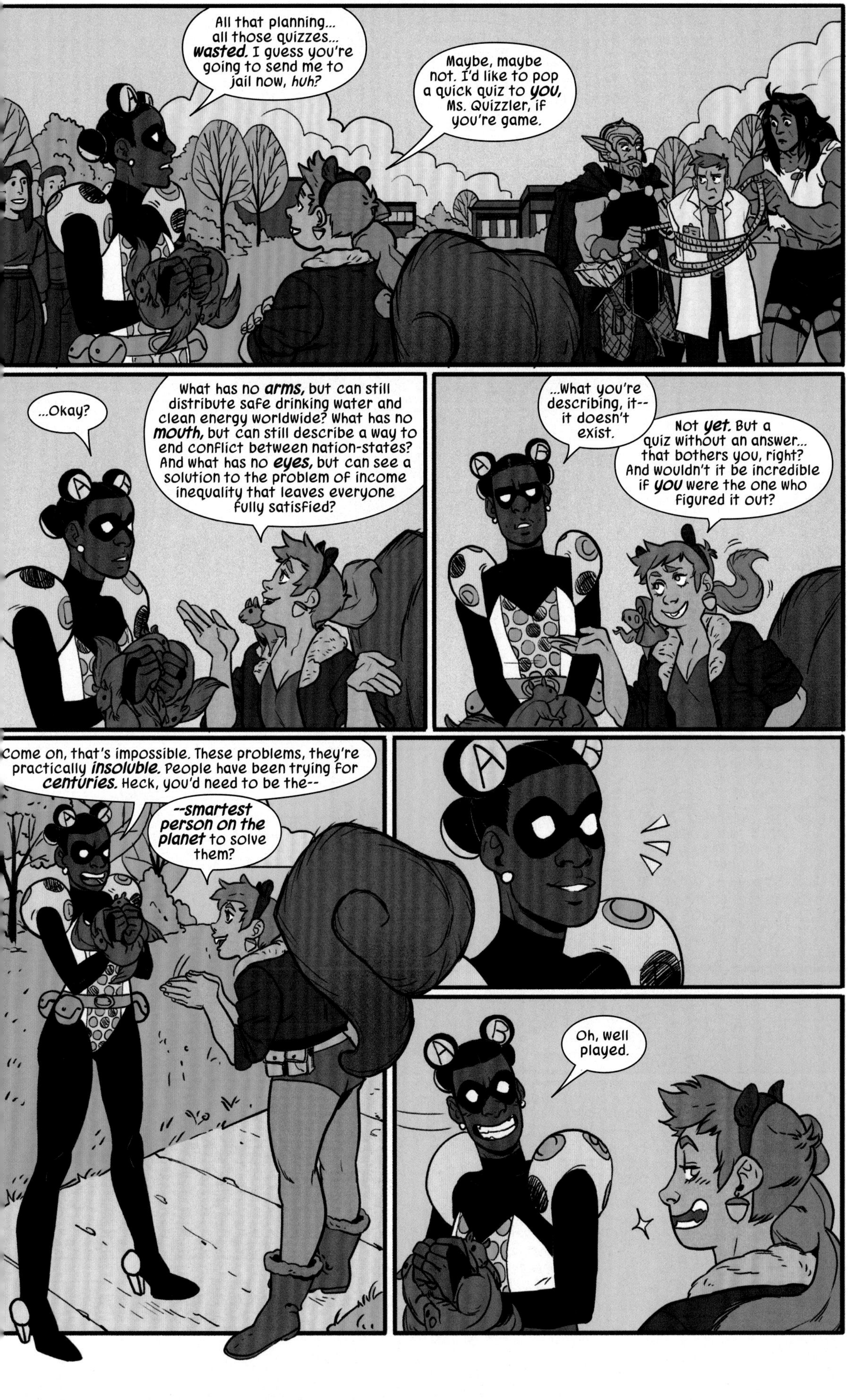
All that planning... all those quizzes... wasted. I guess you're going to send me to jail now, huh?
Maybe, maybe not. I'd like to pop a quick quiz to YOU, Ms. Quizzler, if you're game.
...Okay?
What has no arms, but can still distribute safe drinking water and clean energy worldwide? What has no mouth, but can still describe a way to end conflict between nation-states? And what has no eyes, but can see a solution to the problem of income inequality that leaves everyone fully satisfied?
...What you're describing, it-- it doesn't exist.
Not yet. But a quiz without an answer... that bothers you, right? And wouldn't it be incredible if YOU were the one who figured it out?
Come on, that's impossible. These problems, they're practically insoluble. People have been trying for centuries. Heck, you'd need to be the--
--smartest person on the planet to solve them?
Oh, well played.

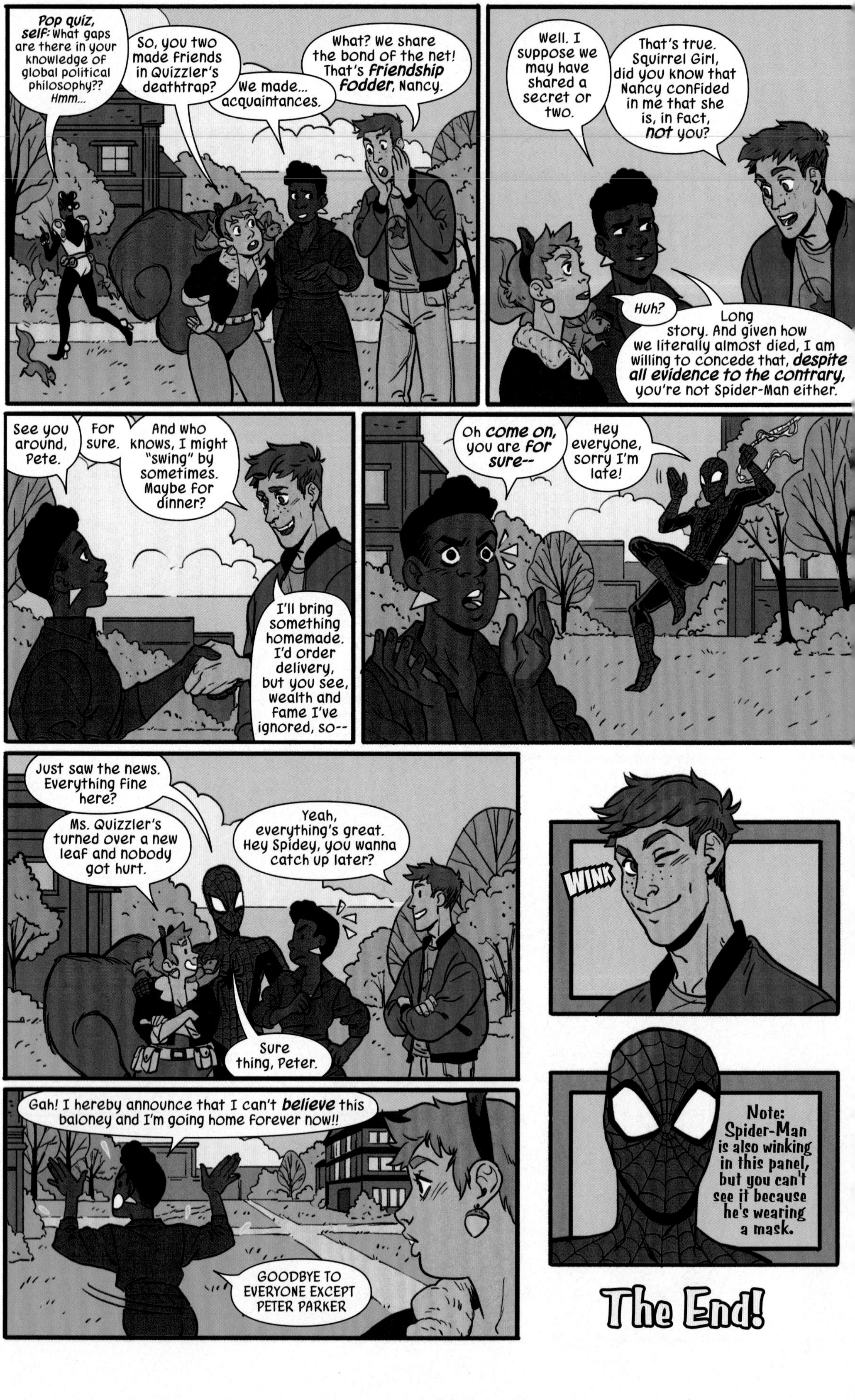

Pop quiz, self: What gaps are there in your knowledge of global political philosophy?? Hmm...
So, you two made friends in Quizzler's deathtrap?
We made... acquaintances.
What? We share the bond of the net! That's friendship fodder, Nancy.
Well. I suppose we may have shared a secret or two.
That's true. Squirrel Girl, did you know that Nancy confided in me that she is, in fact, not you?
Huh?
Long story. And given how we literally almost died, I am willing to concede that, despite all evidence to the contrary, you're not Spider-Man either.
See you around, Pete.
For sure.
And who knows, I might "swing" by sometimes. Maybe for dinner?
I'll bring something homemade. I'd order delivery, but you see, wealth and fame I've ignored, so--
Oh come on, you are for sure--
Hey everyone, sorry I'm late!
Just saw the news. Everything fine here?
Ms. Quizzler's turned over a new leaf and nobody got hurt.
Yeah, everything's great. Hey Spidey, you wanna catch up later?
Sure thing, Peter.
WINK
Note: Spider-Man is also winking in this panel, but you can't see it because he's wearing a mask.
Gah! I hereby announce that I can't believe this baloney and I'm going home forever now!!
GOODBYE TO EVERYONE EXCEPT PETER PARKER
The End!

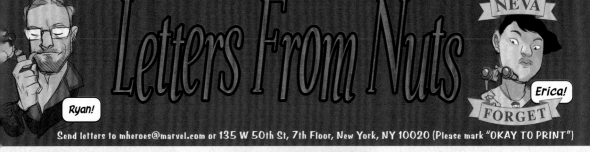

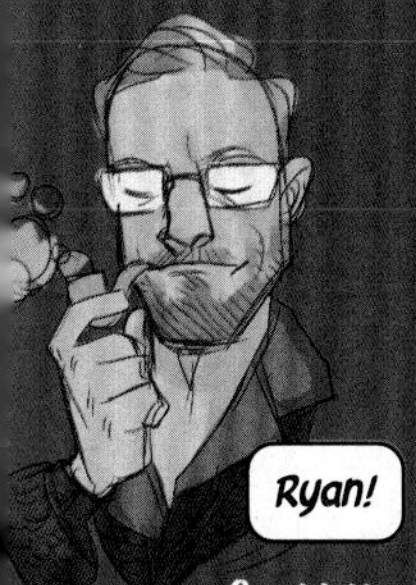
Ryan!

Letters From Nuts

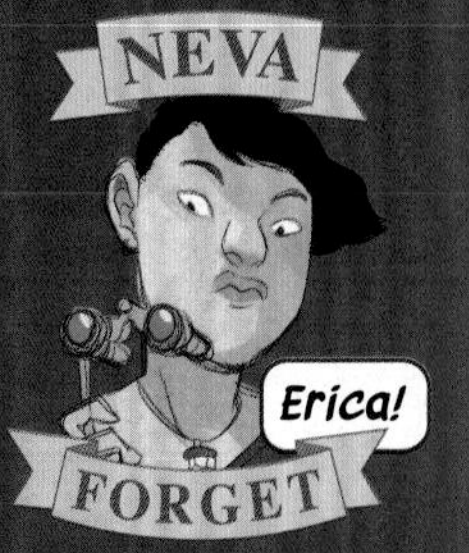
NEVA
Erica!
FORGET

Send letters to mheroes@marvel.com or 135 W 50th St, 7th Floor, New York, NY 10020 (Please mark "OKAY TO PRINT")

Hey, everybody! Before we hand over the letters page to Ryan, we first wanted to give a quick shout-out to our guest artist this issue, Naomi Franquiz! Isn't her art--and her take on Doreen's world--great?? Check out her website (naomifranq.com) and pick up *Misfit City* from Boom! for more of her terrific work. Naomi will be back NEXT MONTH for a very special issue! Ryan has details on that issue at the end of this, but first…your letters!

Dear Letters from Nuts Team,

Hello from a longtime SQUIRREL GIRL fan! I've been meaning to write for a long time. After a lot of coercion from me, I finally convinced my mom to buy me a SQUIRREL GIRL collection. I love it so much! I also have the novel. We have squirrels in our yard. Ours really don't bury the seeds, corn and peanuts we leave out for them and the birds. They kinda pat the grass down over the nut and then hop off to grab another one. Right now in Meridian, Idaho, where I live, it is really rainy, so when the squirrels come, their tails are all soggy, and they look a little like drowned rats. I feel so bad for them! I have a bit of a personal request: Can you add in a hamster-themed hero to buddy up with Doreen? I think that would be so cool. I have attached a picture of my hamster. Her name is Milkey Way. She has never bitten anyone. She is feisty though, so apologies for any blurs. Thanks!

Breana N.B.
7th grade student

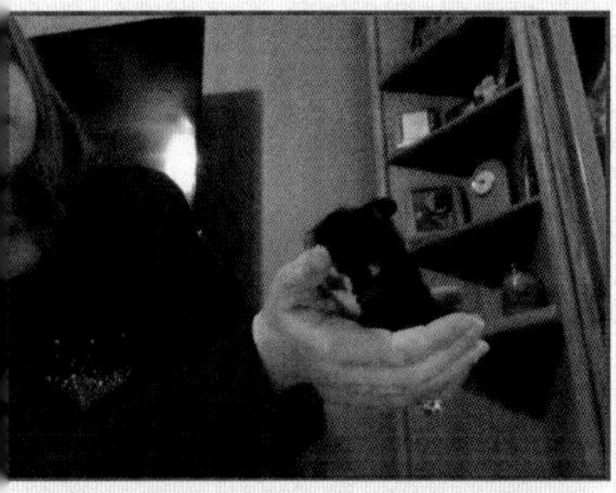

RYAN: Thank you, Breana! I've seen people with pet squirrels, and they don't always bury nuts either--sometimes they just climb up on someone, "bury" the nut in their hair and move on. It's ADORABLE. Milkey Way and I have something in common: I've never bitten anyone either! If we ever introduce a hamster-themed hero, she will definitely not bite people. It is extremely rude.

Dear Squirrel Team,

I was Squirrel Girl for the comic convention in our town (Santa Clara). We designed this costume and my grandma helped make it. Have you ever dressed up as Squirrel Girl? I figured out why I started liking Squirrel Girl--because when I was 5, I read the first comic of THE UNBEATABLE SQUIRREL GIRL and she had a pet squirrel named Tippy-Toe. I loved both of them! My dad has a bobblehead of Squirrel Girl at his office for work and Tippy-Toe is beside her. My mom thinks she is a great role model.

Maddie

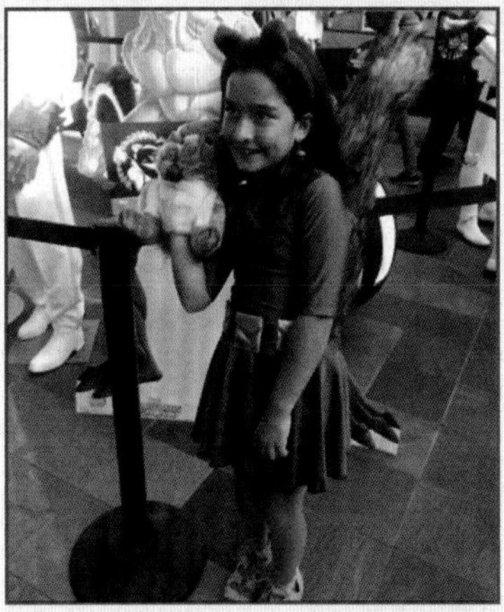

RYAN: Maddie, such a great costume! And I think it's awesome you've been reading since way back with our first issue. Our 50th issue is coming out next month (it's only #42, but we did eight issues before starting with a new #1), so that is a lot of comics! I think I have the same bobblehead that your dad has on my desk. It's good that she nods, because I can ask her "Is this a good issue that I'm writing?" and she nods yes, and I say, "Okay, phew, thanks, Doreen."

Dear Ryan and all the other nuts,

I wanted to find a way to introduce the Marvel Universe to my 6-year-old daughter, Callie, and SQUIRREL GIRL was just the right thing. It's the best balance of kindness and butt kicking. Sometimes the topics are heavy, but I don't have to worry about misogyny, homophobia, racism or other bad vibes. Callie loves the book and wanted to wear a Squirrel Girl costume for Halloween. (See attached.)

Including the letters pages in the trades makes us happy and Callie was eager for me to send a picture.

Thanks for telling great stories that we can share,

Isobel and Callie

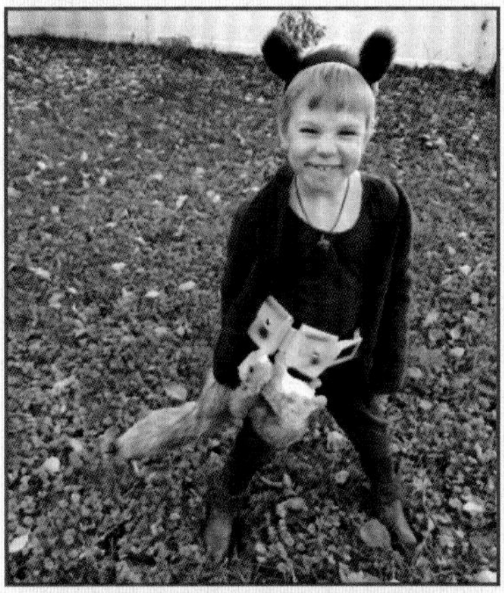

RYAN: Isobel! Callie! A GREAT COSTUME! And Callie, you've got a great attitude to go with it. You've correctly identified that "kindness + butt kicking" is the SQUIRREL GIRL secret sauce, and I'm glad you've been enjoying it so much!

Dear Squirrel Girl Crew,

Just wanted to say that I have greatly enjoyed your book. The storytelling and artwork are so well-crafted and they served as inspiration for a cosplay photo shoot I did with my friend Kamryn of KAMIcomics. We shot on location at Treaty Oak Park in Jacksonville, FL, and it was the perfect backdrop for the character. Kamryn has a great fondness for Squirrel Girl, and her attention to detail when it came to making her cosplay really shows. After our shoot I was further inspired to make the attached Cosplay Cover with a photo from our shoot. I don't know if Marvel has plans to make more official Cosplay Variant Covers, but I felt it was still worthy to share with you.

Thank you for all you do!
Mark Pariani

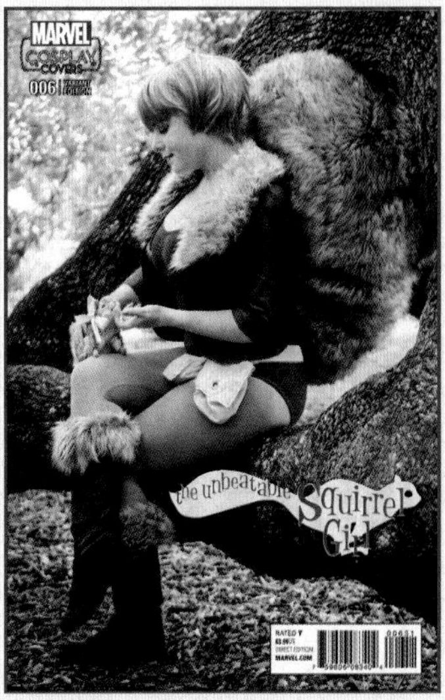
MARVEL
COSPLAY COVERS
006
the unbeatable Squirrel Girl

RYAN: This is me going on record as saying THIS IS A GREAT IDEA--we've got so much great cosplay here in the letters pages, it makes sense to put some of it on the cover too! I love the mockup you did and of course Kamryn's costume is super amazing. It's always such a thrill to see the character come to life like this--thank you so much for sharing!

Okay, Ryan, hear me out:

Ryan Reynolds plays Deadpool on the big screen.

Nolan North is frequently the voice of Deadpool in animation and video games.

So if you, Ryan North, were to write a Squirrel Girl/Deadpool crossover, the previous two facts, combined with that new fact, would suddenly become fascinating!

Bonus points if you can work in a cameo from baseball legend Nolan Ryan.

Keep making me laugh,
Jeff Gilligan

RYAN: Alternately, what if I use a pseudonym when working in acting and voiceover but only ever replace one of my names? WHAT IF THAT THING I JUST SAID WAS REALITY??

Dear amazing SQUIRREL GIRL team,

Thank you for yet another amazing volume! I love Derek's new take on Squirrel Girl and her friends. You might recognize me, I sent a letter before, it was in the column for #36 (that was amazing to see in the letter column!). Ryan: I decided to follow up on Cat Brat and drew her:

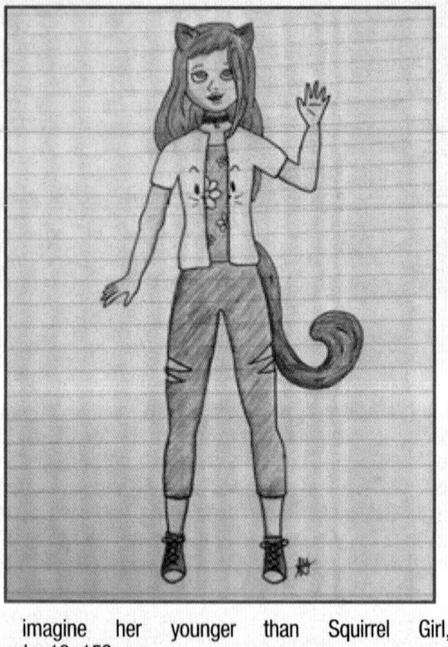

I imagine her younger than Squirrel Girl, maybe 13–15?

Thank you for this amazing comic, keep writing and drawing.

Ruby, A.K.A Cat Brat

RYAN: RUBY! Of course I remember Cat Brat. And your drawing of her is everything I imagined! I like that she's got a little cat collar on too--it's a fun theme detail! I'll make you a deal right now: I'll keep writing and drawing if you keep doing the same, okay?

It's Christmas Eve at the moment, and I should be wrapping presents for my twin daughters. However, I'm compelled to instead send some holiday greetings to all of you that make THE UNBEATABLE SQUIRREL GIRL happen! I am going to finish the gifts directly after writing this, so I didn't push that off to the side totally. Just temporarily.

I generally don't send a letter so soon after my previous one, but I had to go with my feelings this time around. It may not seem like much to run the words and pictures that we send to y'all. For us though, it's something special we get to share we each other as a family. Something very neat that we have been able to do for years now.

So, with that said...when I saw the family photograph snapped of us from this evening, I immediately felt that I had to send it in. Squirrel Girl is such a fun part of our lives, and you all mean a lot to us. You feel like family that should get some type of holiday card!

Also, I have a promise to make to Ryan North. I will send you a batch of weird paragraphs within the next year at some point. I don't want you to think I chatter nonsense for everyone else, and not for you. That is not the case. You will have your dish of strange.

Thanks for everything, Squirrel Providers. Much love!

Darrick Patrick
Dayton, Ohio

P.S. The photo I'm including is of our full little crew. From left to right, it's Logann Patrick, me, Niki Wooten and Nola Patrick. If I waited until tomorrow, I could snag a shot with all of their new Squirrel Girl gear that's under the tree. Another time!

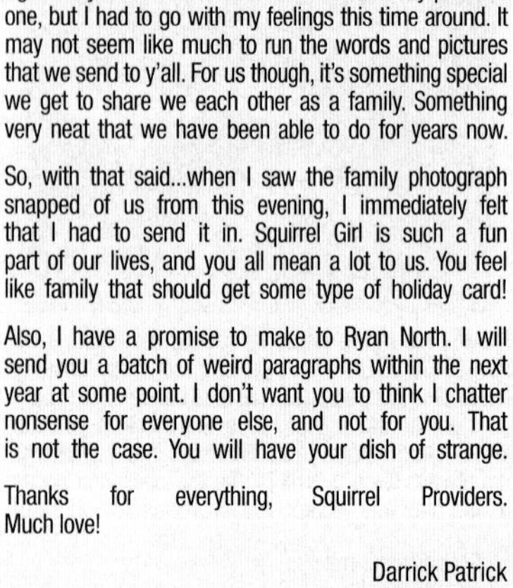

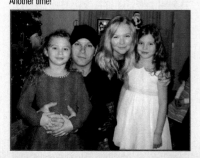

RYAN: Darrick, happy holidays to you too, and thank you for this card! It's been great to see your family grow every few issues. I don't think there's another Marvel comic that has a letters page as engaged and loving as this one, and you're a part of that--so thank you!! And I have never been promised "weird paragraphs" before and I look forward to seeing what they contain!

Hello Squires of the Squirrel,

It seems that my fanatic following of SQUIRREL GIRL was destined. The first time I heard of the Central Park Centurion was while playing *LEGO Marvel Super Heroes.* When I unlocked her, I was like, "That's a thing?!" I looked into it, and what do you know, the first-first issue of UNBEATABLE SQUIRREL GIRL was published around that time. Now that is some perfect timing.

I love that the Marvel Universe has a hero that solves problems through the power of friendship. I just finished the SQUIRREL GIRL Vol. 8 trade feat. Silver Surfer. As someone with experience in mediation, I really enjoyed the storyline. Conflict resolution can be really exciting. Forget police dramas; Hollywood should do some conflict resolution dramas. For anyone interested in the subject, I would HIGHLY recommend *Getting to Yes* by Roger Fisher, et al. It's an easy read and you'll lose count of how many times it's helped in your life.

Remember: Whether you're a human, fish or rodent, love is always potent.

Michael Toomey
Kansas City, MO

P.S. Do you have any information on what happened to the New Warriors TV show? Is it going to be part of the new Disney streaming service?

RYAN: Thank you, Michael! I'll have to check out that book--thanks for the recommendation! As for the New Warriors show, I don't have any SECRET INSIDER INFORMATION on it, which is disappointing, but I can say that I've read the script for the pilot, and it's great, and there's a scene in it that's so "Peak Doreen" that I wish I'd thought of it for the comic. So I suppose that does the opposite of what you wanted: rather than giving you concrete information on A TV Show Starring Squirrel Girl, instead I've said nothing but made it even MORE exciting. I hope it happens soon too!

Dear Squirrel Girl Team,

I love your work, I really do. And I love that there is a kick-butt ginger super hero in the Marvel Universe. Heck, I was Squirrel Girl for Halloween last year (pics attached also okay to print) but I have to ask, why did you make the "Hunter of Hunters" into "the Unhuntable Sergei," another run-of-the-mill super hero in New York? Because you know how many super heroes are in New York in the MCU? ALL OF THE SUPER HEROES! Nearly all of the super heroes are in New York stopping crime--did the city really need another one? And the worst part was he was doing invaluable work stopping poachers, something arguably only he can do so incredibly well. Do you know how many Amur leopards are left in the wild? Fewer than a hundred! And they are native to Russia! Kraven could have single-handedly saved that species in the MCU, but instead he is stopping muggers Spider-Man wasn't fast enough to get to that day. *Sigh*

Look, I know you all were going for a full redemption arc, but I don't see why that has to end with him being a run-of-the-mill crimefighting super hero, the MCU is literally bursting with those. But a Hunter of Hunters? A man who takes on machine gun-wielding poachers with a spear and WINS? Come on, guys, that was awesome. Can't Kraven do that and still be redeemed? Can't he be the hero the world's endangered wildlife needs, not the cliché redeemed bad guy we don't need/deserve?

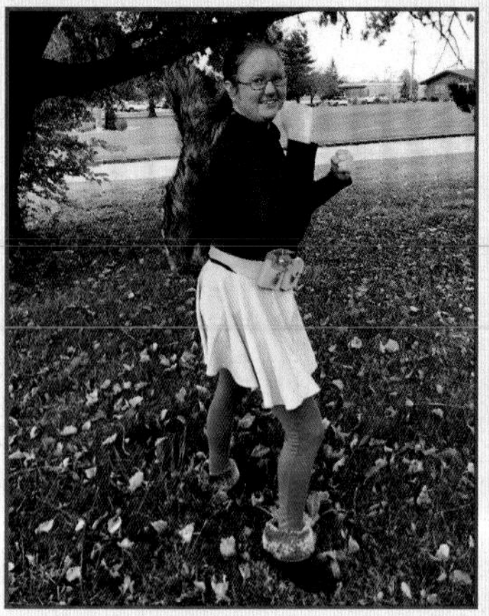

RYAN: Okay, first off, GREAT COSTUME AS WELL. Love it. As for the Kraven thing: This is my fault! I didn't mean to imply that Kraven was abandoning his Hunter of Hunters/Savage Land Protector roles to also fight crime in NYC! Quite the opposite. In my mind he's doing ALL of those things. The man is independently wealthy, in peak physical condition, has lots of free time and we've already seen that it's no big deal for him to charter a jet from the jungle to NYC to go hang out with Doreen. He flies around the world stopping poachers, saving endangered species, protecting his dinosaurs in the Savage Land--and when his travels take him to NYC, now he has some evening entertainment lined up there too. Man--just writing that out makes me think of how awesome Kraven is. I hope we get to see him again soon!

UP NEXT: As mentioned above, it's our FIFTIETH ISSUE! It's a milestone few comics get to reach, and I'm so proud of all of you who have made this happen by supporting the book each and every month, by buying the collections, by taking the book out from the library, by dressing up like Doreen Green, by telling your friends about the comic--you have made this happen! And to celebrate, we're doing something special: getting the whole team back together! Our next issue, #42, is our 50th-issue spectacular, and features a special stand-alone story with the art talents of unbeatable artist Derek Charm, OG SQUIRREL GIRL artist Erica Henderson and artist-of-this-very-issue Naomi Franquiz! What threat could bring these three talents together? Oh, just KANG THE CONQUEROR--a time-traveler from the distant future who has set his mind on attacking Doreen in three distinct time periods! How can Squirrel Girl fight someone who can go back in time and set things up so she always loses? We'll all find out next month--don't miss it!

Next Issue:

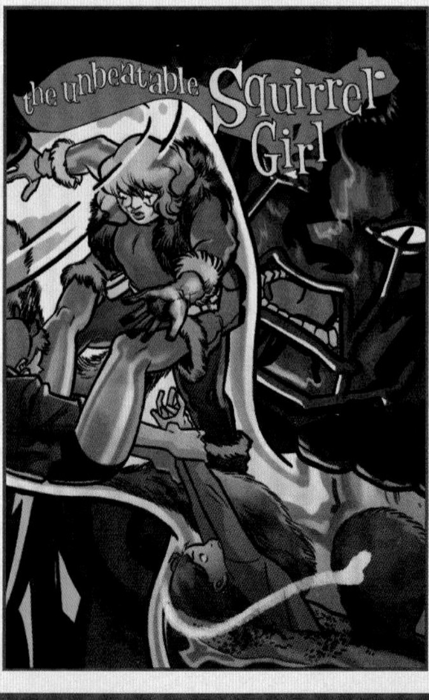
the unbeatable Squirrel Girl

Attention, Squirrel Scouts! Make sure to check out our production blog, **unbeatablesquirrelgirl.tumblr.com**, where we post behind-the-scenes stuff on how the book gets made, along with all sorts of cool things *you* make: fanart, cosplay, whatever!

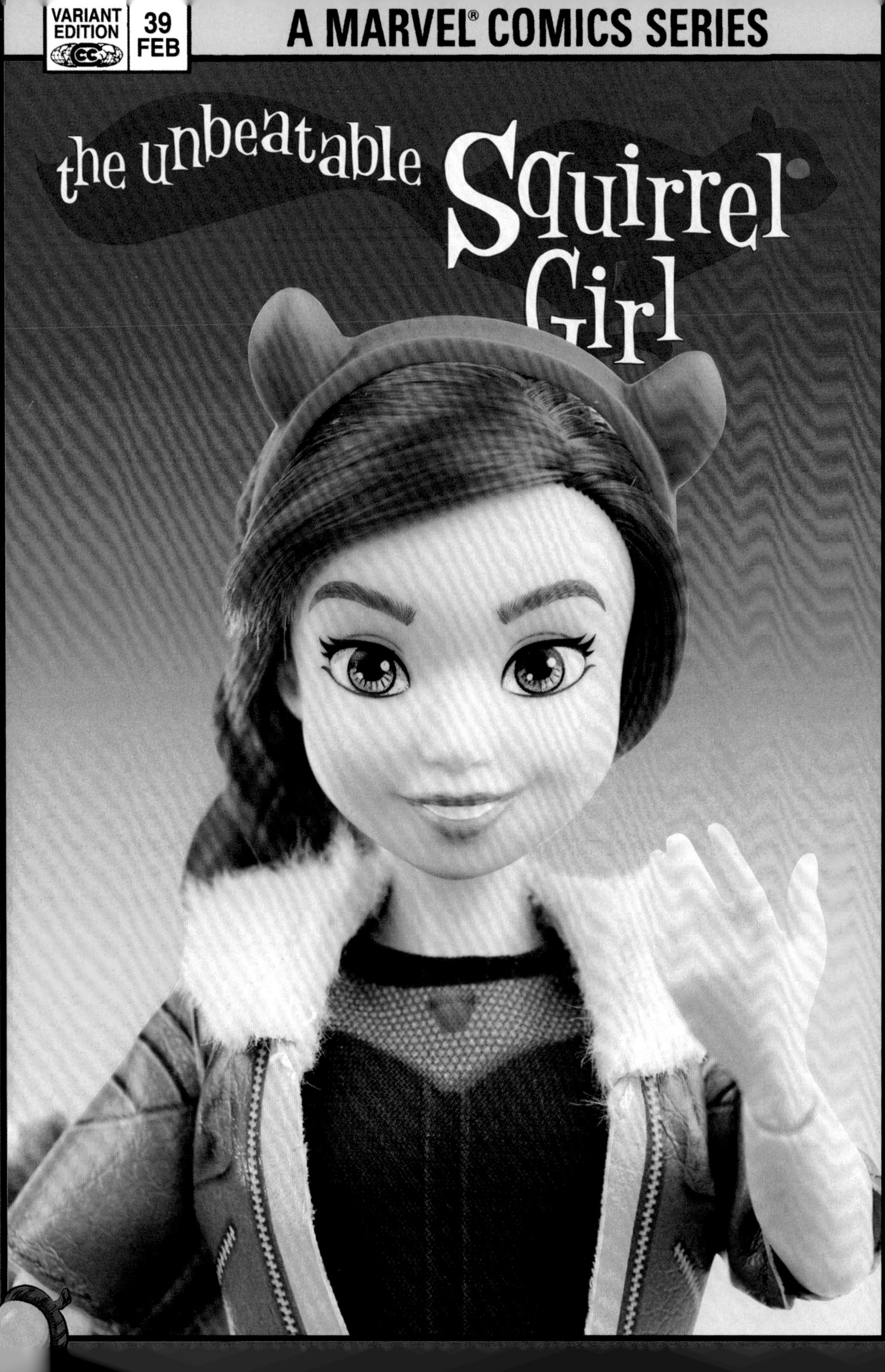
VARIANT EDITION
39 FEB
A MARVEL® COMICS SERIES
the unbeatable Squirrel Girl

MS. QUIZZLER DESIGN AND CHARACTER STUDIES BY **NAOMI FRANQUIZ**

OCTOBLITERATOR

OCTOBLITERATOR
DESIGN BY
DEREK CHARM

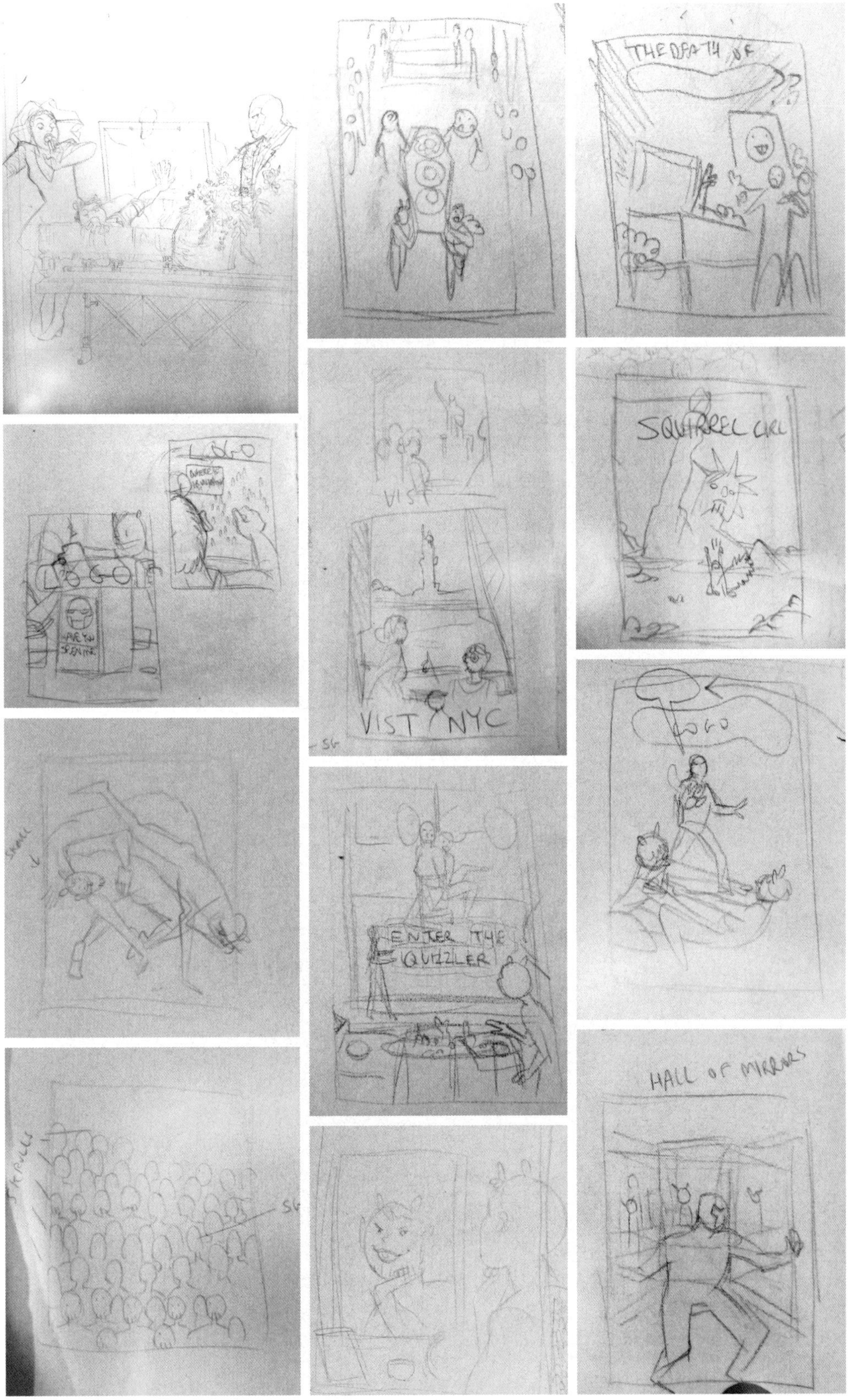
THE DEATH OF
LOGO
SQUIRREL GIRL
VIST
VIST NYC
ENTER THE QUIZZLER
LOGO
HALL OF MIRRORS

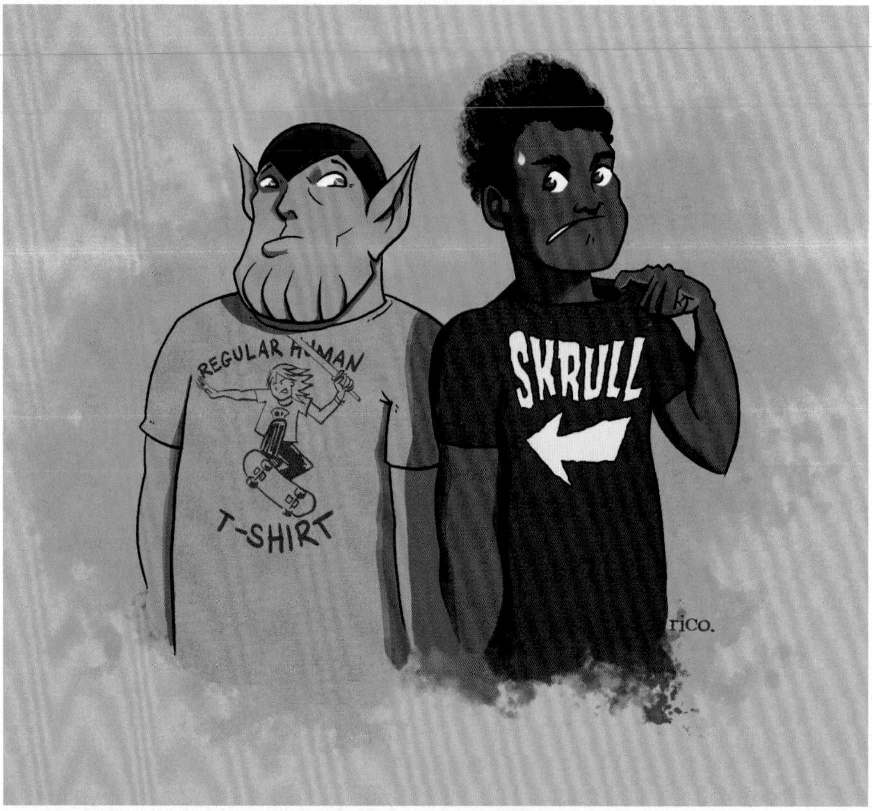
REGULAR
T-SHIRT
SKRULL

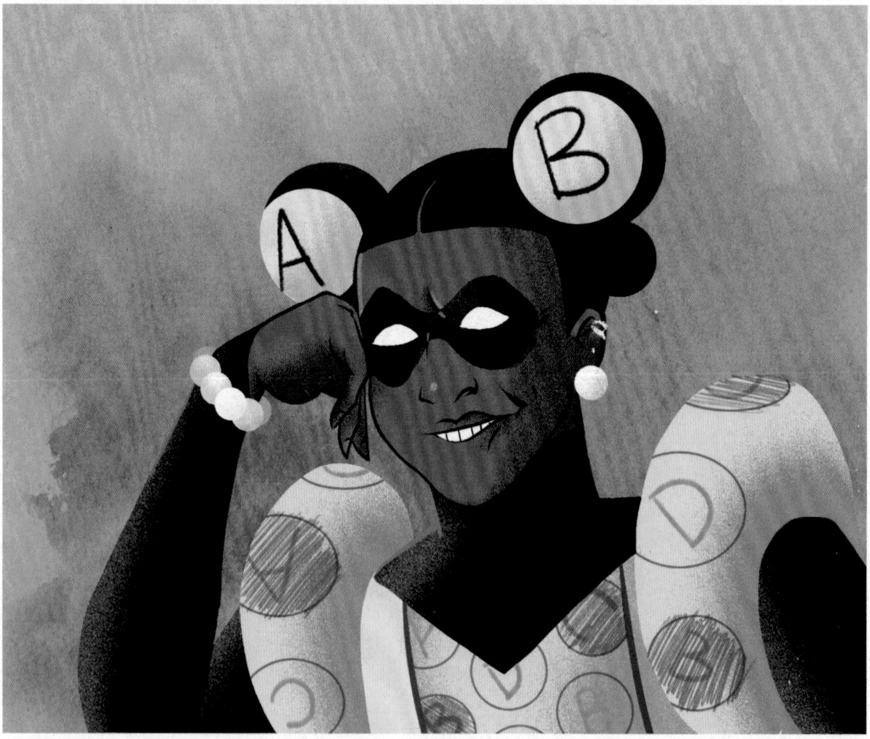
A
B